A Lasting Spring

A YORK STATE BOOK

Jessie Catherine Kinsley. Photograph by Milford Newhouse

A Lasting Spring

Jessie Catherine Kinsley, Daughter of the Oneida Community

Edited by **Jane Kinsley Rich**

with the assistance of **Nelson M. Blake**

SYRACUSE UNIVERSITY PRESS   1983

Copyright © 1983 by Syracuse University Press
Syracuse, New York 13210

All Rights Reserved
First Edition

This book is published with the assistance of a grant from
the John Ben Snow Foundation.

Library of Congress Cataloging in Publication Data

Kinsley, Jessie Catherine, 1858–1938.
   A lasting spring.

   (A York State book)
   Includes bibliographical references.
   1. Kinsley, Jessie Catherine, 1858–1938. 2. Oneida
Community—Biography. 3. Oneida Community—History.
I. Rich, Jane Kinsley. II. Blake, Nelson Manfred,
1908–   . III. Title.
HX656.05K56 1983   335'.9747'64 [B]   82-19200
ISBN 0-8156-0183-2
ISBN 0-8156-0176-X (pbk.)

Manufactured in the United States of America

In fond memory of Louise, Annie's granddaughter

JANE KINSLEY RICH, a granddaughter of Jessie Catherine Kinsley, was born and still lives in Kenwood, New York, home of the Oneida Community.

NELSON M. BLAKE is the author of a number of books on American social and cultural history, including *A History of American Life and Thought* and *Novelists' America: Fiction as History, 1910–1940*.

Contents

Preface

EDITORIAL TASKS have been shared by Jane Kinsley Rich and Nelson M. Blake.

Mrs. Rich, Jessie Kinsley's granddaughter, dated copies of her grandmother's memoirs, letters, and journals, and supplied materials for the illustrations. From her own knowledge of the old Oneida Community and the later Kenwood community, she has provided many of the identifications and explanations contained in the footnotes.

Nelson Blake, a historian long interested in the Oneida Community, advised on the final arrangement of the material and wrote an introduction for the book as a whole and for its several subsections. He has used material supplied by Mrs. Rich and other sources to provide further explanations in the body of the text and in the footnotes. He wishes to thank his wife, Elizabeth, for assisting him in this editorial work.

NMB

My thanks go to Flosie Allen, who passed along to me the J. C. K. letters written to Hope Allen. This was the impetus for the book. My gratitude to Sean Devlin is boundless. I owe thanks to Mark Weimer, Dorothy Woodward Ackley, Laura L. Noyes, and my husband, Wells Rich; and also to Oneida Ltd. for use of a copier and help from people in their photography lab. I am particularly honored to have introductions written by Nelson Blake.

Summer 1982   JKR

Introduction

WHEN JESSIE KINSLEY died at the age of seventy-nine in 1938, a friend offered a sensitive summary of her life. "It was," he said, "A Lasting Spring." The phrase came from one of Jessie's favorite verses in Shakespeare:

> Orpheus with his lute made trees,
> And the mountain-tops that freeze,
>   Bow themselves when he did sing:
> To his music, plants and flowers
> Ever sprung; as sun and showers,
>   There had made a Lasting Spring.
>
> (Henry VIII, III.i.3–8)

Jessie had used the haunting words "A Lasting Spring" as the title for one of the beautiful tapestries that she made from braided silk. Friends could see how well they described her own character, particularly the eagerness and hopefulness with which she greeted each day. Even when she was old and ailing, she found continual renewal. There was always something exciting in the books she read, in the braidings she made, in the birds and flowers that she encountered on her walks, in the friends she talked to, and in the children she entertained with her stories.

How had Jessie Kinsley achieved this serenity that impressed all who knew her? It certainly was not because her life had been free of sorrow and suffering. Quite the contrary. She had been tortured by tragic losses, but she had found the strength to go on, not only to endure life but to enjoy it. Her principal source of strength was probably to be found in the caring community to which she always belonged. First, this was the

xi

Oneida Community, one of the great nineteenth-century experiments in communal living. The old Community broke up in 1880, but a new community took its place, and much that was best in the old continued to flourish in the new. In Kenwood, the section of Oneida, New York, in which Jessie lived most of her seventy-nine years, almost everyone worked for the same company; most of them belonged to families whose roots were in the old Community; most of them valued cultural things — literature, music, art, and education; and most of them placed the welfare of the group above the advantage of the individual.

This is a book by Jessie Kinsley and about her. It is largely made up of her own writings — reminiscences of her early life, fragments from journals that she kept from time to time, and letters that she wrote to her relatives and friends. But it includes also brief passages about Jessie Kinsley as her daughter and granddaughter remembered her and as a historian reflects upon her life. Nineteenth-century social history is rich with communal experiments — New Lebanon, New Harmony, Brook Farm, Nauvoo. We usually tell their story in a familiar pattern — birth, life, and death. But we never ask whether there was any life after death. What happened to the communitarians after the community failed? Did any of the old ideals survive? If so, how did they find expression? The experiences of Jessie Kinsley demonstrate that more than fifty years after the breakup of the old Oneida Community it was still a powerful influence shaping not only one person's life but the lives of a whole group of relatives and friends.

Jessie Baker, known after her marriage as Jessie Kinsley, was born on March 26, 1858, in the Mansion House, a large wooden structure that stood on a commanding site near Oneida Creek in central New York. Her mother was Catherine Hobart Baker, a forty-four-year-old widow. Who was her father? This was a question never satisfactorily answered for reasons that Jessie explains in her memoir.

The place of the birth was highly significant. The Mansion House provided shelter for the Oneida Community, some 576 men, women, and children who were followers of John Humphrey Noyes, one of the most unusual figures in American religious history. Noyes taught the doctrine of Christian Perfection, that true believers could live lives free from sin. Since sin had its roots in selfishness, Noyes organized his disciples into an association where all property was held in common, where each person worked for the good of the whole group, where individual husbands did not claim individual wives, and where parents did not seek special privileges for their children but turned them over to the community for loving care and training.

The Mansion House was the home where Jessie Baker lived for most of the first twenty-one years of her life. Like other Community children, she was sometimes moved for a few weeks or months to other places, sometimes to Willow Place, only a short distance away, sometimes to the branch Community at Wallingford, Connecticut. But she always came back to the Mansion House. This is where she received her schooling, where she did her assigned tasks, where she made her youthful friends, where she had fun at picnics, dances, concerts, and theatricals. And at the Mansion House as she grew into adulthood she was brought into that unique Oneida Community experience known as "complex marriage."

Physically the Mansion House went through a metamorphosis during these years. The rambling wooden structure gave way, step by step, to a grander Mansion House built of brick. But the Mansion House as symbol did not change. Here the life of the Community centered. Here in the great kitchen food was prepared; here in the dining hall the Perfectionists ate their meals together; here they met evenings in the Big Hall to listen to talks by Mr. Noyes and other respected leaders; here they staged entertainments; here they conversed in the Upper Sitting Room; here they read books in the well-stocked library; here they worked and played and slept.

Economically the old Community went through bad times and good. Attempting to support itself by farming, it suffered through early years of great hardship. Conditions improved as the Community developed various industries. It began to preserve fruits and vegetables, to make carpet bags, to market silk thread, to produce chains, and—most profitably—to manufacture steel traps. Last of all—not until 1877—the Community began to make and market silver-plated tableware.

This then was the tight little world of Jessie's youth. But that world was radically disrupted when she was twenty-one years old. During the night of June 22, 1879, John Humphrey Noyes, aided by Myron Kinsley and another faithful follower, slipped out of the Mansion House and made his way to Canada, where he spent the last seven years of his life. Why did Noyes leave the beloved Community, the embodiment of all his ideals? One reason was Kinsley's warning that he might be sent to prison. In an upsurge of righteous indignation, zealots in central New York— forerunners of today's Moral Majority—were demanding that the authorities arrest and prosecute the leaders of the Oneida Community for their alleged iniquities. Noyes had ridden out earlier storms, but this one was much more dangerous because of crosswinds within the Community itself. Noyes was growing old, deaf, and hoarse. He had tried to pass the leadership over to his son, Dr. Theodore Noyes, but the younger man's admitted skepticism in religious matters caused deep divisions within the Community. The members were also disputing over sexual and family affairs, an old guard insisting on strict regulation in these matters and a younger generation demanding more freedom. The danger in the situation was that Noyes's critics within the Community might help his outside enemies to obtain evidence on which he could be indicted for sexual misconduct.

By taking up residence in Canada, Noyes had hoped to disarm his opponents, but the disputing factions continued to make trouble. The old leader received frequent letters from his relatives and friends, reporting on problems and beseeching his advice, both on business affairs and issues involving complex marriage. These inquiries and Noyes's replies were more often than not carried by Myron Kinsley. To quiet outside clamor and settle controversy within, Noyes finally advised the abandonment of complex marriage. Citing St. Paul, he recommended celibacy as the best alternative but acquiesced in conventional marriage as the best course for those unable to maintain celibacy. Acting upon the leader's advice, the Oneida Community ordered the practice of complex marriage to cease on August 28, 1879.

However grudgingly, the right to take husbands and wives had now been conceded, and Jessie soon had one of the most momentous decisions of her life to make. Two suitors were eager to marry her, but she could not choose between them. In her perplexity she wrote a letter to the most respected authority she knew, John Humphrey Noyes. The leader advised her to reject both of them and marry Myron Kinsley instead. Since Myron was Noyes's most trusted lieutenant during this critical period, the suggested match shows how highly Noyes esteemed young Jessie.

Myron was twice Jessie's age, so marrying him might not have seemed a very romantic course. But Jessie, no doubt recognizing Myron's worth, went along with the idea. On February 8, 1880, the couple were married at New Haven, Connecticut — not far from Wallingford, where Myron was in charge of the silverware works. Myron was forty-four years old; Jessie was not quite twenty-two. Despite this disparity the marriage appears to have been a singularly happy one. In 1881 the couple had their first child, Edith; in 1883 they had a son, Albert; and in 1887 another daughter, Jessie Janet.

Myron and Jessie started their married life in Wallingford, but moved back to the Mansion House before their first child was born. Myron was thus on the firing line when the next great struggle developed within the Community. With the new family arrangements — men with wives and children to provide for — loyalty to the old ideal of common property and work for the group as a whole wilted, and there was a strong demand for private ownership. Once again the leaders in Oneida, and Noyes in the Stone Cottage at Niagara Falls, Canada, engaged in complicated negotiations, and once again Myron Kinsley acted as go-between.

The various parties finally agreed on the transformation of the Oneida Community into Oneida Community, Limited, a joint stock company. All members over sixteen years of age were allotted shares in an amount proportionate to the number of years they had spent in the Community and the amount of property they had brought in with them. Younger children were to be supported and educated at company expense until they reached the age of sixteen when they were to receive $200. The new company came into being on November 20, 1880.

Myron was one of nine directors on the board of the new company and was assigned the job of managing the new shops at Niagara Falls, New York, where the silverware and chain businesses were being transferred from Wallingford. The family lived in Niagara Falls from 1881 to 1890, when Myron was brought back to Oneida. They lived for a time on a farm belonging to the company, then in the Mansion House until 1899, when Myron was sent to Chicago as company representative.

As wife and mother, Jessie worked very hard, particularly in the early years when she had to run an extended household that included not only her husband and her young children, but two grandmothers, several other relatives, roomers, and maids. No doubt, these burdens were related to the breakdown that invalided her for a year in 1894. But the later years of her marriage became easier. The children grew older and required less care; the older relatives passed on; the company made more money, and Myron and Jessie lived better. The years in Chicago provided Jessie with opportunities to see fine paintings, hear good music, and attend the theater—experiences that she loved. In 1902 Myron retired from active work, and the family returned to the Mansion House. In 1903 Edith married her cousin Martin (Mart) Kinsley; in 1905 Albert married Carlotta Cragin, the daughter of one of Jessie's classmates in the old Community school; and in 1907 young Jessie Janet married Chester Burnham, who belonged to another old Community family.

These years of happiness were interrupted by a series of sad events. In November 1907, Myron died, leaving forty-nine-year-old Jessie a widow. Because of the difference in ages this must have been a loss for which Jessie was somewhat prepared. Much more tragic was the death in 1908 of Jessie Janet, struck down by acute appendicitis when she was married less than a year and was carrying a child. For years afterward Jessie's letters and journals recorded continuing grief for this lost daughter. Jessie herself went through another period of illness during which she feared she had a malignancy. This proved not to be the case, and she put her life back on course with the support of her surviving children and her friends. For more than the next twenty years she made her home with Edith and Martin Kinsley. At first the family lived in Chicago, where Martin was now company representative, but in 1912 they moved back to Kenwood, the residential section now growing up around the Mansion House. Here Jessie had three rooms of her own in the fine new house that had been built by Mart and Edith. Sharing the same interests in reading and painting, mother and daughter enjoyed a uniquely warm relationship.

The third period of Jessie Kinsley's life began in 1913, when she made a tour of Europe with Annie Kelly Miller, another widow with strong family roots in the old Community. The two American women made a leisurely six-month trip, crossing the ocean by ship, traveling about the continent by train, sleeping and eating in modest pensions, and relying on horse-drawn carriages and primitive automobiles to get them around the various cities. To Jessie who loved architecture, sculpture, and painting it was a thrilling experience – a chance to see with her own eyes the beautiful objects she had hitherto known largely through books and pictures.

As she made her way through Europe, Jessie recorded her experiences in letters that she wrote to her relatives and friends. She also kept a journal that she decorated with little sketches. Even as a girl she had loved to draw and more recently she had taken painting lessons from Kenneth Miller, Annie Miller's son, who had a studio in New York City but conducted summer art classes in Kenwood.

Jessie was never really satisfied with her own painting. She felt limited by having to work on such a small scale. After she returned to Kenwood, she gradually found her way toward a new and highly original form of artistic expression. She started in a modest way, doing no more than other country women had long done in working cotton and woolen rags into rugs and chair coverings. But she soon made radical innovations. She began to do her work in bright-colored silk which she twisted into braids. These she used like the colors on a palette, sewing them into pictures, decorations, and ornamental borders. Emancipated from the painter's easel, she made large tapestries. By the end of World War I, her work had already attracted the attention of art lovers in distant cities.

Having seen Europe the year before World War I began, Jessie felt all the more keenly the horror of the great conflict that took so many lives and shredded so much of the old social fabric. She had an unusual opportunity to observe the contrasts between prewar and postwar Europe because she spent several months in England during 1919, when Martin was sent there on company business.

The final period of Jessie's life was spent back in Kenwood, a small area surrounding the Mansion House. Her best-loved activity was her braiding on which she spent many hours each day, but she found time to pursue many other interests. She had always been a great reader, and

she now devoured books voraciously. She read both old and new books —
poems by John Donne, William Blake, and A. E. Housman, historical
works by George Macaulay Trevelyan, letters by Horace Walpole, Matthew Arnold, and William Dean Howells, and novels by Thomas Hardy
and Richard Hughes. While Jessie worked on her braiding, Edith would
read aloud to her; while Edith painted or did sculpture, Jessie would do
the reading. It was reminiscent of old Community days when one person
would read aloud while a roomful of men and women prepared fruit for
canning or sewed on carpet bags.

Jessie had a great love for children, not just her own grandchildren but all the Kenwood children, whom she entertained by storytelling
and drawing. They called her "Aunt Jessie," a familiar form of address in
old Community days but now especially appropriate.

She loved the out-of-doors. She worked in her own little garden
and walked through those of her neighbors. She lay in a lawn chair and
watched the bird life that changed with the seasons. She even liked to hear
the shrill sound of tree toads at night — all the more cherished because she
was plagued by deafness and ringing noises in her head.

Despite her loss of hearing, Jessie treasured her contacts with the
old friends of Community days. Evenings she would cross the street to the
Mansion House and attend meetings in the Big Hall. Sometimes an ama-
teur orchestra would play, or other musicians would perform, or lively
discussions would take up issues of current interest. Even on quiet evenings when no special events were scheduled, Jessie would walk over to
the Mansion House and visit with the oldest residents, women in their
eighties and nineties like Aunt Jane Kinsley, or Mrs. Barron, Mrs. Freeman, and Mrs. Norton, widows whose husbands had been prominent in
the old Community. Often the women would get together in the Nursery
Kitchen, a place of happy associations with the old days.

In 1931 Jessie changed her residence for the last time. During the
Great Depression, Mart and Edith sold their house to the company and
moved to an apartment in the Mansion House. Jessie was established in
the Mansion House, too, where she transferred her pieces of silk and her
half-finished braidings. In the new, yet old, home Jessie spent the final
years of her life, doing the things she loved so well — braiding, reading,
walking, writing letters, and visiting with her friends.

Jessie died of a thrombosis on February 10, 1938 — a month short
of her eightieth birthday. In accordance with the custom of the old Community, her friends gathered in the Big Hall and paid tribute to her. Then
they laid her to rest among her relatives and friends in the old cemetery
not far from the Mansion House.

A Lasting Spring

A Girl in the Mansion House

$\mathcal{I}$N 1914, when she was a fifty-six-year-old widow, Jessie Kinsley wrote an account of the first twenty-one years of her life. This provides a unique insight into what it was like to have been born into the Oneida Community, to have passed the years of infancy, childhood, adolescence, and early womanhood there, and then to have had that compact world suddenly disrupted.

For the most part it is best to see Jessie's world through Jessie's eyes, but some historical background may improve our perspective. The story begins in Vermont. Not as sober and conservative as it later became, Vermont was the birthplace of some of the nineteenth century's great visionaries. Brigham Young was born there in 1801, Joseph Smith in 1805, and John Humphrey Noyes in 1811. Noyes's life began conventionally enough. His father was a solid citizen, a businessman in Brattleboro, and a member of the Vermont legislature and the U.S. Congress. Young John graduated from Dartmouth College in 1830 and studied law for a year before coming to the first turning point of his life. In 1831, a year of fervid religious revivals, John experienced conversion and decided to become a minister. Dissatisfied with Andover Theological Seminary after one year, he transferred to the Yale Theological School in New Haven. While still a student, he was licensed to preach in 1833 but soon ran into trouble. On February 20, 1834, he announced that faith in Christ had set him free from sin—a doctrine so unorthodox that his license was revoked and he was asked to leave the school.

Determined to continue witnessing to what he regarded as truth, Noyes lived the next few years as a wandering preacher traveling through New England and New York State. He also sought to win converts by publishing pamphlets and periodicals. The doctrine of Perfectionism that

1

he was preaching was not entirely new. He had predecessors, especially among dissident Methodists, and the northeastern part of the country was speckled with miniature groups of Perfectionists predisposed to give Noyes a hearing.

In 1838 Noyes returned to his home base in Vermont and married Harriet Holton. She was one of his earliest followers and had enough money of her own to help him with his projects. Settling down in the Noyes family home in Putney, not far from Brattleboro, John became the leader of a small but strongly committed group of relatives and converts. One of the earliest to follow him was a young woman named Catherine Hobart, who some twenty years later gave birth to Jessie.

A man of shrewd intelligence, John Humphrey Noyes perceived that other Perfectionists were receiving a bad name through their reckless behavior. What was needed, he believed, was careful organization and co-operative effort in establishing a stable and sinless society. Step by step he guided his Putney followers into a society, at first committed to study and discussion, then to pooling their property and working for the common good. In 1845 the "Putney Corporation or Association of Perfectionists" was organized.

Despite some grumbling about the Perfectionists' unorthodox religious teachings, the group's Vermont neighbors displayed no hostility toward them until the fall of 1847, when news began to circulate about the practice of complex marriage. Threatened by prosecution on charges of adultery, Noyes began to look about for a new base of operations.

Fortunately an opportunity presented itself in central New York, where Noyes was already in contact with a handful of Perfectionists living in various communities. One such group was settling on property belonging to Jonathan Burt on Oneida Creek. Burt invited Noyes and the Putney group to join them. On February 1, 1848, the Oneida Association was organized, and during the following summer and fall the first Mansion House was built.

Although Noyes was a strong leader whose will prevailed on all important issues, he ruled the Community not by decree but by fatherly admonition and advice. Helping Noyes to guide affairs was a group of older members—relatives and early converts to the movement. Committees were created to carry out special duties. The most effective means of control was the practice of "mutual criticism." From time to time each member would submit himself or herself to rigorous criticism by a special committee. Here the person who had shirked in his work, the one who had offended others with his brusqueness, the one who had displayed vanity or jealousy or greed, the parent who had been too possessive of his or her own child, the man or woman who had betrayed "special love" toward some other individual, all heard their faults vigorously criticized. It was supposed to be a loving exercise, but it could be a distressing experience and provided all the discipline needed for most problems. Criticism was sometimes enough to correct the children, although there was no sparing of the rod.

Outsiders often denounced the Community as a "free love" colony, but the Perfectionists indignantly rejected the accusation. Actually under complex marriage sexual relationships were carefully regulated through training, custom, and moral suasion. Noyes was ahead of his time in his strong advocacy of birth control. Having put his wife through the hazards of pregnancy and childbirth five times during the first six years of his marriage—with only one child surviving—the founder had become convinced that it was sinful simply to allow nature to take its course. To separate what he called the "amative" from the "procreative" function of sex, he learned to practice "male continence." That is, he refrained from climax. In a colorful description he likened his technique to a man rowing near a waterfall. "If he is willing to learn, experience will teach him the wisdom of confining his excursions to the region of easy rowing, unless he has an object in view [propagation] that is worth the cost of going over the falls."[1] Within complex marriage the men were under strong communal pressure to practice male continence, particularly since the struggling Community could not afford to support a multitude of unplanned-for babies.

The need to restrain youthful exuberance and teach the disciplines of male continence led to another of Noyes's doctrines, that of "ascending" and "descending" fellowship. This meant that the older women should provide the sexual initiation of the boys and the older men that of the girls. This crossover of the age groups was presumed to serve a religious as well as a physical purpose. In this as in other matters, it was elevating to the less spiritually developed young people to have close association with their spiritual superiors.

Relations between men and women were in theory entirely voluntary. The man usually took the initiative; the woman was at liberty to accept or reject him. As Jessie explains, negotiations were carried on through a third party, usually a particular older woman selected by the leaders for this responsibility. This custom served an additional purpose. Noyes and other Community leaders had reliable sources of information about the so-called "social life" of the Community and could admonish the members who might be straying into dangerous paths. "Exclusive love," that is, always associating with the same partner, was condemned.

A method of birth control so dependent on self-restraint could

---

1. Maren L. Carden, *Oneida: Utopian Community to Modern Corporation* (Baltimore: Johns Hopkins University Press, 1969), p. 50.

not be expected to be 100 percent successful. Those who row too near the falls will occasionally topple over into the rapids below. The wonder is that male continence worked as well as it did and that the number of unsanctioned births was kept remarkably low. But mistakes did happen, and one fortunate one resulted in the birth of Jessie to Catherine Hobart Baker in 1858. Whoever had faltered in his practice of male continence showed an understandable reluctance to confess his error. Not until Jessie was seven years old did a troubled male admit that he might be responsible. And when she grew older Jessie suspected that yet another, and a much more prominent man, might be her father.

During its first twenty years the Oneida Community admonished its members to refrain from having children. A few babies were born by mistake, and a few others, because of special circumstances, were brought into the world with the approval of the leaders. But for the most part the moratorium on childbearing continued until the late 1860s, when the Community became much more prosperous. Noyes and his fellow leaders then decided that the time had come to put into practice his long-held theories about scientific breeding. Just as sheep could be improved by selecting the heaviest and wooliest for breeding, so humans could produce healthier and more intelligent children if only the parents were carefully chosen. "We see no reason," Noyes wrote, "why 'in the good time coming,' every child that is born should not be a 'genius' . . ."[2]

In 1869 the Oneida Community began a challenging experiment in what Noyes called "stirpiculture"—derived from *stirpes,* a Latin word meaning stock or race. Noyes himself chose the earliest candidates for parenthood; later special committees made the selections. During the next ten years men and women chosen for their superior qualities produced fifty-eight children. The offspring were not always the geniuses that Noyes had hoped for, but they were a remarkable group, well above average in health, energy, and intelligence. Indeed, many of them grew up to hold important managerial posts in Oneida Community, Limited.

If the old Community exerted strong moral pressure to restrain the hit-or-miss propagation of children, it took just as much care in their rearing. Nursing mothers kept their infants with them until they were weaned; after this the toddlers were cared for in the nursery during the daytime and returned to their mothers evenings. From age two to ten the youngsters lived in the Children's House. For a time this was a separate building; later it was one of the wings of the Mansion House. Here the children slept, ate their meals, and played under the supervision of "fa-

2. Constance Noyes Robertson, ed., *Oneida Community: An Autobiography,*
1851-1876 (Syracuse: Syracuse University Press, 1970), p. 344.

thers" and "mothers" charged with this duty. No effort was made to cut completely the parental bond; occasionally the child would spend time with its own mother or father. But parents who clung too closely to their offspring were criticized for "philoprogenitiveness." Probably Catherine Baker was believed to possess this weakness. This would explain why Jessie and her mother were often separated, with one being sent to the Wallingford Community and the other kept at Oneida.

Formal school started at the age of seven, sometimes earlier. Adults designated as teachers instructed not only in the traditional reading, writing, and arithmetic, but in other matters important to the community—Bible study, self-criticism, singing, playing musical instruments, and performing simple tasks like wiping dishes, piling wood, and picking butternuts.

Compulsory classes ceased when the child was twelve and began more serious work for the Community. But voluntary classes in a wide range of subjects—algebra, Latin, French, geography, astronomy, Bible study, art appreciation—were provided, not only for the teenagers but for adults as well. Indeed, an extraordinary appetite for learning was one of the Community's most striking characteristics. Several of the most promising young men, John Humphrey Noyes's eldest son Theodore among them, were sent to Yale College to complete their education. Unfortunately, a college education and an enthusiasm for the theories of Charles Darwin sometimes weakened simple religious faith, a development that contributed to the break up of the old Community.

But the seriousness with which men and women arranged their personal lives, accepted or abstained from parenthood, and turned over their children to the Community did not mean that Oneida was a joyless place to live. The truth was quite the contrary. Looking back on these years, Jessie Kinsley used a metaphor probably suggested by her braiding. "I know," she wrote to her daughter Edith in 1914 "that the religious fervor developed a narrowing fanaticism in some; yet quite quickly a bright line—the philosophy of playfulness and artistic endeavor—began to grow in the warp of religious life." The play spirit brightened each stage of existence. The Community children rolled hoops, swung on swings, dug into piles of dirt, and were taken on swimming expeditions to nearby streams and lakes; the young people played in orchestras and bands, sang in choruses, danced, played baseball and croquet, and staged plays and operettas; the older people watched and often participated in these activities. They read to themselves and to each other. They organized picnics. They even tried to lighten their work with the play spirit. They sometimes marched to the fields to the music of fife and drum and organized "bees" to perform communal tasks.

In the crisis of 1879 and 1880, great changes came about. Noyes retired to Canada, complex marriage was ended, and communal ownership gave way to individual holdings. Yet if much was lost, much was retained. The Mansion House still stood, continuing as a place where many of the old families still lived and ate together. People still gathered in the Big Hall for discussion and entertainment; children continued to go to school there; adults organized classes in literature and art; musical groups performed to amuse themselves and their neighbors. Much more than in other places there was an extraordinary sense of community. Within that loving atmosphere Jessie centered her entire life. She lived brief periods in other places; she traveled in foreign countries; but her heart always remained in the Mansion House. Here she had been born and here she would one day die.

MEMORIES OF YOUTH: MY FIRST TWENTY-ONE YEARS

My Mother

Early Summer, 1914

Dearest E. [Edith Kinsley, Jessie's daughter],
    Here are some memories of my *young* days — of my mother, my sister, the girls of my class and other friends. I shall not try to carry my recollections much beyond your birth, for I have letters to attach to these pages, and you have your own remembrances — those will serve to fill out a picture of later days better than I could make.
    My mother, Catherine Elvira Hobart (Baker), was born in Putney, Vermont in 1814. Her parents had moved to Putney from Keene, New Hampshire, shortly before she was born. Her father was Peter; her mother was Susan (Hall); her brothers were David, Henry and Ralph; her sisters were Adaline and Fanny. Catherine was the sixth child. This Hobart family, with the ancestries of Hall, Chamberlain and Clark, had its roots in Keene.
    The family's move from Putney to northern Vermont, near the town of Montgomery, was a fascinating story that Mother used to tell us. The journeying by the "Onion River" left a deep impression in her mind, and the name has held fast in mine. I know the old log house, too, and the wide fireplace where Mother learned to read. These are a part of my life because of her stories.
    One night, all the children climbed the ladder to the attic. There,

Adaline heard a howling and sent little Catherine flying down the ladder to ask Father, "What is it? Oh, what is it?" There followed a hunt because the wolves had killed ten sheep. The cry of "Wolf! Wolf!" as the hunters saw the wolves dash out of the forest, still rings in my ears as it did in Mother's. When she went to school that morning she passed a wolf lying gaunt and gray before Mr. Lusk's door—dead. "Perhaps that's the last wolf in Vermont," Mr. Lusk said.

Another story was about a whirlwind that tore [its] way through the forest, laying trees about like Jack-straws, while Grandmother Hobart and her children, lying flat upon the ground behind tree stumps, watched the roof of their dwelling fly away. Mother remembered her mother's loud outcry when barrels full of feathers were exposed: the feathers sailed aloft in eddying circles, lost forever.

The most thrilling story Mother told me (though now it seems commonplace) was of a stranger who came asking for food when she had been left at home alone. Strangers were few in that wild north country, and the child was frightened but she provided bread and milk for the traveller, and together they ate of this as they sat on the wide door-stone. The man talked of Jesus. My private conviction was that this strange, gentle person was Jesus himself. When he went away he left Mother a little *treasure:* a story book—good little stories about good little children.

In Grandfather's house there were few books, but, with no memory of the time she learned to read, Mother made those books her constant companions and could recite whole pages from Young's *Night Thoughts, Pilgrim's Progress,* and *The Bible.* (This early habit led to a wider association with books later.) Other knowledge came from within a drafty log schoolhouse behind a hill, and industrial education widened at home. Fanny, Adaline and Catherine spun and wove wool and flax, helped to fashion the family clothing, cooked and cleaned, helped Father and the brothers with the haying and at "sugar time." By and by the older boys married, and, alas! Adaline died.

It was when Mother was eighteen that she first united with a church—the Episcopal Church—and henceforth most of the important events of her life were connected with her religious development. She remained an Episcopalian until a revival quickened fervor and she thought she found a greater earnestness in the Methodist congregation. When the Hobart family returned to southern Vermont—to Mother's birthplace in Putney—a second revival, called the "Finney Revival"[1] brought her again

---

1. Charles G. Finney, the most popular evangelist of this period, conducted a series of revivals in the Middle Atlantic states and New England. The revival in Putney was not conducted by Finney himself but by another preacher using Finney's methods.

into spiritual unrest. It was then that she heard a young reformer, J. H. Noyes, preaching *perfection.* She found that that word, *perfection,* under his interpretation, was the message of Christ. From that time her heart and mind were dedicated to that word, and her life thenceforth was bound to the lives of Mr. Noyes and his followers. Thus, after a time, she forsook the "world" and her family and became a part of a larger family, "The Putney Community" of Perfectionists. When the Putney Community dissolved she soon joined the new organization of Perfectionists at Oneida.

J. H. Noyes

Like my mother, John H. Noyes was a Vermonter. He was born in Brattleboro, some nine miles from Putney.

His father, John Noyes Sr. (who had accrued wealth and honor in public life), had married at the age of forty a young woman of nineteen, Polly Hayes, sister of Rutherford Hayes, of Brattleboro, Vermont. To Polly and John were born nine children. Their first son was named John Humphrey Noyes — J. H. N. The three *younger* children were Harriet, Charlotte and George, and they only will appear with their leader in these recollections. Harriet became "Mrs. Skinner"; and Charlotte, "Mrs. Miller."

To Polly was due the family move from Brattleboro to Putney when her husband retired from business in 1823. Putney had been a favored seat of revivals, and it was here where she hoped she would "best promote the spiritual improvement of the family." The children were at various times thereafter sent away to school; but their mother gave her heart and mind constantly to prayers for their conversion. "And Mother gathered the harvest of her prayers and labors," wrote Harriet. "For all of her children were converted in 1831, among them her oldest son, John, who had just graduated from college and had spent a year in the study of the law. He changed his plan of life and entered Andover Theological Seminary."

After two years of "rapid progress" and "discoveries of Christian experience" at Andover (viz. his theory of the second coming of Christ in A.D. 70), John went to New Haven, where, says his sister, the "professors of theology led the van of the army of young converts in New England." At Yale his own experience reached an important crisis. He declared himself free from all sin through faith in the gospel and the promises of Christ, becoming, as he wrote his mother, "a fool for Christ's sake," of "no reputation," a "Perfectionist."

Even in those days of stage coaches, the news of Mr. Noyes's conversion to Perfectionism went rapidly over the land, carrying with it a power which shook the churches and made the sincere everywhere examine anew the foundations of their faith.

Mother Again. Oneida Community Beginnings. My Birth

In 1838 or '39, when Mother first heard J. H. N. preach in the chapel in Putney, the "travail of his spiritual birth," as she might have phrased it, was over. Since 1836 he had been living in Putney, publishing a paper and founding a "school" that grew within eight years into the Putney Community. Mother joined the school for Bible study and in 1846 she left her home and went to live with the Noyeses and the Cragins[2] in the Noyes House.

The forty communists had already "ceased to say 'mine' and 'thine' respecting houses and lands and goods," and the spirit which followed the teachings of their leader swept away the claims of selfish ownership as it had with the early Christians. No man said "that aught he possessed was his own." Continuing my quotation from the old *Circular,*[3] "The same spirit which swept away property distinctions stayed not in its course until even the selfish claims of marriage were also swept away" . . . "Mutual Criticism became a Community ordinance. In the midst of their revolutionary changes in respect to property and marriage, heart-searching criticism held sway, and the members were eager to avail themselves of this 'ordinance,' so strong was their desire for personal improvement" . . . "The school grew in numbers — the disapproval and jealousy of the churches was aroused" . . . "Soon a hot fire of persecution was raging" . . . "In a short time the prosperous, happy Community was scattered."

Before the end of the Putney Community, however, my mother married James Baker. Mother had heard of the new social theory before her marriage, but not so Mr. Baker. Mother helped to reconcile her husband to it by "prayer and supplication," she told me. They were married after the theory had made some stir. Mr. Baker was a native of Putney.

I can think of nothing more fortunate in Mother's life than her joining the Community. It was like coming into a new world, like entering

2. George Cragin and his wife, Mary, were early converts of John Humphrey Noyes and original members of the Putney group. Carlotta Cragin, a descendant, married Jessie Kinsley's son, Albert.

3. The *Circular* was a Community periodical, published frequently.

college for life. In my imagination I contrast what might have been her development in her own little Putney sphere with what came to her in the Community. Perhaps she would have taken up (as my Aunt Fanny did after Grandfather and Grandmother Hobarts' deaths) the occupation of servant in a family and so had an honorable career, yet a less complete development.

These communists suffered poverty and persecution, gave up everything for a cause, sought a new home in a wild place, entered into strange new ways; yet their spiritual and mental growth was accelerated by their leader, through the enthusiasm of their numbers and the constant giving and seeking of the gifts of the mind and heart.

In Putney they arose at five in the morning to study the Bible, and almost immediately criticism was started. At Putney, and later at the Oneida Community, there were study classes in all branches of knowledge so that the old as well as the young were constantly at school. As always there was the printing and publishing of a paper, and later, schooling in business when manufacture was taken up. I know that the religious fervor developed a narrowing fanaticism in some; yet quite quickly a bright line — the philosophy of playfulness and artistic endeavor — began to grow into the warp of religious life. Bible study was made a game. Work was made a game. Later, when the Putney Communists had moved to Oneida, men and women went to work to the sound of a fife and drum. There were Shakespearian plays. There was music and games and dancing. Whole days were given up to festivities to mark some special occasion, such as the 20th of February ("The High Tide of the Spirit," which was the anniversary of J. H. N.'s first confession of Christ as his savior from all sin). Often the house was illuminated to finish the gaiety of the day.

A great festival was made by the Oneida group when, in 1858, the laying of the first Atlantic cable by Cyrus Field was accomplished; the band played at sunrise on that day. Breakfast was followed by games, and dinner, by a lecture. Supper was served to the entire family under the old butternut tree, and the day was finished by a grand illumination.

All the problems that Mr. Noyes, his family and the Community met and partially solved were, in a little way, Mother's problems. Insofar as her temperament allowed, her's, too, was the gaiety, pleasure and growth.

Nine months after her marriage came the disruption of the Putney Commune, and Mother went across the Connecticut River to Mrs. Samuel Lord's where, on December 23, 1847, my sister, Mary, was born.

Mother and Mr. Baker were among the first to go to New York State to join the Burts at Oneida Creek where the nucleus of Oneida Community was forming. They arrived there in April, 1848. Mary was a tiny child of five months (she weighed only twelve pounds when a year old). The conditions in the Burts' log home and the new shed-like building (hastily put together to shelter the incoming communists) must have been hard for the women with young and sickly babes. We can imagine the journey, too, and something of its hardships. I saw once in the *Circular,* in a year much later than 1848, an account of the arrival of the Vermont party of which Mother, with baby Mary, James Baker, and Mr. Burnham[4] were a part. I think the tale was told by Mr. Burnham in a letter, and the letter was a chapter of some life or reminiscence. I have looked for this again to quote from it but did not find it. It was a vivid account of the state of the roads and of the condition that the poor travellers found themselves in after a tramp through the clay — covered with mud to the hips.

I can give you no clear picture of Mother's appearance at the age of thirty-four. Her first photograph was made many years later in 1863, coincident with my own earliest childhood memory of this best loved person. She was then fifty. But I know that her short figure was slender: her weight was one hundred-one pounds. Her hair was straight and black, abundant, and fine. Her skin was clear. Her eyes were gray. Her nose was rather long and prominent. Her mouth was good in line, but the teeth were soon to go for want of dental care. Her brow was large and well formed, as was her head. Eyebrows and eyelashes were dark. She toed in and may have been awkward. Her feet and hands were small and beautifully formed.

I have always wished for a likeness of James Baker yet I do not know of one. He died when Mary was nearly nine years old — two years before I was born. His death was the result of an unhealed wound in the leg — a wound caused by the kick of a colt. Modern medical skill would have cured him, but the deep sore knew no disinfectant, the bone wasted away, and then came consumption. In imagination he was for long my dearest father, for Mary let me share her love.

In 1851, Mr. Henry Allen Sr., his wife and family joined the Community. In a truly pentecostal spirit they gave up their family home in Wallingford, Connecticut, to be thenceforth a Community home, a branch of the Oneida Community. It was to this branch that Mother and Mr. Baker had come when death took away the latter. Mary, I think, was there too. That was in September, 1856. On the last sad day, several hours before death really came, there was a sudden sinking. Mother was resting. Mrs. Hannah Hatch[5] was by the bedside. "Oh, James, James, do not die,"

---

4. Henry W. Burnham, a former Congregational minister and one-time "Millerite." Millerites expected the second coming of Christ in the near future.

5. Wife of Eleazer Hatch. Eleazer came to believe that he was Jessie's father.

Catherine Hobart Baker

she cried. "Wait a minute till I can call Catherine!" To be asked to *wait* at such a moment touched Mr. Baker's quick sense of humor. He rallied when Mother reached him. He was laughing instead of dying.

My sister, who was left fatherless, was undersized, almost dwarfed. I have a curious recollection of coming suddenly on this fact when separation from Mary had added inches to my height, and I found myself much astonished to be looking down upon her. As a consequence, no doubt of early physical ills, Mary was a slow, laborious scholar; but as to wit she was very keen. Good humor and laughter, quick repartee, and fun followed her. Her energy and good judgment gave her trusted positions in business which she filled well. Her amiability gave her love. She was plain, for her mouth would not close over her teeth; but her eyes were fine, and her face revealed a noble, faithful spirit. She gave love lavishly. Sometimes this seemed for her a misfortune, for love thus given is not always valued at its worth, and Mary came upon many disappointments. However, I cannot remember her as long depressed. Her spirits were buoyant.

But to go from Mary to Mother during the years before my birth —well, I imagine from what I heard through Mary and others that a certain amount of fanaticism had become a part of her life through intense religious zeal and may have warped for a time her really lovable nature. Mary said Mother was austere and severe—sometimes harsh. Those were tremendous days, when great hardships were endured for what was supposed to be the Cause of Christ and communism, when individual desire and thought was under the discipline of criticism. And criticism was *sometimes* used as a flail to beat down instinct, instead of turning it by praise as well as blame (*as intended by Mr. Noyes*) into a flame that should light a way to that dream of "heaven on earth."

What, then, came to soften and mold Mother, to make her the sweet and lovable woman I remember? My unlooked-for coming, I think, so late in her life (Mother was forty-four), and my following childhood. Perhaps my warm, happy love for her was a more potent means than suffering to change any harshness or crabbedness of her overwrought spirit into loving thankfulness. I have no memory of harshness.

The policy of the Community had been to forbid the propagation of children during these pioneer years. A "mistake" was considered a serious detriment to the society. Alas, then, in the summer of 1857, Mother became conscious of wrong in her own person, though without intent, and innocent of knowledge when the mistake occurred. There had been some failure of Male Continence.[6] For several months she had not imagined a child was to come but attributed her illness to her age. When, however, her condition was assured to her, I suppose it would be hard to imagine her mental distress. Added to the distress of the mind was the physical want of good food, for the Community was poverty-stricken still, and the tables were bare of appetizing food. Beans and potatoes, molasses and bread (without butter) were the common diet.

Perhaps "poverty-stricken" is an inaccurate phrase to use about the conditions in 1858, though food and clothing were indeed scarce. For some time after 1848 the new Community had lived on its capital. Many new members—in 1850 there were 205 members, in 1848, only 87 members—brought funds and energy, but until manufacturing was successfully started there was no sure income. Between 1849 and 1857, $40,000 was sunk. A free paper was published from the first, and as early as 1849 the first so-called "Mansion House" was built of wood and farm lands were purchased.

In 1855 an expensive branch commune in Brooklyn was given up and all its members came to the Oneida Community. Then, too, the first large orders for traps came in, and all effort was concentrated on their manufacture.[7] Men and women together worked at the forge and the bench. There was no hired help.

As the trap industry grew there came the need for new machinery, new factories and new water power, so that, in 1858, and for several years later, there was still keenly felt the pinch of poverty and the need of money.

In 1863 the new brick mansion was built, and for the first time help was hired for the farm work; the bag work was hired out.

During the nine months of Mother's pregnancy, many hours were

6. A Community practice to prevent unwanted pregnancies. Obviously, over a thirty-year period a few unplanned children were born.

7. Sewall Newhouse of Oneida Castle had invented the Newhouse trap before joining the Oneida Community in 1848. He taught the Community men to manufacture the traps. For many years it was the Community's most successful business.

spent daily at the bench in the trap-mill, pounding out springs and flattening pans.

I was born on March 26, 1858 — a matter of three slow days.

Mother shared a room with three other women. Later she moved into a more commodious room in the "Middle House," then the "Children's House." Even this room was fully shared by other occupants, for Mrs. Waters and little Edith were equal boarders by day and night, while in trundle beds in the same room slept three little children.

Mrs. Waters (Louisa Tuttle of North Haven, Conn.) had married Hial Waters of New York. She was younger than my mother — a warmhearted, handsome woman. Edith was three months my junior. Out of our mothers becoming so closely united in one small room grew a great affection among us all that lasted a lifetime. It was not a Community custom for husband and wife to occupy the same room. My mother was always "Mother Baker" to Edith; "Mother Waters" was a second mother to me. We were too young when Edith's father died to remember him but often heard him spoken of. Sometimes Edith saw his relatives who came to visit her from Norwich.

I think Mother's troubles about me continued, for I was not strong or well, and she feared my ill health might be "The Judgment of God" coming upon her for a lack of reconciliation to my coming into her life, and that my death might ensue as a just "punishment." Superstitious fears of this sort were not part of her later life, for she became a philosopher whose faith and creed were broader and more reasonable.

Then, however, came suffering so great upon Louisa, her roommate, that for a time at least Mother forgot her woes.

Louisa's husband, Hial, caught typhoid fever when their daughter, Edith, was only three months old. Mother watched the sick room and brought word when Louisa was unable to be there because of her young babe's needs or when it was feared that her anxiety would injure the sick man. When the fever brought death to Hial, Mother's whole thought was to comfort her friend.

When our mothers had weaned us from the breast we went to live in the Children's House. At the same time our mothers became caretakers in the children's rooms. There was no real children's house set aside for us — only certain contiguous rooms in the Middle House were assigned for our use: playrooms, schoolroom, bathroom, nap-room, etc. At night, until we were somewhat grown, we slept with our mothers. Living in the Children's House did not change or lessen our love for our mothers, rather, I imagine that love was strengthened. We were disciplined if we became too attached or "sticky" to our mothers, and they certainly suffered the discipline of "philoprogenitiveness."[8] Yet who can say that such experience was unnecessary in a society where it was *undertaken* that no man nor woman should claim aught as his own—neither father, nor mother, nor wife, nor child, nor brother, nor sister. Yet we may imagine the pain of the struggle with the *fundamental* instinct of *motherhood*. The aim in this strange association, framed on the "Bible pattern" and called "Bible communism," was to assure the children that their parents were the *entire* Community; and, as to the older people, the feeling was ingrained in them that they were mothers, fathers, grandparents, aunts, and uncles to *all* of us children. Nevertheless, it was found a comfortable and pleasant thing for a child to have a special "Community father" where any, by death or inadvertence, had missed a *natural* father, to connect him in an objective way with the great group.

I have now reached a point, I think, where henceforth much of this narrative will be made out of my own scattered memories, and these will have association with people and names so familiar to you that only in a few instances shall I undertake characterization. The familiar names will drift in and out and hold my stories together.

Your grandfather, Albert Kinsley, was an early friend. My first recollection is of seeing cars[9] flash by the end of Main Street in Oneida while he held me in his arms. Charlotte Leonard, who loved little children, had saved her pennies, and I was taken by her to Oneida to have that little picture taken which she has given to you.

Myron, your father, twenty-two years my senior, used to tell of trotting me on one knee, Edith Waters on the other.

Edith had a Community father after her own father died—that is, someone was chosen by her mother to take a kindly and special interest in her. My mother chose no Community father for me. I was seven years old when Eleazer Hatch, who previous to that time had been doubtful of his responsibility for my existence when earlier questioned by my mother, suddenly became convinced that I was his daughter. He was under a conviction of "sin" and in condemnation of spirit and said he knew such an experience would be just his luck. Mother felt some concern about this late claiming of me, but, as I was delighted to have a father, she allowed the relationship, and I asked for Mr. Hatch's name. So then my name was no longer Jessie Baker but Jessie Hatch, and to my great relief, I was rid of the suggestive rhyme . . .

8. Excessive love for one's own offspring.

9. Trains on the New York Central Railroad.

Little Jessie Baker —
Take her up and shake her.

No doubt it was a strange matter to have a father thus come into
my life, yet I did not then think it strange, I am sure, and verily felt I had
found the best father in the world. He was a slight, light-footed, blue-
eyed father, several years older than Mother — often moody, sometimes
quick-tempered, always quick-witted. I had known him in the Children's
House as "Father Hatch." Through this change I might now lay especial
claim to him, beyond all other children. A great satisfaction indeed!
Moreover, Father Hatch was loving and kind, and our status as father
and daughter was a tender, happy one until his death in 1888. Except on
one occasion, no ordinary father and child *could* have been happier together. Of the one misunderstanding I will speak later.

Becoming a Hatch thus, summarily, did not at once admit me to
the Hatch family inner circle, which contained Mr. Hatch's three children, Cornelius, Annie, and James and their mother, Hannah Hatch.
There must have been heart-burnings, but time made them all friendly
and loving to me (capable, dark-eyed Mrs. Hatch as well as her children).
Annie became the dearest of sisters. You will later see how her love and
mine was tested. I am sure your memory holds Annie as a part of our
family, and the picture of her bright hair, blue eyes, high forehead and
somewhat plain countenance is still yours. Perhaps, too, you found her a
student: quick, keen and clear-headed. She was twelve years my senior — a
tender-hearted woman of changing moods.

As a child I remember my mother praising me for letting her go
from me, and for going from her room back to the children's rooms by
myself *without crying.* I remember, too, Edith's passionate wails for her
mother.

"Mother Waters always gives Edith something when she goes
home," I told Mother. "You never give me anything."

"Well, what would you have me give you, dear child?"

"A herring, Mother."

Mother laughed, but I remember the herring she later gave me
with the warning that it would make me thirsty.

In the spring Mother always gave me bitter tea of poplar bark or
wormwood to help my appetite; and when a cold or a fever attacked me,
she put scratchy mullen leaves about my neck and made me sweat by putting wet sheets around me and packing me away among blankets. Oh,
how hateful that was!

There is a very early memory of riding on Mr. Daniel Nash's
shoulder over stile and over field to the "high banks" where he guarded a

crowd of boys who were going in swimming. When Mr. Nash himself plunged in my screams came, and great fear still haunts that picture.

The Indians came over the hill to our big kitchen. The squaws brought baskets strapped to their heads or hanging behind their shoulders, and sometimes, too, their little brown babies in papoose cases (a padded board). They stood the babies up beside the wall like a framed picture while they begged for scraps from the kitchen. I had a very bad dream once of being carried off in a squaw-basket. The Community treated the Indians with much consideration.

There was a great honey-suckle vine on the north side of the old Mansion House. Its yellow and purple blossoms cast an overpoweringly sweet odor into the "Little Yard," our children's yard which was at the right where there was the children's entrance to the apartments in the Mansion House. Nearby were cellar stairs. When I had to go down those stairs for shoes that the boys had blacked, I sang loudly up and down, to warn my fairies to keep the witches off.

One day my Father Hatch's granddaughter, Leonora, (you will hear more of her later) burst into the children's room out of breath with running. "Come! The doctor is cutting *your mother's head off!*" We clasped hands and flew down the long passage to Mother's door. The door was open. Mother was swathed in sheets and towels, and blood ran down from her hair. "There," said Leonora. "I told you so!" Yes, a strange man with a knife and one arm around my mother's shoulders seemed to be sawing at her head.

"Run!" whispered Leonora. "Run for my grandmother."

At first we ran silently. Then the horror overwhelmed us and we began to scream. But it was only a few steps from Mother's room to Grandma Langstaff's. She quieted our fears and led us back. I found my mother's operation for the removal of a wen over, and the doctor going. He laughed at me. She pitied me tenderly when she saw that I was still shaking with fright. "I wonder how that door came open," she said. "It's too bad that you have had this experience."

I remember death coming near when Aunt Sarah Campbell came to my mother's room for help, crying, "Oh come! I fear my father is dead — he is so strange!" *Unnoticed,* I followed my mother's hurried flight upstairs, where I saw the old gentleman, Riley Burnham, indeed dead from a quick heart failure. But death came nearer to my *affection* when Mrs. French died, and when Mr. Ransom Reed died, for I had been a favorite child to both of these dear people.

Another friend was Mr. Ellis — a friend to all children. Sometimes we made fun of this gentle person — of his strange, cracked voice — but we loved him too. He was fond of nature and all its beauties, and in long walks to the woods and hills he cultivated our fancies and opened our eyes.

We children were sometimes rude, I think, to Mr. Perkins who had a palsy—his head was ever shaking from side to side. Often we watched while he and Mr. Newhouse skillfully opened oysters in the court under the balcony of the old Mansion House. Once Mr. Perkins insisted that Marion Burnham and I eat a *raw* oyster. I cried. Marion was very angry!

We sometimes ran about in the laundry near the court, playing at hide and seek, and were tempted into going further into the nearby kitchen. This was forbidden. Once Edith Waters and I were whipped when found on the tabooed ground. We children were bidden to be quiet near Harriet Hall's room and, for a long time, near L. F. Dunn's room. These two were nervous invalids. Finally, the "Dunn Cottage" was built for L. F. D. at the bottom of the lawn.)

We saw a very stout Mrs. Toby with long skirts and great hoops, though *every other woman* wore a short dress with pantalets. Mrs. Toby, Grandma Burnham and other elderly ladies wore caps; my mother and most of the women and girls had their hair cut short about the neck.

There is another flash of memory out of the indistinct past from which so many impressions have vanished. I stood by a window. On a stairway beyond a partition I heard sudden angry shouts and a struggle. Then the noise was on the porch (I think it was in the Middle House). Then from the window came into view the sight of a man thrown by other men into a snow drift—violently thrown, without excuses. I saw the man emerge, pick up the things that had been thrown out with him, and walk away sending back loud, angry words and burning glances, shaking his fist as he shouted. That was the last act, I believe, of "The Mills War"[10]—a tiny war in our midst whose history I do not know, nor can I philosophize on its merits. A bad man was said to have been summarily cast out.

The Girls of My Class. My Stay at Wallingford

Lily[11] says we went to school first in the old Burt House, across from the Mill. I have a faint memory of the long bench in front where I sat. Lily says that Annie Hatch taught that school. There was rotation in all Community work. I remember Miss Pomeroy, Mr. Underwood, Har-

10. The Community decided that William Mills had a licentious interest in some of the younger girls. No one else was dismissed in this way.

11. Lily Dale Bailey Hutchins, later Mrs. John Cragin. Carlotta Cragin was the daughter of this marriage.

riet Worden,[12] Portia Underhill, Mrs. Charlotte Miller,[13] Mr. Freeman, Mrs. Dascombe and others, at one time and another, teaching our school — sometimes in the "Tontine," sometimes in the "Seminary."

We loved Harriet Worden as a school teacher. She read aloud to us *Dred* and *Never Too Late to Mend*. Mr. Underwood's pedagogic instincts did not allow us frequent reading in school, but when he *did* read, his reading was dramatic. We learned to pare potatoes and trim apples under the tutelage of old Mr. Levi Joslyn and Mr. William Perry. They were ever below stairs engaged in this prosaic business, and they were able to take away the thinnest skin possible from a potato or an apple. To sew, we were taught by Miss Pomeroy and Aunt Sarah Campbell. We ran on many an errand for Aunt Sarah.

I see I am here using the familiar appelation of "Aunt," attaching it unconsciously, in the old Community manner, to many names. We used "Uncle" and "Father" and "Mother," too, thus unconsciously in the old days when there were no "specialized" relationships: "Uncle John," "Uncle Dunn," "Mother Waters," "Mother Noyes," "Mother Miller," "Father Noyes," "Father Hatch." We did not use "Sister" or "Brother" as I remember, and the terms were, all of them, unused by many — though in that case, "Mr.," "Mrs." or "Miss" were coupled with the name. All we children, I think, used "Miss" in speaking to or of the younger women, and the old ladies were many of them given the title "Lady": "Miss Emily," "Miss Harriet," "Miss Ann," "Lady Burnham," "Lady Noyes" (Polly), "Lady Thayer" (Betsy). After a long time I became "Miss Jessie." When I had married Myron it was quite shocking to hear him forgetfully introducing me to a stranger as "My wife, Miss Jessie." And Beatrice McKeon to this day calls me, lovingly, "Miss Jessie."

Our class learned to sing with Aunt Helen Noyes. Rose [Hamilton] and Edith [Waters] would take the bass in the part songs, Flora [Whiting] and Mabel [Joslyn] the tenor, Lily [Hutchins] and Marion [Burnham] the soprano, Leonora [Hatch] with Edith perhaps, or Rose *and I* carried the alto. Not that *I* was depended upon to carry anything: my singing was a timid pretense. I could never be sure of getting the right note. When we had grown proficient, we sang at "Noon Meetings" and in concerts.

Now I will sketch briefly the routine of life in the Children's House. We could not become spoiled in that home of many children, yet

12. In 1870 Harriet Worden bore John Humphrey Noyes's stirpicult son, Pierrepont Burt Noyes, who, for many years, was the chief executive for Oneida Community, Limited.

13. Mrs. Charlotte Miller neé Charlotte A. Noyes, the founder's sister.

we were not neglected. Our routine was to be called at six o'clock, run to one of the children's rooms for our clothes and a dash of water, then to breakfast in the big dining room of the old Mansion House. After breakfast there was children's "Morning Meeting," where the Bible was read aloud, and we were talked to and admonished; then to work in a bee[14] somewhere, probably out of doors. School followed work until noon. After dinner there was the grown folks' Noon Meeting, and perhaps we would be called in to sing one of our songs. Then school again; then playtime when often we visited our mothers in our mothers' own rooms until supper at six; after supper, play-time again until the meeting hour of eight. Oh, the stories of those evening hours when the folks were off at meeting, and we were entertained and then put to bed by two grown-ups who took their turn at this task, and by some unknown system were chosen. The best story-tellers were Charles Joslyn and Charles Cragin, or Chloe Seymour and Harriet Worden; but there were many others almost equally as gifted and remembered. We were in bed before the "Evening Meeting" was over at nine o'clock. Of course this routine varied with the age of the child and the season of the year.

Indeed we were a happy lot — far happier than are children made tyrants by petting, or nagged by anxious and over-worked mothers. I cannot say that our individuality was much studied. Some energetic, mischievous children suffered. I was timid and anxious to please.

The force that managed the Children's Department were a "Head" and six, eight or ten helpers. (My work in later years was often as a caretaker in the Children's House.) A day for these hard-working Children's House people was from twelve noon to twelve midnight, so that they were free a half of each day for study or recreation.

Both in the school and in the Children's House were children older and younger than I. One strongly welded group was known to those who formed it as "Our class of girls." There were seven girls in the group at first (later there were more): Rose Hamilton, Lily Hutchins, Leonora Hatch, Marion Burnham, Mabel Joslyn, Edith Waters, and Jessie Baker Hatch. Carrie Bolles was added first when she came to the Community, a girl of nine years (her family joined Oneida Community in 1865). Later, Ida Blood, Isabel Brooks, and Lillian Towner came and joined our group of close friends (poor little Emily Kneeland only hovered on the edge). Because Harley Hamilton sang with us he was sometimes called a member of the class. Edith Waters was not the oldest girl of the class but she was the leader. She made a gratuitous puzzle for a stranger who asked

14. Bees were a pleasant way to gather together and work on some project — gardening, sewing, bag making, etc.

Jessie Catherine Kinsley, age 6

her name by saying, "My name is Edith Waters; my father's name is George Hamilton, and my mother's name is Louisa Tuttle." (This was when she was a tiny girl: George Hamilton was her foster-father, and she had heard her mother called by her maiden name.) Of course strangers were always puzzling over Community relationships, but this was an unnecessary confusion.

Edith's mother was wonderfully skillful and executive. Edith was like her with perhaps even greater strength of character. Edith could pick more berries than any other girl (two quarts to my one) and not a green berry in her box. She could clean knives "like lightning," we used to say. The table knives and forks were steel and we used brick-dust and cork to polish several hundred every morning. Edith's needle was swift, too, and dexterous. The broom went fast and thoroughly in her hands. As type-setter in the printing office she could not equal either Carrie or Marion but she did much work. She grew tall and straight. She was gay, light-hearted and beautiful—dark-haired, dark-eyed and fine featured. Her voice was that of a contralto. She sang well, and she and Leonora and Carrie played almost equally well on the piano, though I believe that Edith was more proficient for her years. Most conscientious and truly re-ligious, she could think for herself—and the power to think was what made her our leader.

Rose Hamilton and Lily Bailey were born the year before Edith and I. Rose was dark; Lily was fair. Rose was a dwarf and hunchbacked; Lily was vigorous. Rose sang bass; Lily sang soprano.

How well I remember Rosy's long sickness which began, I think, in her fifth year. It was rickets. I remember her water-bed and her mother's care of her. We were all her knights as long as she lived, neverthe-less, Lily was her mate and special protector. Rose had a good mind, un-like her dwarfed body, and her spiritual power was leaven to our class. She was a peacemaker. She was jovial. Lily was jovial, too. I wish I had her memory. She would make a racy and interesting story full of incident, where I remembered so little. Rosy died when she was nineteen. She was at Wallingford at the time.

Lily's marriage brought her two children. Her daughter and my son married and have made us grandmothers of the same dear babes. We are, however, more than related by the marriage of our children—the old tie of Community sisterhood still holds.

What a happy, graceful, and vivacious little girl was Leonora Hatch. She loved Edith just as I did. She found book learning difficult. She was passionate, headstrong, and was subjected to much criticism. Life carried her along on dramatic wings. She fell headlong into loves and later into marriage. She was always a pioneer. Drama, almost tragedy, has always been her portion.

Marion Burnham's birthday was one day ahead of Mabel Joslyn's, in May, 1859. Marion was a curly-headed, roly-poly child—quick of action, quick to learn. Mabel Joslyn was slow. Marion was full of energy and will-power, of a fiery temper—though her little tempers blew quickly away and left us always in generous sunshine. Mabel, though she had a firm will, was not willful, but she was serious-minded. Both of these girls were singers. Mabel's voice was much benefitted by training af-ter 1879. There are some natures in which the child-like qualities are not lost in maturity—Mabel's was of that character, simple and direct. In 1899, when she died at the age of forty, her hair was white. Marion mar-

ried Dr. Noyes and bore him a son, Raymond. A second marriage,
through which Dr. Noyes remained her friend and helper, brought her another son, Richard Nolan.

Most of the mates of my youth (those now living) are grandmothers as I am. An unusually close association such as ours must have
had its psychological effects on our lives, and in fact it has left links that
disassociation has not broken.

I will leave personalities now and go on with my desultory memories of events.

The years 1860 through 1864 were the years of this country's Civil
War. Our Community men did not go away to fight, partly because the
draft passed us by through accident, and partly, too, because they were so
imbued with the importance of their own socialistic endeavors as to *believe* those endeavors to be "quite as significant" or, I quote, *"More important to their country and to the world than the issues of Union or Slav-
ery."* However, Myron, your father, told me many years later that he was
almost persuaded to "forsake all" and enlist with many of his Vermont
cousins in a regiment going South from his native state. The struggle in
him was *so* great that, looking back on it, he could hardly understand
what held him. It was not, he thought, a lack of courage or the instinct to
fight, but the conviction of his parents and his own youthful belief in the
divine mission of communism to right all the wrongs of humanity, and to
bring about ultimate unity and equality for all men — to allow no North,
no South, no slave and no master.

Times were hard on *us* then, financially, as well as for the rest of
the country. Wool was high and cotton *priceless* and not to be found on
the market. Mother had the care of the bedding in the Community. Washing and carding cotton with hand-carders to thus repair quilts and com-
fortables occupied much of her time. I forever found her card-card-
carding or piecing bed quilts out of old dresses in the upper rooms of the
"Tool House."

One day she was crying. The cards were flying back and forth
over the cotton. I was anxious and frightened. "What is the matter,
Mama?" "Oh, child, our President — our President Lincoln has been
shot!" How little that meant to me. How lightly that war passed over me,
leaving hardly a memory.

In 1863 came a terrible scourge upon the Oneida Community.
Diphtheria carried away several young people. One hundred and twelve
persons were sick. Seventy-two of them were severely sick. Five died. My
sister, Mary, was very sick, and while Mother cared for her, I, who was
less dangerously ill, was nursed carefully and lovingly by Miss Chloe Seymour. Chloe had lost her only child, a remarkable boy, in October, 1862,

and I can remember hearing what I called "tears in her voice" as she sang to me quaint Scotch songs. I was in tears often because I hated the frequent swabbing of my throat with alum and water or burnt alum. Finally ice was used. I loved ice and soon got well. There were no more deaths from diphtheria after ice was used.

In another sickness, in 1865, Maria Barron mothered me. I loved her, too. I think Mother was then in Wallingford. That year was an unfortunate one for Mother. She fell down a flight of stairs — stairs that were too perpendicular and dark to be safe — and broke a bone in her left foot. The injury was diagnosed as a sprain, and no doctor was called in. The result was a long lameness of seven years during which the bone knit together with ligaments and Mother went upon crutches. She returned to Oneida Community from Wallingford Community in 1866 or '67 greatly depressed, and I was her greatest comfort. Sister Mary was then very busy. Alas! the powers in the Children's House and my Father Hatch felt sure that some passing illness of mine was due to Mother's "bad influence," and I was sent to Wallingford. How happy I was to go and only childishly sad to leave Mother. It was years afterward that I realized what Mother suffered by this separation, and from what she was tempted to feel was a deliberate cruelty toward her.

A picture of me was taken by D. Edson Smith in the South Garret of the Mansion House on the day I left for Wallingford, in August 1867. While I was in the attic excitedly posing for my picture, my class of girls were sitting on a row of trunks below, crying and criticizing *Harley* because he did not cry over my going. Harley wrote to me apologizing for *not crying*. He said *"I would have cried if I could, but I couldn't."*

You may imagine this journey an astounding event to me. Moreover, I made it in company with two most distinguished Community people, Mrs. Harriet Skinner and Mr. Hamilton.[15] I rode upon a railway for the first time and was car-sick. At Albany we left the stuffy train and went down the Hudson River by night on a boat full of golden stairways, deceptive mirrors and red, plush furniture. I slept in an upper berth after an evening of intense excitement. When we arrived in New York, as mythical and unrealizable as Arabian Nights to me then, we spent some days at the St. Mark's Place Apartments rented by the Oneida Community for its agents.

That first morning I remember that we stumbled upon G. D. Allen[16] on a crowded street as he was hurrying, a bit late, to meet us at the

15. Harriet Skinner neé Harriet H. Noyes, the founder's sister. Erastus Hamilton, trained in Syracuse as an architect, supervised construction of the Mansion House and was for many years Noyes's right-hand man.

16. George D. Allen was the son of Henry Allen, Sr., who donated his Wallingford property to the Oneida Community. George became one of Jessie's suitors.

wharf. I discovered him as he went past us unseeing and otherwise un-
seen. Well, he congratulated my bright eyes and then took my shrinking
hand and kindly led me through the din and across streets that seemed im-
passable. This is my first memory of George. I did not know then how
much he would afterward mean to me. I wish you children had known
him so that you could join your memories with all my knowledge and
make as true a picture of him as you have of your father. He was a man
well worth knowing. He was not perhaps a man as large intellectually as
his sister, Harriet, or perhaps even his brother, Henry, but he was *noble,
good, true, great-hearted,* like your father: a *Community knight-errant.*

When we left New York City to finish our journey to Wallingford
we took the Sound boat to New Haven. Of course I was a little sea-sick
but I saw some porpoises! At New Haven I saw something perhaps more
exciting: "Boyle." My summer readings with my Father Hatch had made
the names of Mr. Noyes's old Perfectionist friends and antagonists familiar: "Dutton," "Boyle" and "Weld." As we passed through the New Haven
Station, Mrs. Skinner said, "Look, Jessie, there is James Boyle."[17] I saw
a dapper, elderly man with white, hanging hair, a straight back and legs,
in colonial costume—more distinguished to me, perhaps, by this odd
costume of three-cornered hat, flaring coat-tails, knee-breeches and
buckles at knee and ankle, than by his face, though I believe that, too,
was interesting. A young lady was hanging on his arm; they made a fine
picture.

I had been a thin, pale child, but the change to Wallingford im-
proved my health. I grew tall and began to put on a little flesh and color.
At Wallingford I did not find children of my own age. Flora Whiting,
Rosamond Underwood and Arthur Bloom were there but they were older
than I; while two boys, Ormond Burt and Harold Noyes, were younger.
Soon I entered upon various duties and, curiously, while I had lessons of
Augusta Hamilton in the morning, in the afternoon I taught Ormond and
Harold to read, to spell and to cypher. How far was I advanced in these
rudimentary branches of learning at nine? I do not know. A good
memory makes mental tasks easy, but I was not a precocious child. I imagine the boys had a more efficient teacher in the forenoon. Yet reading
was already a delight. In the sitting room of the Allen House I was inclined to curl up with a book in the corner of the black, horse-hair-covered
lounge where I would remain for hours, if not routed out by someone
who noticed my pale face and sent me out of doors. I imagine that almost
any book was grist and eagerly gone through. At Wallingford all kinds of
books were accessible. At Oneida the Children's House was rather remote

17. From 1834 to 1836 James Boyle of New Haven, and John Humphrey Noyes
published a religious journal called *The Perfectionist.*

from the Library. *Swiss Family Robinson,* bound volumes of magazines and *Adam Bede* left their impression on me at Wallingford.

Not all of my duties were attractive, nor were they carried out to the satisfaction of a big family of grown-up people. It was a great change from the Children's House. A small, perpendicular flight of stairs—the cause of Mother's dreadful lameness—was my care; also the inevitable emptying of slops, some "devil's work" in the printing office, and the aforesaid delightfully *important* work of *teaching* Ormond and Harold! I also helped Miss Mary Prindle make a great many beds. One new and delightful task was *washing clothes.* At Oneida Community, I believe, there was already machinery in the laundry. At Wallingford there *may* have been washing machines, but I remember only the long set tubs in the middle of the room with Susie W. and a dozen others bending over them from either side, and the odor of steam and soap and suds. I would secure a stool beside Augusta and with my hands in the suds, up and down on a board I scrubbed my white stockings and other people's handkerchiefs. This task came only on Monday mornings. It began very early and ended in the clothes-yard where I "passed pins" amid the flapping sheets. Many busy hands made light work.

Quite my most *hated* task was wiping dishes, morning, noon and night. Again Wallingford was behind Oneida: no fine, self-emptying, copper-lined dish-washing receptacles, no rinsing frames—only pans in the kitchen sink with adjoining shelves—so the need of wiping, wiping, wiping dishes, a hateful and *fearful* wiping, because *I broke things.* Here I helped Mrs. Abbie Burnham, Aunt Ellen Miller, and Flora Whiting. The sound of crashing crockery was hard on Mrs. Burnham's nerves: "That child breaks everything she touches! You *must* be more careful, Jessie!" or "There now! Oh, what a careless girl! Why *do* you break things? Flora doesn't." A dreadful spirit seemed to be with my hands. Perhaps my *subconscious* self took revenge for timidity and *monotony* by these loud crashes. At last I broke something in Aunt Ellen's room, and then I pulled a shade down so hard in Augusta's room that it fell out of its fixtures and smashed the choicest of possessions. Public criticism did not exorcise my little devil, though it was meekly received. Finally dear Aunt Ellen Miller (so loved by your father and George Allen both) found the psychological cure. She took me aside and told me she knew that I did not mean to be naughty and careless; I must begin all over again to be good and careful, for she was going to give me a fine present if I went one whole week without breaking a single thing! The *spell* was broken. I earned or, rather, gained from Aunt Ellen a bottle of cologne!

It was glorious out-of-doors at Wallingford: a mountain, a river and woods filled with great rocks. There were barns, too, to play in, and sheep pens to watch. A favorite game for Ormond and Harold was to drop into the sheep pen, attract the attention of the ram, and then, before the latter could assault them, they would run to the gate and climb to the top bar. One day Ormond was overtaken and knocked down by the ram as his dash brought him near the gate. I was a perfect coward, but my sense of responsibility sent me over the gate to rescue Ormond who lay quite stunned. I succeeded in getting him on his feet and part-way over the gate before the creature charged again. This time he banged Ormond's legs into the fence and made him howl. Ormond also insulted a cow with a bit of verse caught from elocution class . . .

> How, now, shall we turn Turk?
> Let's kill, slay, slaughter!

To this invitation the cow responded with a hook of her horn under the boy's eye, making a tear that, fortunately, was not disfiguring.

Another adventure was connected with Ormond. One warm day, Constance (Mrs. Reeve) took Ormond and me to bathe in the Quinnipiac, a wooded stream running through meadows at the foot of a long hill called "Mt. Tom." We put on aprons for bathing suits, and Ormond, six years old, and I, ten, remained in a shallow bay cut off from the main stream by a chained log, while Constance, with a parting word to us to be good children, ran along the river bank for some way upstream, there to drop into the swift current and have an easy swim down again. An old boat attached to a tether floated out into the stream beyond the log. Ormond secured an oar from this boat and threw it over the log. It began to float away down-stream. In a flash, with indignant scolding of Ormond, I went over the log to catch and save the oar. The water was deep, but I was a good swimmer, and all went well until I reached the oar and grasped it with both hands, exulting. Very promptly I went to the bottom of the river. Water filled my nose and throat, and as I came to the surface, I used my hands, *not to swim*, but to clear my face. Getting one breath, I felt myself going down again and with a scream and my mouth *wide open* I went under water a second time. Then it seemed I could not get up: my breath was gone. I was in a panic. But I rose again with a scream and went down a third time. Then I felt something touch my back and I found myself under the boat. How I got out from under the boat and gained hold of the rope to which Constance found me speechlessly clinging, I do not know. My next memory is of being rolled about by Constance on the floor of the bath-house. I was weak and sick for some time but I held my tongue about the adventure, as I promised Constance I would.

I remained at Wallingford over a year and then returned to Oneida in 1869.

Return to Oneida Community. School. Graduation from Children's House. Second Visit to Wallingford. My Sister, Mary. My Clothes

In 1869 the Middle House, which had stood between the old Mansion House and the newly built brick Mansion, was moved down the front declivity of lawns and across the road to a new site. The next year the old Mansion House was torn down.

A long South Wing was to be added to the new Mansion House and this, like the Middle House, was for some time to be called the Children's House.

After the Middle House was moved across to the East side of the road, it was thereafter called the Seminary. The Seminary has been moved this year (1914) again toward the old Mill and is called the "Elms." Helen's and Kenneth's baby[18] has been born under the roof that covered so many Community babies.

In the Seminary I went to school with the other girls. Mrs. Bushnell was our teacher. She was a natural evangelist, filled with religious fervor, and often school would become a revival meeting. In the course of one of Mrs. Bushnell's earnest talks I became convicted of unbelief and sin. I can remember the terror and pain of my mental state. At this time I had been reading aloud with my Father Hatch Mr. Noyes's *Religious Experience*. Both in school and during the Children's Meetings in the Children's House I had learned to "Confess Christ." The formula, "I confess Christ in me a good spirit," had been a concise prayer that made my conscientious little soul contented. Now, for some reason, that prayer was not enough. I felt afraid of the devil and sin; I think they were almost synonymous. I do not well remember intermediate experiences but I do remember this great pain, and then one day suddenly saying aloud in school, "I confess Christ in me my savior from sin," and bursting into tears. Mrs. Buhnell was by my side in a moment, full of exhortation and comfort. But with those words had come the understanding of Faith. Christ *in me* seemed the surest thing in the world; there was no more doubt of keeping out the devil. Christ would keep him out; all good was

18. Louise Miller, born on June 9, 1914, was the daughter of Kenneth Hayes Miller and Helen Pendleton, his second wife, both artists living in New York City. Kenneth's grandparents were John Miller and Charlotte Noyes Miller, the founder's sister. Kenneth's father was George N. Miller, a leader in the business affairs of the Community; Kenneth's mother was Annie Kelly Miller, the daughter of Daniel and Lavinia Kelly, early joiners of the Community.

The Mansion House, c. 1900

right at hand. I was as happy as a lark. Fear was gone completely. I had several times of earnest conviction later, but this, the first, was most vivid.

Before I left the Children's House, I went to Wallingford for a second visit. I left my mother feeling much better, but not yet cured of her lameness, as she was still walking with crutches.

In the Children's Meetings at Oneida Community I had sometimes been criticized in a general way. I felt very *grown-up* when at Wallingford Community I was advised to "offer yourself for criticism." Although my throat was choked with crying when my criticism was finished — for I had been told of faults — yet the loving praise given was stimulating and I was really happy. I count all of my criticisms — except one, perhaps — as Pierrepont does his whippings, as blessings. "Mutual Criticism" was a curious Community custom. One offered one's self for criticism voluntarily or was *asked* occasionally, perhaps several times in a year or even as often as once a month. I imagine that when the ball of criticism was set rolling in a group of critics it was sometimes too easy to throw in the *accusations* (as well as the praise) and say, "I have thought of that in B____." or, "I have noticed *this*."

Once H. suffered a severe criticism of which notes were taken. The notes filled eighteen pages. He went to Mr. Noyes with them.

"In spite of it all I am a good citizen," said H.

"Yes," said Mr. Noyes, "You are. And don't you know that in a spring freshet there is always a lot of floodwood — don't be discouraged." He said Mrs. Miller would meet him after a criticism. "Cheer up" she would say, "Be happy — we all love you."

I think such helps over hard places have been remembered longer than the criticism.

It is a fact that all the members of Mr. Noyes's family and all whom they *loved* came under the fire of criticism (legitimately administered — not back-biting). Beyond all others in the Community, Mrs. Miller, Mrs. Skinner, George Noyes, George Miller, Helen Miller, Tirzah Miller and their associates were continually in the flame. Helen said she sometimes felt she had not a moment's peace.[19]

I suppose criticism made of Community life a sort of "training-school," like, yet unlike, those schools for teachers where their work and ways with pupils are observed, and then later commented on and criticized by fellow students and professors. Mannerisms, ways, faults, improvement, merit — all were subjects for comment and advice in a Community criticism. The system was devised by J. H. N. and a group of students at Andover when the former was there at school in 1832. He took his turn of criticism there, found it excellent, and so transplanted the process to Putney and then to Oneida Community. J. H. N. was not exempt from criticism in the early days of the Community as he became later when — as Emily Kelly tells me — he said that in his case criticism became a farce. In the *end,* in Canada, he asked Myron for a criticism.

I remember the mental chaos I would find myself in when, after a criticism, I would leave the friendly group of critics, which I myself had requested to convene, and go away by myself to take thought and cry a little. "I am certainly a fool," self-depreciation would clamor. "I do believe I have improved in control of my tongue, for Miss Harriet thinks so, and Miss Emily says I am more careful." These were the voices of comfort. "Oh, I must try harder to toe-out and stand straight!" "And I am sorry I hurt M's feelings about that box." "Perhaps what Miss Chloe says about my temper is true, too." "But, oh! how glad I am George M. said that there was no lack of *desire in me to do right.* Yet how *can* I be as good as I want to be!" There was great relief in prayer, in the *hope* that "Christ

---

19. Mrs. Skinner was Harriet Noyes, another of John Humphrey Noyes's sisters. George Washington Noyes was J. H. N.'s brother. Helen and Tirzah Miller were daughters of John and Charlotte Miller.

within" might thus be helped to shine through the faulty cover of the "outer man."

The first winter of my second stay at Wallingford Community saw me living week after week in New Haven. There was a little home there for the students going to Yale. I was nearly twelve years old — small for my age — and I went there to serve as table waiter, to run errands and to help busy Mrs. Burt and Emily Kelly with other household duties. It was most annoying when sweeping off the front porch or the iron balcony to find myself observed by a row of little boys who made remarks about my *Community* costume of skirt and pantalets. At the weekend the house was generally closed, and all went up to Wallingford Community for over Sunday. W. A. Hinds[20] was a student and plagued me by saying that I was really not worth much since the conductor on the train thought me too small to ask for my ticket. I remember Mrs. Burt and Emily Kelly there, and George Miller and Charles Cragin and Charles Burt. This must have been in 1870–'71.

During the latter part of my stay at Wallingford, in the summer of 1871, I was afflicted with fever and ague. Many of the people at Wallingford Community were likewise afflicted with chills. I suppose mosquitoes brought the infection, and the infection itself was thought by some to be an importation from the South when the soldiers came home, for before that time, Wallingford had been a healthy locality. This sudden virulence could not have been due to the new lake making breeding places for mosquitoes, since the Community were only *surveying* in 1871. The lake was not flooded until 1872.

Everyone was kind to me through this sickness, though no one took especial care of me. I roomed with Annie Hatch. Annie, though a victim of ague too, would cover me with blankets during my chill and give me water through the hours of fever. In the morning I would crawl out and be about until four in the afternoon, then again would come the chill, the following fever and often I was in a delirium. My spleen enlarged; although emaciated, my clothing at the waistline would not meet by six inches.

At last, in September, 1871, I returned to Oneida Community with the "Refuse Lot," guided by J. H. N. who had escaped the chills and fever.[21] We were sorry bits of humanity. Our clothing was certainly pecu-

---

20. William A. Hinds became one of the most prominent business leaders, first in the Oneida Community and later in Oneida Community, Limited.

21. In 1870 Mr. Noyes's brother, George, died at Wallingford from spleen enlargement disease. Joel Higgins, Sophronia Higgins's brother, died of this trouble in November 1871. (Jessie Kinsley's note)

liar, we were sallow and sick and quite as typical in appearance, I would imagine, as "poor white trash." I wonder what our fellow travellers thought of us. Mr. Noyes was kind and unperturbed. I remember him in a seat forward of where I was with Annie, sitting with folded arms: thinking. Thinking in his case was indicated by a rapid up and down movement of his eyebrows that wrinkled his forehead. I do not remember all who were numbered in the Refuse Lot—Annie Hatch, Alice Ackley, Mr. Herrick, Ormond, Mr. Bradley (two others, I think). I had my usual shake and fever as we journeyed west. When we arrived at Oneida Village we found our friends knew not of our coming, and upon Mr. Noyes devolved the necessity of borrowing mules and an omnibus to get us over the four intervening miles to the Community home. In the darkness, inside that omnibus, we sick folk felt apprehensive, for we somewhat doubted Mr. Noyes's skill as a driver of mules, but outside on the box he was jubilant, and we did arrive safely in due time.

The change from Wallingford to Oneida and the administration of quinine (taken also with *criticism* as an *antidote to evil*) worked a quick cure for most of us. I have a vivid memory of Edith Waters shouting with me at the ague devil as it gave me a final shake, to "Get out! Get out! Let Jessie get warm!" Most devils have a reputation for being over-warm.

I was glad to get back to Oneida Community—to live again near Mother, Mary and Edith. My mother was kind and wise: she always held both my love and confidence. Mary and I were separated by ten years in age, yet I had grown taller than my diminutive sister. She became my second mother and, though she held places of responsibility in Community work, she found time, when my clothes were no longer made in the Children's House, to help me with their making and mending.

Now in memory I come to a momentous change, much greater than the one from Wallingford to Oneida: my class of girls were graduated from the Children's House. There were no exercises. We were simply told that we were old enough to be good citizens of the big Community and were to go often to Mr. Noyes's sister, Mrs. Miller, or to Mabel's mother, Harriet Joslyn, for *counsel.* We were advised also to "offer" ourselves frequently for criticism.

It was now, too, that I grew closer than ever before to both my mother and my sister, though not without the danger, I suppose, of accusations of "philoprogenitiveness" or "idolatry" if our love seemed to manifest itself as a *special love.*

Graduating from the Children's House brought to our group a coveted honor. We attended the big Evening Meeting. We no longer heard stories during the "Children's Hour." At eight o'clock, with our sewing or tatting and our lighted lamp, and with all the gathering crowd of older people, we found our seats in the Hall. We went to little octagonal tables and beside these we sat down to sew and to listen. Most of the women were busied with sewing. The men sat about in groups or rows. Near the center of the Hall the "news reporter" and the "letter reader" and Mr. and Mrs. Noyes or other executives took seats near a larger lamp-lighted table. I think the old hymn books were passed about, and there was singing and an accompaniment played on a small harmonium. Sometimes my class of girls (with Harley) sang a part song or glee. (More often, however, we sang at Noon Meeting, another family gathering after the mid-day meal, more—as I remember it—a *social* gathering, not quite so serious or long as the Evening Meeting.) Then the news reporter read a quick report of news gleaned from weekly and daily papers, followed up by a reading of the *Wallingford Journal* and letters from our men abroad on the road or from strangers. How often the news reporter found in the papers queer garbled tales of our own Community life. The most amusing letters read were from people who wanted to "join."

Sometimes business discussion was next in order, but usually business was left to the Sunday morning "Business Meetings." At other times there was an especial public criticism to which the unaccustomed, timid hearts beat fast. The last half hour of the Meeting was, as a rule, a time for religious expression. Mr. Noyes frequently had something to say in the form of a "Talk," and his thought was commented on by others. Meeting ended, not with a *set* prayer but with our own peculiar form called *"Confessing Christ,"* when we would express our desires and emotions in confessing Christ in us a guide and leader. It meant a tremendous screwing up of courage for me to speak aloud in meeting. But occasionally, when I heard my dearest Edith say quite loudly, "I confess Christ in me a soft heart," then I would follow with the same prayer, or, "I confess Christ in me a *good spirit,"* or, "I confess Christ my *helper* neither to give nor to take offense." A warm glow would follow this effort along with a sense of being able to be a better girl; and I judge there was nothing more sincere than these little prayers, not alone to me but to others as well. They came bursting forth from many hopes and experiences.[22]

More about J. H. Noyes, His Wife, Sisters and Other Leaders of Oneida Community. My Sister's Child and Other Children

In the preface to the publication in book form of J. H. N.'s *Home Talks,* the editors, Alfred Barron and George Miller, make this comment

---

22. Evening Meetings bore the character I have described both at Oneida Community and Wallingford Community, as well as at the smaller homes: the Villa and Willow Place. (Jessie Kinsley's note)

about the talks: "The *spirit* of the Home Talks has always been the life and breath of the Oneida Community." As with my mother as well as myself, for a long time these talks did, in a certain sense, become life and breath.

Family Communism

Communism, dreadful bugbear as it is on the large scale, is the fundamental principle of every family. The man keeps no account with his wife, but cares for her as for himself. Man and wife keep no account with their children but regard them as their own flesh. This is the theory, at least of the family compact. Thus all children are born in communism and for the sweetest part of their lives are nourished and brought up in communism. They come in contact with the opposite principle of trading selfishness only when they begin to leave the family circle and mingle with the world.

Communism is really the very essence of home. The man who turns back in imagination from the desert of common life to the oasis of his childhood and sings, "Home Sweet, Sweet Home" is unconsciously thinking of communism and longing to return to it.

The communism which begins with marriage does not stop at the first generation, but reaches the grandchildren and, like a light shining in a dark place, is reflected back to parents and grandparents, and glances far and wide among uncles and aunts and cousins until it is lost in distance.

And we must not imagine that this family feeling which thus radiates unity in little circles over the world, has its seat exclusively or even chiefly in consanguinity. On the contrary, its very beginning is in the love that arises between man and woman as such without blood-relationship. Husbands and wives are related to each other only as members of the human race; and yet their love is the source of the love between brothers and sisters and cousins and kindred. They are the real founders of the family community. So if the old saying is true that "blood is stronger than water," we must add to it that "love is stronger than blood."

Thus it appears not only that we are all born and brought up in communism, but that one of our very strongest natural proclivities in adult life is for *communism with non-relatives* and the founding of small communities. With such germs in our nature and education, it cannot be so difficult as many imagine for us to fall in with the spirit of progress (which is really the spirit of Pentecost) and allow science and inspiration to organize family-communism on the grandest scale. It will be but returning home; only we have to give up the old one-horse wagon for two, and go by the great railroad train that carries a meeting-house-full.

His speech was not too rapid. It was without much ornament of elocution though forcefully enunciated— of a "searching penetration," a "subtlety in common sense," an "experienced wisdom," and a "destructive tolerance" that would make it remarkable in any company. Inside of all expression, moreover, and finding voice sometimes in his talk, was his own belief in his "divine commission." There are memories of him in his room — early memories and later ones. These are complex, both welcome and unwelcome, bound up with emotions and experiences of many years.

In his room in the North Tower, and later in the room made for him in the new wing (a very plain, unfurnished room with his mother's beautiful old clock for a striking ornament), people of the society sought him for counsel, went to him with complaints or new plans, stayed to play a game of cards or dominoes and sometimes went to him for love. His many children went there. There, as well as in Meeting, he gave the discourses we called "Home Talks."

Beginning at this time (1870 or '71) and at intervals during succeeding years, I read aloud to "Mother Noyes."[23] As I have told you before, we were taught to hold J. H. N. very sacredly in our thought as inspired of God, and there were other leaders that inspired awe, but Mother Noyes was the very center of affection and reverence. Mrs. Harriet Skinner wrote of her, "Her spirit is inside of the Community character, and has done more to inspire it than any other human influence except Mr. Noyes." I think Mrs. Noyes lived in a world filled with faith and hope. She saw a providence in everything that happened. She once told me that her "peace was like a river." I think Mr. Noyes admired her more than any other person and her devotion to him was complete — in fact their understanding of each other seemed not to fail. As I remember her then, she was not bent, her step was somewhat shuffling though quick, her heavy gray hair was short and curly and worn straight across the neck at the back. Her figure was of medium height and weight, her dress was the pantaletted short dress, always of calico; her eyes were deep-set in a somewhat rugged face — full of intellectual thought and spiritual beauty. You can imagine what those hours of reading meant to me. I think Mother Noyes loved me, too — I cannot remember that she ever sharply criticized any of us girls. Sometimes the other girls joined our reading, but more often we two were alone. We read the Bible through more than once. Often we read J. H. N.'s talks. Sometimes we read poetry or history, sometimes novels. I read aloud easily. Mother Noyes sewed. There was a very practical side to this association, too, for she taught me to sew and *mend* especially.

Her room was a storeroom of *useful* things as well as of books and papers. Its nooks and corners were full, the bureaus and stands piled with boxes, the bed covered with clippings and writing material.

23. "Mother Noyes" was Harriet Holton Noyes, whom J. H. Noyes married in 1838.

In later years, at the Stone Cottage in Niagra Falls, she read Greek and Latin and Hebrew and studied botany—and once, when there, I asked her what new thing she was studying: "Oh, now—well, now I am chiefly learning the lessons of old age, and you must know they are good lessons."

My memory of Mrs. Charlotte Miller is of a gentle teacher who made English History delightful—a loving friend who always made criticism seem like Love, and a gentlewoman who wanted me to keep my hands clean and to stand straight, sit erect and "breathe deep."

My association with Mrs. Skinner was never on the intimate footing that daily reading and studying gave to my connection with Mrs. Noyes and Mrs. Miller. You will see later how she helped my marriage-romance. I once had preserved several lovely letters from her but I must have lost or destroyed them. After my marriage, she sometimes visited Myron and me.

There was unspeakable reverence for the beauty of her character in my heart. I wanted to be like her. I am sure all three of these women would have left with you, could you have known them, that rare savor that clings in your memory for George Miller. They could criticize without personal animus; they could reconcile a sore heart to see its fault; they could stimulate ambition to rise out of littleness of spirit, both for itself and others. They were great hearted and made you feel great hearted. I think Mrs. Fanny Leonard and Sarah Dunn in a minor degree were in the same way noble as leaders in the Community.

Another word about my sister Mary—in 1872 she was one chosen by the Community to bear a child. This gave her great happiness for she loved the father of her child and adored children. But misfortune came, for the fine boy whom she bore was stillborn because of hard labor. Dear, dear Mary, what a sad heart was hers—what suffering!—the greater, too, since she was told by the doctor that successful child-bearing would be impossible for her. The father of her child was afterward married to the mother of his later offspring (when the Community break-up came), but his will toward Mary was always to be kind. When she was dying in 1887, he comforted her by a visit of farewell. She gave him her watch to carry home to his wife.

Letter from the "Girls" (Classmates). We Enter the Social Life of Oneida Community. Theodore R. Noyes. Beginning of the Great Disaffection

After graduating from the Children's House our lives—I am speaking of "my class of girls"—were as well ordered as were the lives of other Community women. We were given work in the printing office, the kitchen or laundry, and after a few years we went back into the Children's House sometimes as caretakers of the children there. The scheme of work was planned out as your agents' work is planned, by people of ability in that line (often by Sarah Dunn, Mrs. Thayer and Louisa Waters). In work there was change and rotation which kept life from becoming monotonous. Then there were frequent bees. We were called early to pick peas or berries, and again in the evening we went into the fields or raked the lawns in merry companies. I remember one spring when my class of girls were house-cleaners, with Cornelia Worden (Wayland-Smith) as head laborer. She taught us not to miss dirt in corners but to work upon honor. We went swiftly forward over a great field.

Out of school hours there was much baby-tending for us young girls, for in the late sixties little groups of *stirpicultural* babies began to arrive in the Community circle. These were the outcome of high hopes for race betterment, and as may be imagined, were *sometimes* the signs of obedience and self-sacrifice on the part of the parents — but they were splendid children (only one excepted). Beginning with Horatio's class, I suppose there was hardly a baby that I did not roll about in a baby carriage, or mind at meal time to relieve a mother. I think I must have shown aptitude for this work, for later I was one of the Children's House workers month in and month out — that was more often my work than any other. If I had *only* kept my diaries of that time full of tales about these babies and children.

Ordinarily our work was done separately. We roomed with one or perhaps two of the girls, or with some older person. (I remember sleeping on a very rolling, hot feather-bed with Mrs. Bushnell, who had first taken off her wig and then taken out two sets of teeth.) Many causes made frequent changes in the Community life: one could ask for movement to Wallingford, the Villa, Willow Place[24] or New York City if he desired. The rooming committee must have had some problems to solve.

Very often Edith and I were roommates. Already then Edith must have shown symptoms of consumption (we called it catarrh), for a wise doctor told her to sleep winter and summer with wide-open windows.

We still went to school. Later we joined classes for elective studies. There was High School started under Dr. Noyes and Joseph Skinner — I do not think it lasted long. Mrs. Dascombe had a sort of Young Ladies School with us, and we must have been ill-mannered for I remember before she came, that there were great expectations of good to

24. Willow Place was located about one mile north of the Mansion House. The trap factory was located there. This is now the city of Sherrill, New York.

come to our *manners* from association with her. But there was some disappointment in this expectation, as Mrs. D. hardly commanded respect from us for good manners or good sense.

The girls who took up musical studies were given time for practice. Aunt Helen and Mrs. Bloom taught us to sing and play the piano. The piano was put into the Dunn Cottage at the back of the lawn where practice could be exercised upon it all day long without disturbing sensitive nerves.

Letter written to Carrie at Wallingford. I was fourteen.

O. C. July 29th, 1872

Dear Carrie,

I have a little time so thought I would write to you. I guess you are busy now by the amount of work the journal reported.

Croquet is all the game now. Folks go out and play all the time. It is so nice to have Father back again, he is quite well. Edith, Marion and myself room again over to the Villa.

Mr. George Miller goes over to the Villa to meeting every night and stays all night most always, is it not nice? I practice every day. Mr. George brought *My Summer in a Garden* here and I have been reading it. I *laughed* and *laughed*.

Clock is striking ten, singing school time. Must *stop*.

Jessie

Religious training and a naturally reasonable disposition made me anxious to do right, and also made me fearful of *"self-seeking."* I was, I imagine, a little afraid to be especially happy over anything and often asked for criticism as a devout Catholic would go to confession.

There came a time when we entered the social life[25] of the Community. I will not speak too intimately of that. Looking back upon it, I do not wholly understand it, nor do I unreservedly approve of all of that experience. I see faults of a grave nature. Perhaps there was "self-seeking" in the conduct of some; nevertheless, the thought to *forestall stolen loves* and to make *desire legitimate* was, I believe, the purpose of those in authority — those who managed our lives — while in our hearts was innocence and struggle for unselfishness, and toward Mr. Noyes, loyalty as to one almost *divine*.

I was sixteen when I loved G. A. [George Allen] The love began

25. Sexual life.

Jessie Catherine Kinsley, 1874

in a romantic way and was a part of my happy life for years. At length I saw him become interested in a woman greatly my superior in looks and in mentality, and because I would not then strive for what I thought would be selfishly sought, we drifted apart. I cannot tell you much about this part of my life in the Community because it is too strange to be understood. With my present growth I cannot, as I said before, look back upon it with understanding or gauge the depth of my own innocence. That I was truly innocent, simple and modest, I believe for a certainty. Other girls may have had exciting experiences. I may have been a prig. Surely I was a Puritan *trained* to seek first the Kingdom of Heaven in every action. (I do not mean that I succeeded.) I cannot remember being criticised for special love. I loved G. [George Allen] and C. [Charles Cragin] and O. [Orrin Wright]. Yet always with reserve; unreserved love came when Community life was over and I married Myron, your father.

 Dear Edith, if imagination carries you back into the unusual past that I cannot describe, you must think that religious devotion was a part of it all. In its religion you will find the key to this Community life. We applied religious phraseology to everyday life curiously and, if I mistake not, without hypocrisy (truly without hypocrisy to those of us who knew no other existence, no other explanation). The fulfillment of Complex Marriage was an "Ordinance"—a loving "ordinance of fellowship"—

more earnest than the kiss or the everyday handclasp, no doubt, but simple, sacred, without guile or unrestrained passion: "a communion of spirit and body." "What we love in a particular tune is *music,* what we love in love is God" — that was a Community saying, too. I have no doubt that these ideas helped in the making of unselfishness, and I suppose they helped make the discipline of Male Continence possible. Of course, as I have said before, grave mistakes were made, and all experience did not reach the heights of religious hope, but *Christ first* was fundamental in theory and led to "Ascending Fellowship." When Miss B., then our mentor, one day very seriously introduced this subject to us, she called it "Godly Fellowship." "We are all brothers and sisters," she said, "and the wiser ones lead the less wise through 'Ascending Fellowship' into love." See the "Law of Fellowship" since published in J. H. N.'s book, *Home Talks* (p. 103) from which she quoted, as I remember. She was very serious, simple and loving, and we were blind young things.

When first this strange, mysterious, uncomprehended means of Ascending Fellowship was entered upon, no sex instinct was consciously awake in me, nor was any apprehended for a long time. Perhaps this will seem strange, but it is true. There was obedience and loyalty and some curiosity. I know the moment when pleasure awoke in me like a miracle, out of a romantic episode made possible by Mrs. S. [Skinner]. I promptly fell in love then and knew indeed that I was loved, yet covered all in my heart with prayer and gave no occasion for criticism for Special Love.[26]

So you see what a grave little thing I was. In fact I believe that all Community women were conscientious — by this I mean that they all *tried* to be unselfish. The *marvel,* though, in Community life was the unselfish spirit of the men toward one another, and their freedom from the instinctive desire for sole possession. I know how unselfish they were, and Myron, your father, knew. A concrete instance that occurs to me is one that your father told me when we were once talking about the past after our marriage. When he was a young man quite desperately in love with E. M., he acted as third party and carried love messages to her from Z. Z., who was his rival in sports as well as in love, but not a *hated* rival.

I will add here a word about the practical arrangement for sexual relationships. The man did not solicit the woman directly, nor the woman the man. When a man imagined that he would be welcomed, he then ventured to ask a third party — usually an older woman — to arrange (not in his presence) a meeting for him with the desired one. And thus you see,

---

26. A Community term for exclusive romantic attachment. The fear was that such bonds would lead to "the marriage spirit" and/or distract individual attention from collective social goals.

the women of the Community had the freedom to say "no" or "yes" easily, while the third party also arranged for the place of meeting.

I doubt not that there was struggle against jealousy in the hearts of some men, but your father told me he was *never* jealous, and I do suppose his experience was not an exceptional Community experience.

Since it is true that at the time of the break-up we communists seemed to grow suddenly selfish in many ways, I wonder if there was not an afflatus, renewed through criticism (criticism that was almost always upbuilding rather than destructive) that made us go beyond ourselves—our natural selves—and took from us the desire for selfish *rights* and gave to us truly what was called the "Pentacostal Spirit."

And now you must think of my life going on from day to day, the days and weeks making months and years, with each day filled with its round of duties and amusements, with changes of rooms and roommates, with migrations from the Villa to Oneida Community to Willow Place to Wallingford.

There were seasons of ill health, but no serious illnesses. Mother was a very great friend. Sister Mary became ever more dear to me. Our class was less and less an integer—more broken, more individualistic. My education was one of intermittent growth. I was a constant reader, but my choice of matter was not wise nor deep. In books I found passionate pleasure. Often I was an actor in a play, or acting as part of a committee to produce entertainment.

Card-playing and dominoes were allowed amusements. Mr. Noyes resented the luck or skill in cards or dominoes that made him fail to be a winner in a game, as I amusingly recollect. There was music and dancing and skating. There was croquet and baseball and picnics and rides.

There came the time when I was called upon to *give* as well as to receive criticism. Very simply and ignorantly I observed character with no knowledge of psychology. Evening meetings meant heart-searching and confession of Christ.

And always there were the changing and the steadfast lovers—some heartache, much happiness. What seems now to have been a strange experience was then but natural. One formed no habits to dull the edge of love except, perhaps, as one was obliged to maintain too rigidly the principle of Ascending Fellowship. I touched the little world of the Community most intimately, the great outside "World" not at all or only the fringes of it through excursionists and constant visitors whom I imagined uninteresting.

Once a touch of skepticism came and went within my mind. I had been reading *Vestiges of Creation,* a sort of John-the-Baptist book, in that it preceded the great light of Darwin's *Origin of the Species* with an exposition of creation and the evolution of matter. In this touch of skeptical thinking I must have been reflecting the more serious skepticism already at work among the older group of young people. Charles Cragin[27] gave me *Vestiges* to read. There were momentous changes going on, but I was not in their midst in any sense; still they were too great to be wholly outside my life and meant too much to the future of the Community.

I do not know when religious doubt came to these young thinkers. It must have been when the Darwinian Theory of 1850 to '54 had much later penetrated — partly through college life, partly through the purchase of books — into our little circle. Well, consternation came finally to Mr. Noyes and the older part of the Community when the disaffection became known. Much was at stake. Mr. Noyes had begun to think of his successor; he was growing old and his hope was in his son, Theodore, who confessed openly to changes in *belief*! There was a long discussion in meeting about 1875 in regard to the succession. I think that I was sick at that time and later went to Wallingford — my memory has no sure record of that discussion, only an imperfect one. The naming of Mr. Noyes's successor was postponed. A year or two later, Theodore *was* given the position.

Doubt begot doubt. Perhaps this was the beginning of the end. You see, in the minds of that young class of students, there was doubt of God and immortality and the religious system, the base of our social ethics. And then doubt grew in the minds of *many,* regarding Mr. Noyes's ability to long be a leader. Doubt grew of his impartiality toward his son. There were doubts of J. H. N.'s "inspiration." Later, in the hearts of some, came doubt of the goodness of his intentions and of his acts. All these things anticipated the great climax of 1879, but you will see how little I sensed the real meaning and depth of the fomentation going on for the end came to me as a great unbelievable shock! During the years 1874 through '76 we went as a community into an investigation of spiritualism in order to help the young, if possible, to find faith in immortality. It was most exciting. Ann Hobart proved to be a good medium. Dr. Theodore Noyes led the investigations. I attended several seances in the "dark room" in the North Garret where we sat around a table, and people *shook* — but I was not a medium. Dr. Noyes and other young men attended seances abroad, in Vermont, New York and other places — they reported remarkable experiences.

After a time Mr. Noyes became reconciled to Theodore and had reason to believe that he was less skeptical.

---

27. Charles A. Cragin, one of the young men whom the Community had sent to Yale University, was beloved by Jessie and her "class of girls."

If I felt unable at the beginning of this narrative to give you a true picture of *Mr. Noyes,* now, when I would like to sketch a likeness of his son, Theodore, my pen is just as impotent. Both were big men—the father far greater than this son, but I have always believed that Theodore did not find his right development. He would have been a great educator. I think it was my timidity and lack of wit and brilliancy—perhaps it was my trying to be so good—that made me unattractive to the doctor; maybe he was in rebellion against the docile, lamb-like, self-searching character that Community life developed. He did not notice me. I stood greatly in awe of him. I longed to sit at his feet for knowledge and I have vivid memories of his being a wonderful teacher. Later, after the break-up, I think perhaps Myron and I misjudged him. But long afterward, Edith, when you were grown and he joined our reading class, we became *brother and sister,* and, as you will see, he thought his father was my father. I loved him as much as I admired him.

Certainly, if one looked among the men of that time for a leader, as his father had need to look, there was no one—no one except Theodore—who seemed made of the great timber needed for that place. All other men dwindled. So he was tried later but found wanting. I am sure that Doctor Noyes proved himself in his leadership of Oneida Community, Limited. From somewhere I hope there will sometime come a true picture of the doctor.

Wallingford Again. Edith Waters and Charles Cragin

In 1876 I went to Wallingford for a third time. Edith Waters was there, Marion Burnham, Ida-Kate Kelly and Ida Blood—girls of my class. Edith and I both loved Charles Cragin. There was no jealousy between us though I knew that Charles loved Edith better than he loved me. I roomed with Beulah and Helen Miller in the Upper House. When Beulah's baby, Dorothy, came, I helped her care for the baby and almost felt she was mine.

My work was in the Printing Office. I did not set type or run a press or "overlay" or do any of the expert or intricate work of the then large printing establishment, but I learned to sew books and to inspect the printed sheets as they came down on the great machine, and I often bronzed.

At Wallingford the farm and the old barns (scenes of play and adventure for me in 1869) were under Charles Cragin's supervision. He was "through" Yale College and was doing "scientific" farming, scandalizing older farmers with his schemes and ventures. Into a small two-room building called the "Barn Office," he put a studio. A cobwebby little back room was made to hold a camera — not a common article then — arranged for light, and, in one corner, a dark room. Perhaps all of Wallingford Community sat before his camera. One day *he* posed and let *me* "take" his likeness: you could see the keen gray-blue eyes, the thoughtful creases in the forehead and the deep lines about the mouth. No picture gives the key to his personality. I can't tell you how wonderful I thought him to be then, and how beautiful. He was alive with quick intuition, vivid, clear-thinking, strong, unselfish, filled with subtle thought for others — of the little things that make happiness. Yet he was absorbed to the point of intensity in work that was his own, and whatever work he undertook became his own. As I remember him, he was quite unlike his brothers George E. and John. Perhaps he was a master of the power of flattery with a vivid sincerity to back it. Soon after the time of which I am now writing, his superabundant energy started the spoon business, now grown to such high proportions. The factory was at the foot of the hill, and his studio was moved there. Then followed, not long afterward, the exodus of the Wallingford family to Oneida Community, which took Edith away but left him. Later, fever and ague, overwork and finally a sickness which ended in his death. Of his death I shall write on another page.

Doctor Noyes came to Wallingford while I was there, and Ann Hobart Bailey, too (she was Mrs. Sophia Skinner later).

We young people had study classes throughout the winter of 1876–'77. How interestingly Doctor Noyes taught history and astronomy! Ann was in charge of the young girls — "Mother of our class" we called her.

In 1877, when Mr. Noyes finally gave his leadership to his son, these two young people, Theodore and Ann, came into remarkable prominence. Full of new ideas, they vibrated between Oneida and Wallingford and led our quiet Communities a strange life. Women like Mrs. Dunn and Harriet Skinner, once leaders, men such as Mr. Hamilton and Mr. Woolworth, were put under severe criticism and taken from responsible positions. Methods for control of intricate Community relationships, without the old appeal to the conscience, but by a tabulating card-index sort of system, were tried with policing and espionage.

I will not try to enter into further account of that Community-wrecking time. It was inevitable when Mr. Noyes grew old that he should wish to put his brilliant son into leadership; but, as I have before shown you, the time was not propitious. Theodore was not wise enough then, nor was a society, founded on a belief in the divine Christ, satisfied with a man who was an "unbeliever." Dissatisfaction grew apace. Many who had before found fault with Mr. Noyes found more fault after this change, and perhaps there were strong men like Mr. Hinds and Mr. Towner[28] who felt that they could better manage affairs than were then being managed. People grew restless.

Your father [Myron Kinsley], whom I then so little knew, left the Oneida Community. When, many years later, he told me about his going away, he said he felt sure the Community would break up, and he hoped to make a home to shelter his family and friends. He married a wealthy woman under whose fascinating influence he had come while yet in the Community. This seemed a terrible thing to his friends and family, and a terrible experience followed, for he found this woman an adventuress and he lived with her only one day. Broken-hearted, broken in spirit and pride, he went west, and later, because Mr. Noyes loved him and loved his father, Mr. Noyes used his loving influence to bring Myron back and gained forgiveness for him from the Community. Myron came home on probation. He went to Wallingford to live and he worked in the kitchen. I was at Wallingford and I remember how troubled and sad he looked. (Myron's daughter, Josephine, was four years old. I had not entered into Myron's life at all.)

O. W., Frank Tuttle and I were made "Entertainment Committee" at Wallingford. Later O. and I were continued as Entertainment Committee at Oneida Community. It was hard work and I was not very strong, as I was again afflicted with ague. I returned to Oneida Community in 1877, about the time that there was an exodus of forty from Wallingford Community to Oneida. Only twenty were left to combat the ague, although a large new dwelling house had been built at Wallingford the year before. Among those who were left at Wallingford were *Myron* and *Charles Cragin.* I think in that year — perhaps it was in 1878 — Mr. Noyes resumed his leadership.

Before I left Wallingford, I was, for some time, "journalist." That is, I wrote the sheets chronicling the daily happenings at Wallingford Community. These were sent, semi-weekly, I think, to the other communes and read at Oneida Community in the Evening Meeting. At Oneida Community the old *Circular* had given over its life to a new paper, *The American Socialist,* whose aim was "to make a faithful record of social progress everywhere." At Oneida Community there was a lively literary club to work for the *Socialist,* and into it I was introduced and became a member (by one whose name I will not give, since his perspicacity was so at fault) as "the future novelist of the Community."

28. James W. Towner, at various times minister, soldier, lawyer, and judge, joined the Oneida Community in 1874. He became the leader of a formidable faction challenging the authority of those loyal to Noyes.

I remember that I put myself through higher arithmetic and ge-
ometry and studied Latin with Dora Campbell. When I was in straights I
went to Edwin Burnham with my mathematical problems. Sickness and
work and changes from Oneida Community to Wallingford Community
had interfered with my studies and alas! my education was fragmentary
and meager. Now, too, there were few study-classes.

Earlier in this narrative I have stated that schooling was possible
for everyone in the Community, young and old, because of the study-
classes that were always kept going. Mr. Levi Joslyn had taught French;
Mr. and Mrs. Noyes taught Greek, Latin and Hebrew; Doctor Noyes dis-
coursed on Astronomy, Physics and History; and many more wise ones
had taught various branches of knowledge. I do not know why the classes
had ceased to exist unless from disintegrating conditions at work which I
did not yet recognize. Although I was a lover of books like my mother, I
did not come into enjoyment of poetry until later, and could not be a com-
rade to Mother who was then in her intense passion for Browning,
Shelley, Wordsworth and Coleridge. Mother, I remember, was then studying history, too, with Miss Sweet and Mrs. C. I think she digested her
reading well. She was an interesting talker, her memory was well stored
and her words were especially well chosen, with a diction that seems now
to me to have been a part of her time — graceful and somewhat stately, like
the minuet, if one may compare dancing with language. My Uncle Ralph
Hobart had a like quality in conversation, wherefore inheritance may
have had a part in this characteristic of my mother.

In 1878, two heart-crushing blows came upon me. On the second
day of that year, Charles Cragin died; just six months later, my darling
Edith Waters died. Charles had worked hard in the bad climate of Wallingford, terribly subject to attacks of fever and ague for which he took
great doses of quinine. Finally, a desperate fever — typhoid fever it was, I
believe — swept his life away.

Edith's death came in July. She had been to the seashore and to
Verona Springs in search of benefit for her failing health, yet she did not
improve. She had consumption and, alas, we did not know then how
great a cure might lie for her close at hand in a life out-of-doors. Here is a
description of Edith. You will see that I did not write it, but it so truly fits
her that I insert it here. It has stood for *her* in my mind since first I read
it . . .

Thou standest before me a tall slim maiden somewhat thin as
befittest thy seventeen summers. Where thy flesh is bare it is tanned a
beauteous color. Thy lips are of the finest fashion. Surely he who did thy
carven chin had a mind to a master work and did no less. Great was the

Jessie Catherine Kinsley in the Mansion Library

deftness of thine imaginer, and he would have all folk who see thee wonder at they deep-thinking and thy carefulness and thy kindness. Is it so that thy thoughts are ever deep and solemn? Yet I know it of thee that they are hale and true and sweet. — Wm. Morris

To me the pain of Charles A. Cragin's death was great. This man who had awakened love in many and gave love so wonderfully held my love, too. It was heartbreaking that he should die, far away, young, suddenly, when Edith was ill, too. But my pain was as nothing compared to the pain of those two who had borne him children — this I now know better than when my heart was aching. And then to have his death followed by the reading of his diaries before everyone — everyone! — those diaries so full of passionate and pathetic love for my precious Edith, who was too ill to know much of them or of the criticism they received. Moreover, they seemed to me then wild and strong, almost wicked. Oh, I cannot write of this tragedy of love, though if I had the genius of a Marie Clare, I might try to do so. This must be a simple narrative. I am not the one to write of things so complex, which I look back upon through the years with mingled feelings of pain and wonder, admiration and regret.

Your Father (M. H. Kinsley). The Terrible Year, 1879. My Personal Affairs and Problems at the Break-Up of Oneida Community. Mr. Noyes Goes to Canada. Letter from Annie Hatch. I Go to Wallingford

And now, before I enter upon the year 1879 with its rapid changes and big events for the Community as a whole, I want to tell you of the man who, within a year, would enter my life as its greatest factor — the man of whom Mr. Noyes, when writing to me of marriage in November 1879, used these words: "The *best* man — one who would deal most kindly with you and be the best father for your children." Edith, were not those words well chosen for your dear father? How our loves clustered around him! His strength and tenderness made him the very center of our lives. What infinite kindness he showed me — what love to us all! He *was* the *"best father for my children."*

On his father's farm in Fletcher, Vermont, Myron must have had a bringing up that was calculated to make his body strong. He was notably strong as a youth. His father was sheriff of his county and a legislator and much occupied at a distance from Fletcher, so that the farm work was left to the four children and their mother. If you had heard your grandfather, Albert, tell stories, as I did, of his ancestors, then you would have heard of strong men, fighters in the Revolution and battles of 1812, workers, men of energy and fine judgment, lovers, fathers and friends of sensibility and tenderness. Your grandfather was to his family — children Sarah, Martin, Jane and Myron — what Myron was to us: its *heart* and *center.* I have a passing memory of your grandmother, Maria. I imagine she was very much like your Aunt Jane. Sarah I think was more like her father.

Myron came to Oneida Community when he was twelve years old. Any picture I may have shown you here of Community life, criticism, unselfishness in love, sacrifice and discipline, was *his* environment as well as mine. Your father was especially adapted to this environment then: he was great-hearted, never petty, never jealous — of this I am sure although he did not enter my life in communism. Under the rules of Scientific Propagation, he had one child in the Community, and his love went out to both the mother and child. Of these two, Mrs. Smith and Josephine, I shall have opportunity to speak later.

Your father was a worker at almost every trade: blacksmith,

Myron H. Kinsley and Jane A. Kinsley, his sister

shoemaker, painter, mechanic, cook, nurse, farmer. He was a builder of businesses, a man of energy in every direction—except toward book-learning: his education there was neglected. There were opportunities, after his first year in the Community, for him to study, as well as for other boys, but in that direction he needed pushing and he always said that work held him too close to allow him to break away, and *sleep* held him strongly after hours of labor. We remember how eager he was for *our* benefits of education in books, in music and in art. *Life* educated him in a noble way. Contact with Mr. Noyes and his family was culture. He was an idealist; he had imagination—spiritual imagination.

If he was not a knight seeking adventure, adventure sought him. Every emergency saw him rise to meet it. He has told you of the boat, the "Pat Rogers" that burned and sunk; of the capture of "Holden"; of the tornado at Wallingford in 1878 when forty were killed and many rescued[29]; of Charles Mills and the "Mills War," too; of the accident on the

29. The *Pat Rogers* was a Mississippi River steamboat. Myron saved a woman and child from the disaster. Holden was an agent for the Community who absconded with

Hudson; and of the stolen horse at Niagara Falls. There were innumerable minor incidents, and many calls for quick courage and clear sight in business and in everyday life, wherever your father happened to be. In this year, 1879, came a *great call* and your father heard it; I think it would not be exaggeration to say that *he saved Mr. Noyes and the Community from a disaster whose extent we can not estimate.*

Now I come to the events of 1879.

I do not know when I began to sense the inevitable—the terribly inevitable disruption coming to our Community. It was a nightmare. Perhaps I felt the terror near, nevertheless for a long time I shut tight my eyes and believed that if I but clung fast to Mr. Noyes and believed in his inspiration, I would help him and the Oneida Community to pass the danger point. I remember O. saying to me, "It's coming; it's bound to come; we are going to have a terrible smash-up." "Oh, O.," I said, "You only *help it to come* when you say that! Think of the women and children! This Community cannot break-up." "Wait and see," was his reply.

There were scenes in the Evening Meetings. The disaffected began to sit in the gallery and from there hurl words upon the loyalists. Open scorn, hatred and rebellion were shown in *many* places. You will understand the misery of this if you contrast it with the almost complete harmony of a past extending backward beyond the limits of my life. Except for a glimpse of summary treatment given to Mills in 1864 (and that was a one-man affair), there had been in *my* memory no shouting, no dissensions, no party-feeling nor hatred. Business had been discussed freely and forcefully, of course—severe criticisms had been given and taken manfully, in silence.

All was changed this year. You see, I had not been much awake to the spiritual significance of the past four years. Associates and my living at Wallingford had kept me out of the deeper currents. Those currents set running in 1875 or earlier had become great streams by 1879.

Also, in this year I began to think it possible that Mr. Noyes might be in truth my father. Mother had long before told me that her experience had pointed to him as the person to whom she would the more easily attribute her pregnancy. But Mother would not be sure—could not be—and Mr. Noyes had told Mrs. Skinner at the time that if I was his I would have *red hair.* I did not have red hair.

Well, in the spring of the year 1879, I sprained my ankle severely. My foot was being dressed one day when Mr. Noyes passed by the door and stopped to offer sympathy for my mishap. "Why, you have my riding

---

funds. Myron shaved off his beard, followed him to Boston, and apprehended him. Most of the money was recovered. Myron assisted the townspeople during the Wallingford tornado.

toe," he said. Then followed inquiry and an enthusiastic acceptance of the *thought* that I *might* be his daughter. This incident was told to my Father Hatch, and before I could reassure him of my desire *always* and *ever* to be his loving child, he was hurt and the matter was made much of by the anti-Noyesites. My Father Hatch was never citicized about me in the old days — in fact he did not own me until I was seven — but this was the one, the *only* misunderstanding between me and my Father H.

To go on now with that momentous year: Myron had been trusted again. Mr. Noyes had given him the honored position of superintendent of the silverware business at Wallingford. Annie Hatch was living at Wallingford Community in this year with *great love* in her heart for Myron. Neither of them dreamt an end could come to Complex Marriage.

Myron came to Oneida from Wallingford in June, 1879. Almost at once, through his brother, Martin, he learned how deep was the disaffection, that bitterness and hatred were all about and threatening, and that there was possibly a willingness to cast Mr. Noyes out, to make him prey of the courts and perhaps of the mob. (I do not think that any of this *interior* trouble had been talked of abroad, though it happened that the Central New York Clergy had been actively working against the Oneida Community for months.) Every stone and drift lay ready for a terrible avalanche. Myron felt that the *only* thing he could do was to warn Mr. Noyes. He went to Mr. Noyes's room on the afternoon of June 22nd. Their conference led to their secret departure that night. Otis Kellogg was their only confidant. He took them to Holland Patent and from there they went north by train to the St. Lawrence and to Canada. (Mr. Noyes never returned to the Oneida Community, though his body was brought here for burial in April, 1886.)

I remember that strange morning when it became known that Mr. Noyes had gone away — no one knew where, but gone he was. We who loved him wept, and our grief was terrible; they to whom Mr. Noyes appeared evil, rejoiced. Not until Mr. Noyes sent through Myron to the loyalists secret word of his whereabouts, did our black cloud begin to lift.

Myron's conduct in thus running away with Mr. Noyes was variously condemned. He was called two-sided by the anti-Noyesites: "He had doubted the permanence of Oneida Community" (witness his going away in 1876) and he had "criticised some of Mr. Noyes's actions" and "*then took his side.*" Myron told me that the severest criticism he ever gave in all his life to anyone was *not given behind Mr. Noyes's back* but *to his face,* when, at Mr. Brett's Mr. Noyes *asked* him for criticism. And he told me that Mr. Noyes took this effort on Myron's part — to appraise some part of his past conduct — with thankfulness, without anger, saying that he was glad to see himself through Myron's eyes. Of course he saw that Myron did not hate him but loved him.

From that time Myron was Mr. Noyes's courier. Through Myron came suggestion after suggestion from J. H. N. to the tumultuous, broken and battered Community.

Myron himself named the first Council — the new governing body — and he had the wisdom to put into this group some of the more rebellious and bitter enemies of Mr. Noyes. I quote from a letter sent by me (no date) to my sister, Mary, at Wallingford: "It was good to have the matter of the Council so satisfactorily settled. I was glad to cast my vote in favor of having the new one chosen by Mr. Myron. He is one among many we may trust, and I love him for his goodness and for the help he gives to Mr. Noyes. I thought the new selection excellent."

Things began to look more hopeful for a peaceful settlement. Then came the proposal of August 20th from J. H. N. to discontinue our peculiar practice of Complex Marriage, and for that change there was almost unanimous agreement after discussion. On either August 26th or 28th, the change took effect. In Mr. Noyes's letter making this proposal he courageously told us what would be left: "We shall hold our property and businesses in common as now: We shall live together in a common household and eat at a common table as now: We shall have a common children's department: We shall have our daily Evening Meetings and all of our present means of moral and spiritual improvement: Surely here is Communism enough to hold us together and inspire us with heroism for a new career."

In accepting Mr. Noyes's suggestion that we give up Complex Marriage we accepted it with *honesty of spirit and action,* and the entire Community went back to conscientious practice of the old worldly standard of marriage and morals, though our own standard had seemed to us so much better and higher and more unselfish.

[In 1934 Jessie added the following comment to her manuscript.]

One not understanding Community discipline and spirit might perhaps think of this ending of Complex Marriage and the interval of days between August 20th and 26th (when the final day came) as a time of self-seeking and excess. But that thought would hardly represent the truth, I am *convinced.* They were serious days and glad days, too, when plans for and engagements for regular worldly marriage were made and final farewells spoken; and sad days when old marriage ties, now to be once again held sacred, and new marriage engagements would stand up sharply between loves; between the continuance of loves, even between the continuance of love where children had been its fruit. Imagine the heartache that spread from sister to sister, from friend to friend. My sister, for instance, had been chosen as one to bear a Community child under "stirpiculture." Her child was *stillborn*. But now she might not marry that young father whom she loved, and who still loved her, because he now had a living son, and both love and duty led him toward marriage with the later mother. There was no excitement so far as I knew, but too much pain and suffering realized by all these people now separating, whose relationships had been most close. Our men were good men, and our women were good, too; and thoughtfulness for one another was uppermost. I only had one engagement in those last days. Mrs. Norton, older and wiser than I am, agrees with me that they were solemn days. — J.C.K.

Immediately after August 26th there were many marriages. I think you can imagine the heartache and the pain that came like a bitter wind across some lives. I do not understand how the misery was borne. With simple ceremony, marriage after marriage took place, and here and there left pain and sorrow.

For myself, I was afraid O. [Orrin Wright] would want to marry me; afraid, for, though I had loved him a long time, I felt sure when I thought of marriage with him, that in time my nature would grow assertive and tyrannical. The fact was that I did not love him as I thought I loved him or I would have put every doubt aside to cast my lot with his. George Allen, when he found (after a time) that I had denied O.'s desire to marry me, began to come to see me again. After a time I almost promised to marry George — in fact I said "yes," I would, and then in a few hours asked my promise back, saying that I couldn't — I would surely wrong both him and myself by keeping my promise and entering upon marriage where, on my part, there was not perfect love, and, on his part, perfect agreement in thought. For weeks following then, from friends to both O. and George there came persuasion and argument to shake my perturbed spirit and obstinate belief that I could not marry either of these men, who, by the way, remained very good friends to each other through it all. George wrote to Mr. Noyes, and asked for Myron's assistance in seeking Mr. Noyes's good word for him, for he knew how greatly I trusted Mr. Noyes. At last I wrote to Mr. Noyes — I wish I had my letter. I put all my doubts and troubles before him. I told him that I thought perhaps I loved both O. and George, told him I wanted to be married and have children, but I wanted my marriage to be one "born in heaven." Would he only tell me what he could, out of a wise heart that would help me to do right? Here is Mr. Noyes's reply, which I copy as the original is worn:

November 13, 1879

Dear Jessie:

Let us be cheerful over these perplexities. There is a way out known to God if not to us, and as you say He will give us light in due time. Don't let us hurry.

I got a letter from George D. Allen asking my consent some weeks ago, it was dated October 25th. I had heard through Harriet (H. Skinner) about his wishes, and also about Orrin's. Deeply as I was interested I did not think it right to say anything until I heard from you. Remembering the intimate relations between you and Orrin, I have thought it pointed that you and he might fall into the current and I should not have quarreled with you if you had. Nor should I have quarreled with you if you had married G. D. A. without saying a word to me. . . .

But you may be sure I was very glad that you have not hurried and that you have turned toward me for counsel. I wish your letter could be read to the whole Community. It is splendid, every word of it, in every way. I hope the marriages of ages and generations to come will be modeled on it, not in respect to the personal appeal to me, but in respect to the earnest longing which it breathes to find out and do the will of God.

I write at once to acknowledge your kind treatment of me, but I cannot make much answer till I have thought and prayed and got light from above.

My first thought is that I do not like to decide between Orrin and George, for it would be an ungenerous thing for me to prefer G. after long witnessing Orrin's devotion to you and G.'s estrangement. On the other hand, I dislike saying *No* to G. not only because it would be attributed by many to personal grudge; but because I am afraid there would be some personal feeling mixed with my judgment of him at present, arising from the fact that in his letter, *after reducing all his differences with me to the single point of doubting my inspiration in special directions,* he proceeds to say, "*Jessie and I may always differ about that matter,*" from which I am compelled to understand that his position in reference to the present difference between him and me is unchanged. If this is so, if his estimate of me and yours remains as they were even a few months ago, I cannot for my life see how you and he are going to live happily together in the close relation of marriage. I cannot see why the same honorable feeling which has prevented him from association with you heretofore for fear of disturbing your relations with me does not still stand in the way. I do not see how mere suppression of thoughts on the subject will secure the sympathy necessary to permanent happiness in the constant intimacy of wedlock. I dwell on this point as I intimated above, because it causes thoughts and feelings which I do not wish to harbor if there is anything personal in them, and therefore I must take time to study them before saying Yes or No.

My most satisfactory impression is the charitable one, charitable to both G. and O., that they are changing and improving and ere long either of them, or both, [may] be worthy of your heart and hand, and that they can *prove* they have changed for the better. I don't know but it is best to wait and see which changes most and fastest. At all events, I must wait before I decide between them and I advise you to. Do not be afraid that I shall keep you from being married and having a baby. I sincerely hope you will have five or six babies, and for this very reason I wish you to have the very best husband that can be found. And I have faith that God will find that husband for you. He found me a wife in wonderful ways and you are a true daughter to me in thinking that He will find you a husband.

I have said nothing about your intimation that you would like to have me choose for you without reference to the claims of G. and O. It has set me thinking. I will only ask you for the present what your feelings are about the *age* of a candidate. If you must have a young man the choice would be more limited than it would if you look simply for the *best* man—one who would deal most kindly with you and would be the best father for your children. My father was forty years old and my mother twenty when they were married, and I have always thought their children were the better for the difference.

I am pleased with Theodore's marriage, partly because of a similar difference in age.

I hope you will now write me the other "half" of what is in your heart about these matters. I, too, might say I have not written half of what is in me, but I must hurry this off as it will be four days on the way and you will be waiting. I will send your letter back to go with this if you show what I have written to anybody. Perhaps I shall want a copy of both sometime. I trust your discretion showing our correspondence.

Yours lovingly,
J. H. N.

P.S. Mr. Pitt admires your letter.[30]

When I read the latter part of the letter, and then its postscript, I thought Mr. Noyes's reference to marriage with a man older than myself might mean Mr. Pitt. So I wrote again at once to Mr. Noyes, saying I could *never* marry Mr. Pitt (Myron was in Mr. Noyes's thought, not Mr. Pitt).

---

30. Theodore Pitt was living at the Stone Cottage at Niagara Falls and acting as Noyes's secretary.

To my second letter Mr. N. made no direct reply but instead sent word to Mrs. Skinner to bring Myron and me together if she could, telling her he hoped Myron would sometime marry one of his daughters, and that Myron was scrupulous of making any advance in attention toward me because of his friendship for George Allen.[31] I had been shy and afraid of Myron always; he had hardly looked my way (once, only to be kind to me when I had the toothache, he brought me some remedy as I sat by the nursery-kitchen fire). Yet for years he had been in my mind as a hero — and if we girls, speculating in private on worldly marriage, put the question "Who would you choose?" my reply was invariably "Mr. Myron." He was a sort of Othello — fine looking, too; he always appeared well to me. Now again, in this hour of Mr. Noyes's need, he had been the man of action.

Mrs. Skinner sent word to me to come to her room. I was puzzled. There I found Myron. Mrs. S. put our hands together and said, "John and I wish you two might learn to love one another." I knew this would be easy for me but I did not know then quite how Myron felt, and he, too, was puzzled about me. Yet I am sure those few moments of broken conversation, with Mrs. Skinner standing near us, were momentous moments in our lives.

Orrin and George were still showing me attention, both saying that they could never give me up until they saw me married. I told them of this word Mrs. Skinner brought from Mr. Noyes. They were not pleased. They *could not* believe I would love Myron.

And Myron was amid complications. There was the mother of his Community child, Mrs. Smith, to be guarded from pain. I am sure that there would have been for Myron only *one* way toward a future marriage (if that were possible) and that with Mrs. Smith, had she been *free*. But of course there was D. E. S., her husband, whom she and Myron both loved, and to whom she was bound.

Further, there was the friendship between Annie Hatch and Myron, now broken in its intimacy by the giving up of Complex Marriage, yet a tender bond that could not be rudely shaken. And so I have now come to the letter from Annie to me: a touching letter that will show you clearly the heart of a Community woman. It is a noble expression of unselfish love — most unusual, too, as the world goes — and it shows quite clearly, I am sure, dear Annie's goodness. I have not my reply, but I know

---

31. Myron was not yet free from his connection with Mrs. Clark, although divorce proceedings were under way, for she, when Myron left her, had almost immediately married another man, writing to M. not to betray her to her third husband. (Jessie Kinsley's note)

my desire was to be unselfish toward her, too, and under no circumstances to take from her Myron's brotherly love.

Wallingford, December 23rd, 1879

My Beloved Sister,

What a long time it has been since any letters have passed between you and me, but it is not because I have forgotten Sister Jessie — you have been in my mind a great deal and I have loved you.

I have heard of the trying situation in which you have been in respect to this knotty problem — marriage — and have felt a sister's sympathy for you. And believe me, dear Sister Jessie, that I was delighted when on the evening of Myron's return from seeing Mr. Noyes, I was asking him what you were going to do and after his telling me your state of indecision I told him that *he* better take you; I was delighted to hear that Mr. Noyes had suggested the same thing to him. Myron asked me if I were honest in saying I would like him to take you and I replied, Yes I am — I should not have a pang about it.

And it is true, Jessie, that I should be happy to have him marry you — and it really would not cause me *suffering*. I have loved Myron very much since I have been here, and do now, but since the change of base in social affairs I have felt like holding onto my love for him loosely, and have had no expectation in respect to him.

I have taken care of Myron's clothes and his room, and have cared for him in a great many other ways that, of course, I shall miss in giving him up; but I have prayed God to reconcile me to anything that might take place and I felt that God had kindly answered my prayer when I found (and with some surprise) that I felt so good about and ready to fall in with Mr. Noyes's choice. I should rather have you than anyone I can think of, and perhaps I show my selfishness in that way. Since I have known of the proposition, and before it got to you, I have had happiness in thinking of giving my care of Myron to you, and of letting you have my room right next to him, and many other things.

When we gave up Complex Marriage, I was tempted to think that all of my sorrow, pain and discipline in reference to special love would be lost, as I felt that I was just getting where I could love unselfishly, but now I see that the work done in me is to be severely tested, and I find it easier to yield up a love that is very dear to me than I probably should if I had not had the discipline that I have had. I feel very thankful for the way in which God shows me his love, and my heart is peaceful and happy.

It is really my hope that you will accept Mr. Noyes's proposition. I believe you will find in Myron the qualities of a true and noble man — and will easily learn to love him if you do not already.

Marry Myron if you feel in your heart that you can do so with love and respect; and you shall have your sister Annie's best love and blessing with it. Do not listen to any rumors you may hear, for I am sincere in this letter, and I write it without Myron's knowledge of it. I am not at all afraid I shall lose his brotherly love.

Your true sister,
Annie

You will see that Annie's letter was dated late in December, and it was not yet the first of the coming year when George Miller came to Oneida Community from Wallingford. He had recently married Annie Kelly.[32] He was working in the factory at Wallingford Community *with* Myron. He, too, had heard of Mr. Noyes's and Mrs. Skinner's desire and he was *determined* to bring me into Myron's life, so he carried me off, *by permission of the Council,* to Wallingford.

Wallingford, December 28th, 1879
Annie Hatch to Beulah Hendee Barron

Myron comes into my room evenings and he and Darry [Dorothy Barron Leonard] have gay times. I feel real reconciled to his marriage, but I wonder how I shall really feel when it is done. I trust God about it. I heard that Jessie feared she would make me suffer in case she accepted Mr. Noyes' proposal, so I wrote her a letter giving her my hearty sympathy and good will.

I Marry, 1880. You Are Born, 1881. I Return to Oneida Community and Meet Mrs. Smith and Others. Life at Niagara Falls. Mr. Noyes Dies. My Sister Dies. Summing Up. End

On this journey to Wallingford with George Miller, Constance Reeve went, too. We were fearfully and wonderfully clothed, Constance and I. In New York City Myron met us. Again, I at least must have looked like "poor white trash." My dress was not the simple pantaletted dress of the Community; it was *long;* moreover, it was immense—twelve inches lapping at the waist, since Harriet Worden had worn it once, and she with Stella. It was a *public travelling dress for us all!* I could not once remove my somewhat better-fitting coat at table or at the theater. My hair was short and covered by an old-ladies-bonnet, tied under my chin. Yet neither

32. Annie Kelly Miller was to be Jessie Kinsley's companion on a tour of Europe in 1913.

Myron nor George betrayed embarrassment over us. Their knowledge of the world must have made them more conscious of our dress than we were, yet they treated us like princesses with great honor.

At Wallingford Myron and I were much together, talking and reading and walking. Annie Hatch was heavenly kind and sisterly. Myron's divorce from Mrs. C. was not yet attained, and he could only hint at future hopes. Love, however, came to me with a vehemence of which I had not dreamed. At least my heart was awake.

One day in January, 1880, came word of Mrs. Clark's sudden death in Syracuse. Although this left Myron free, it brought back the past, and he cried for hours. After a few days he asked me to marry him.

My curious habit of saving pieces (my fad in Community days) has continued into my married years, so here is a piece of my wedding gown, and over further I shall put others, not because you will value them — nor can I much value them now — but because they are concrete bits out of a bygone time connecting me in memory with persons and events — a little piece of the past, a substantial piece of the past alive in me.

This wedding dress has a greater personality than any other. I even remember exactly how it was made and how strangely it felt about my knees and ankles which were so long accustomed to pantalets.

It was on the 28th of February, 1880, that Myron and I went to New Haven, with sister Mary to give me away, and dear Annie Miller and George to witness our marriage. We returned home to find a feast prepared for us by Annie Hatch and other friends. Happy months followed. Myron was a busy man, but full of tenderness for me, and Oh! I loved him.

Our state, financially, was one of communism, and before having children we were supposed to get permission from the Council to be fruitful. Marion Bloom told me once that she remembered how wicked she thought I was, because I did not ask permission. In *your* case, *Edith,* you were a happy "mistake."

In the summer of 1880 I went to Oneida Community to prepare for your coming. We had no money of our own then to buy clothing for you or furniture for our room. We were all still living in a state of communism of property. Everything was obtained through the furnishing committees, and, indeed, you had a funny outfit of handed down baby garments.

The changes I found at Oneida Community were those I could not have adjusted myself to easily without Myron. I was returning a married woman, pregnant, loving deeply, and so momentous were the changes, especially the changes in personal relationships, that, but for Myron, I realize how childishly unable I might have been to meet them.

Myron H. Kinsley   Jessie Catherine Kinsley, 1878

Not a year had passed, and I came back to live in the family with Myron, George, Orrin and the mother of Myron's child. I want to say how unselfish Orrin and George were toward Myron and me. Community *training told,* and all through the years that followed they were our good friends. Yet it was long before I could meet O. or G. face to face without a pang of memory—not desirous memory, oh no, but remorseful memory, as though I had ill-treated them, and their love for me might then be turned to hatred. George soon showed great-hearted interest in my welfare and happiness with Myron. Orrin tried to, but I am sure he felt hurt for years. Both of these men soon married happily. Mrs. Smith's situation was trying and difficult. Mr. Smith was already anxious to leave Oneida Community and go west. She was fearful of a roving life with him and with her two children, Deming and Josephine.[33] Moreover, she wished Josephine

33. Mr. Smith was a social enthusiast. He had taken Mrs. Smith into more than

to live near her father, Myron. This child was too unlike Mr. Smith to readily enter his life, though he would have had the best intentions toward her. Mrs. Smith had been much opposed to the marriage between Myron and me. She wrote Myron a long letter taking him seriously to task for selfishness toward George. Yet when our marriage was accomplished, she told Myron on one of his visits at Oneida Community, that she had nothing against me. Nevertheless, I did not know her well; we had seen very little of each other in the days gone past. It became Myron's loving task to put us on the clear road to love and honor one another.

I am sure that we both felt Myron's great-heartedness on the day that he brought us together when I reached Oneida Community. Mrs. Smith's was the harder part. She had had to give up wholly any share in the love of the man who was the father of her young child. Her situation with regard to Mr. Smith was unsettled, and if Myron was to share their child, then I would be the foster-mother during many months and I was *so* young for the task! But personally toward me, she was beautifully ready to be loving. We both cried in that little room where we met. How *could* I be good enough for my position? Quite quickly and wonderfully, however, Mrs. Smith and I grew to be sisters. Annie Hatch and I had lived together at Wallingford—I being, in one sense, the sole possessor of Myron—and we loved each other and did not suffer. So, then, Mrs. Smith, under the same restrictions but much more trying circumstances, found that she could love me and trust me with her child; and as my children were born, she also loved them. I have always felt she was a wonderful woman!

Thus I found, with Myron's help, peace and happiness in our old home in its new and somewhat chaotic state. In Josephine (seven years old then) I found a dear little girl ready to love me for her father's sake and soon loving me for *my own love given to her.* At intervals later through the years she was my girl, living in our family and calling me Mother. At Niagara Falls she went to school. I saw her grow up and marry. She was a good girl. I cannot remember a word from her that was not a loving word to me, and she profoundly loved her father—a love he reciprocated as warmly.

In 1880, just before the time of your birth at Oneida, there was much discussion of a plan to change the *form of property-holding* from one of common-sharing to *Joint-stock ownership.* In the following month, therefore, I went with Myron and Frank Wayland-Smith to the

---

one strange community before coming to Oneida Community, and into hardship in the South and West, too. While living in one of these distant places she had lost two children. (Jessie Kinsley's note)

Stone Cottage at Niagara Falls where Mr. Noyes was then living with Mr. Pitt, Mother Noyes and others. Myron and Frank were delegated by the Community to present to Mr. Noyes a working plan for Joint-stock.

While I had a lovely time in that exquisite spot visiting with my then rather unknown sister [in-law], Jane Kinsley, Frank and Myron discussed Joint-stock hour after hour with J. H. N., and it ended with our returning to Oneida Community with Mr. Noyes's acquiescence in this new evolution for the Community.

Then a "Commission" was appointed to arrange for the change — a long and difficult task. Your father, Uncle Martin and your grandfather were all on this Commission with seven others.

In January, 1881, we went into Joint-stock. We all felt pretty poor; and Mother and Mary suffered fear and dread from the change. Myron was worn and busy, moving our business of silver-manufacture from Wallingford to Niagara Falls. I could not trouble him too greatly. I shall never forget John and Emma Freeman for their kindness to my dear sister, Mary, and to my mother, too. Mr. Freeman was then as great-hearted as now. In a year or two Mother and Mary came to live with us at the Falls.

You were born the February following our change into Joint-stock. I had a severe sickness as all did not go right at your birth, and there were hours when the Doctor told Myron that he was not sure of saving either you or me. But at last my first little girl was born. Yet so sick was I that I did not have comfort of any sort for days. Your father, at the end of three days, was obliged to return to Niagara Falls. He left me in safe hands, for his sister, Sarah, and your grandmother, Olive Kinsley, cared for me.

I would like to stop and make you better acquainted with all Myron's dear family from my knowledge of them — make you acquainted with your grandfather's clear insight, with Sarah's spirituality, with Martin's uprightness and humor, with Jane's great ability for self-sacrifice, and with dear Mother Olive who came to be so much to you after grandfather's death. But I must hasten on, for my story is getting too long.

When you were three months old we went to live at Suspension Bridge.[34] Grandfather and Mother Olive went earlier to prepare our home. Jane came over from the Stone Cottage to help. This new home, the first I had lived in out of communism, was a stone house next to the Presbyterian Church at Suspension Bridge. You cannot imagine me as I was then. I was *most* unsophisticated and green. Our hired girl, Maggie,

34. Suspension Bridge, New York, was a village adjacent to Niagara Falls.

Jessie Catherine and Edith Kinsley

was often imagined by strangers to be the mistress, because she wore fine clothes and had assurance. I would always forget to use my money, which I then handled for the *first time.*

It is like recalling a dream to bring back the life in that stone house at Suspension Bridge, with you, your father, your grandfather and grandmother. For a time, Helen, Homer, and little Miriam lived with us. Later, when Homer and Helen had made another home, Clarence Bloom and his mother came and before we moved from Suspension Bridge to Niagara Falls, Annie H. was again a dear member of our family. Life was very full and new in all ways, but the ague which I began having at Wallingford pursued me with chills and fever. In the fall of the year 1881, Myron began building our home on Ferry Ave. at Niagara Falls, and in the spring we moved into that house.

What a happy home that was. There, Josephine became my daughter as well as her mother's. There, Albert was born in 1883. There, Jessie was born in 1887. Your grandfather died in one of its lower rooms in the September before Albert's birth, and my sister, Mary, died after a

Residence of Myron H. Kinsley, Niagara Falls, New York

long, long illness, just two months after Jessie was born. Annie Hatch lived with us there until 1887. Annie and Mary both worked in the factory and they roomed together.

Many others came to live in this house with us off and on besides our own family of Father, Mother, Grandfather K., Mother K., Aunt Mary, Aunt Annie, Grandmother Baker, Edith, Albert, Jessie and Josephine.

It was a happy thing for me and for my mother and Mary, too, that soon after my marriage we were reunited, and that I could do for them what you are now doing for me: to live with them and give each to the other love and mutual help. How much they loved you children! Mother was dear and sweet and patient in her old age. She, too, learned its lessons, as Mother Noyes did, and as we all must, if we can. Had Mother drawn for me a picture of Community life, it would have been a

Clockwise from left: Myron, Albert, Josephine, Edith, Jessie Catherine, and Jessie Janet Kinsley

wiser, fuller picture than any I remember of having here set down for you. Mine is the optimistic outlook of unthinking youth. Hers would have been one out of a mature knowledge. I was twenty-one when my Community life *ended;* she was thirty-four in 1848 when hers began. Montaigne says, "As for me I never see all of anything; neither do they who so largely promise to show it to others. Of the hundred faces that everything has, I take one." I wish Mother had left the "one" face that life showed to her for me to look upon. It would have, no doubt, pictured its trials; separation from and disapproval of friends and family; losses of all sorts and deprivations; injustice sometimes, and criticism; a child without a father;

Jessie Catherine Kinsley, Jessie Janet, and Catherine Hobart Baker

terrible discipline of mother-love; growing old in Community experience; disappointment in love; the pain of seeing her leader grow too old and fail at last. Yet because my memory is clear of a fine courageous spirit, I am sure my mother would not have written a *bitter* story of the personal side of an effort that, in *her dream,* meant a "Union of souls with one another and their Lord."

    Your father and I often took you with us for a Sunday afternoon visit across the river to the Stone Cottage. We were always welcome. Sometimes Mother Noyes came over the river to us. Mr. Noyes loved Myron heartily and appreciated all his good qualities, though I am sure he felt free to advise and criticize us both. I remember he would sometimes ask me if I was making an idol of Myron or of you children. He feared perhaps my becoming absorbed in family and small things and losing intellectual and spiritual vision. I tried to keep God first in my heart and to keep mentally awake. I read often late into the night, and for religious exercise I went often to church in the village. But a large boarding-house, three young children, a milk business and ill-health kept me tied close to details and my mind seemed dull.

When J. H. N. was sick, I went often to the Cottage to enquire about him and I sent him letters telling him of my love and anxiety. He was too sick to write in response but would send word to me by his nurses, Jane and Chloe. One day, toward the middle of March, I think, they gave me this line from him . . .

Dear Jessie,

I appreciate your very kind note, but must be excused at present from attempting any adequate answer.

J. H. N.

This was written when Mr. Noyes was very, very sick — not long before I saw him last. And one day, too, he sent word that I might come into his sick room if I would come only to the *head of the bed* for a moment, take his hand, and not *look at him;* he said I *must not see him,* for he had changed too much. I went in and took his outstretched hand. Then, impulsively, I disobeyed, and stepped around the bed and clasped his head in my arms and kissed his cheek and said, "Dear, dear, Father!" He gave me such a happy, grateful look; and his nurse, Miss Chloe, said that all day he chuckled and exclaimed, "Well, well, that was wonderful." This was the last time I saw him.

And now I wonder, Edith, what impressions you will get from these sheets. From a sketch so trivial on the surface, I have tried to be *truthful.* Of course, this is not a history of the Oneida Community, and I did not deal intimately with certain parts even of my own life.

Mark Twain says all autobiographies are lies. I took no thought for the morrow. I lived quite down at the foot of the hill, where a sweet breeze of faith and contentment blew away hate and suspicion and made me believe that I was indeed living in the Kingdom of Heaven. Now with other vision I look back and some things that I remember are painful. I think you will read, perhaps, this later consciousness between the lines, although I have shrunk from its expression. It enables me to account for the bitterness of spirit that at its end, rent the Community asunder; and I wonder that the end did not come more quickly. Indeed, many mistakes were made. And yet I have faith to believe that here a great example of unselfishness was set to the world for all time and that the future will find that out.

One thing I must not leave you, and that is the impression that I seemed especially good. I was dreadfully faulty. I was quick-tempered, inclined to gossip, too sure in my judgements, jumping to conclusions, sometimes two-sided, and, above all, vain and egotistical — yet timid. For all these faults I was constantly criticized.

I am sure I was happy. I was almost always following some pursuit, not as a means of happiness, but as an ideal.

You children have been my educators. You have helped me more than you know. I rejoice to see you pressing forward with all the young people here toward an *ideal:* an ideal not all of *commercialism,* nor yet of *communism,* but with the creed of character-building, toleration and brotherly love.

Myron gave me this word: "All you have to do is be thankful"; and through many trials I have been able to be thankful, and I hope yet not to get fretful with life, since there is much to learn and to do.

Knowing me well, I think you will not get from these pages the imagination that my thought still moves in the close, self-searching way that became its habit in Community days. I am changed, much changed. And again, you will perceive that I am glad my mother was one to follow J. H. N. upon that strange and courageous "raid into an unknown land," and that I am happy for her experience, and for Myron's and my own.

Your mother,

J.C.K.

Written mostly in the spring of 1914.

Wife and Mother

THE YEAR 1880 when Jessie Baker married Myron Kinsley was also the year when the Oneida Community, a commune where all property was held in common, was transformed into Oneida Community, Limited, a joint stock company in which individual stockholders owned their allotted shares. Although the new arrangement was very different from the old, Jessie still lived in a special world. For the fifty-eight remaining years of her life her relatives and closest friends were all Oneida Community, Limited people. Her husband and her brother-in-law held responsible positions in the new company; her daughter in time married a company official; her son became one of the most important persons in the management. Most of Jessie's women friends were the wives of company executives. And most of them lived either in the Mansion House or in the surrounding area known as Kenwood.

Obviously a new community had sprung up on the site of the old one. After the breakup there was a minor dispersal of the members. A few old loyalists moved to Niagara Falls, Canada, to live close to John Humphrey Noyes. Some of the young bloods went off to seek their fortune in the outside world, but some of these were glad to come back again after a few years. The so-called Townerite group that had been most opposed to Noyes's leadership stayed at Oneida a few years hoping to gain control of the new company. When they failed to do this many of them moved to Santa Ana in southern California. The extraordinary thing, nevertheless, is not that some people drifted away from Oneida but that a majority stayed on.

What held them? The bonds were both psychological and economic. These were people who had gone through a great adventure together. The older ones had committed their lives and fortunes to the Community many years before; the younger ones, like Jessie, had known no other life. So most of them stayed on because they loved the place. But even if they felt no such strong affection, practical considerations dictated that they should remain. In the division of property each member had received his allocation, a bit of cash to carry him through the period of adjustment and a designated number of shares of stock. But few people, if any, received enough from the division to retire and live the lives of absentee owners. With $600,000 as the par value of all the stock distributed among 210 individuals, each would have received less than $3,000 if the principle of equal division had been followed.[1] Actually most of them were allotted considerably less. Jessie Kinsley's share was only $950. Whatever the face value of their shares, the new capitalists could expect only very modest dividends during the early years.

The former Communists needed jobs. In the old Community they had been trained in the virtue of hard labor. For this they had received no wages but had been given room, board, clothing, education, and entertainment from the common fund. Now they were on their own. The men had not only themselves but wives and children to support. Most of them therefore took positions with the company. Some worked in the shops along with other employees. (Except in the earliest years of the old Community it had always employed a substantial number of outside workers and paid them wages. Community members had performed many of the same tasks but had received no wages.) But the former Community members were particularly prominent in the white-collar jobs. They became the officers of the new company, the plant superintendents, and the sales representatives. Many of them continued to live in the Mansion House, but as time went on more and more of them built houses of their own in Kenwood on land that they leased from the company, land that the old Community had used for farming.

The new community was almost entirely composed of people who belonged to families prominent in the old. The name most commonly encountered was Noyes, first in the person of Theodore Noyes, John Humphrey Noyes's only child to survive of those borne to him by his wife Harriet Holton. Other Noyeses were stirpicult children of the founder or were descended from George Washington Noyes, John Humphrey's brother. Another quasi-royal line was the Millers, descended from John Miller, one of the early converts, and his wife Charlotte Noyes, the

---

1. Of the 210 persons allocated stock, only 5 received $5,000 or more. These were people who had brought substantial amounts of capital into the old Community. See Maren Lockwood Carden, *Oneida: Utopian Community to Modern Corporation* (Baltimore: The Johns Hopkins Press, 1969), p. 115.

founder's sister. Other names recurring generation after generation were the Allens, descended from Henry Allen, who gave the Connecticut farm that became the Wallingford Community, the Cragins, descended from George and Mary Cragin, who were among the earliest converts, and the Ackleys, Burnhams, Leonards, and Wayland-Smiths.

The Kinsleys, the family into which Jessie Baker had married, was also very prominent. Albert Kinsley of Fletcher, Vermont, had become a convert of Noyes and moved with the leader to Oneida in 1848. He brought with him his wife and four children, Sara age 19, Jane 17, Martin 14, and Myron 12. Albert was a hardworking, businesslike man, and his sons demonstrated the same qualities of shrewd common sense, mechanical skill, and the ability not only to work hard themselves but to direct the work of other men. All three men had been active in Community affairs in the period just before the breakup. They had followed different courses of action. Martin had sided with the rebels against Noyes's leadership, but Albert the father and Myron the younger son had been staunchly loyal to Noyes. Myron had been a very busy man. In 1878 after the tragic death of Charles Cragin, Myron had been sent to Wallingford to run the silver-plated spoon business only recently begun. During the next three years he shuttled back and forth between Wallingford and Oneida, and then later extended his travels to Niagara Falls, Canada, where Noyes had taken up his residence. In a time of turmoil Myron was a stabilizing influence. Widely trusted, he acted as messenger carrying communications between the absent leader and the Community. But his role was much more active than mere go-between. Often he made the practical suggestion that solved some troublesome problem.

Describing Myron's part, Noyes wrote: "Others can tell better than I how the rickety government which henceforth managed affairs at O. C. was established. My clearest impression is that it was to be run in my name, but was devised and engineered chiefly by Myron with the help of the parties at home, and without much help from me, except as I was a necessary dummy. . . . Myron really ran the machine and did pretty much as he pleased." [2]

The story of the birth of Oneida Community, Limited was not quite as simple as Noyes made it. Several men, including Albert, Myron's father, made important suggestions, and carefully balanced compromises had to be arranged. But the Kinsleys played key roles, and both brothers, Martin and Myron, were among the nine members of the company's first board of directors.

Soon after the reorganization the company began to transfer the

2. Ibid., pp. 115–16.

silver plating and the chain manufacture from Wallingford to Niagara Falls, New York. The Wallingford industries had never been very profitable and that part of Connecticut was considered unhealthful because of epidemics of malaria. The new location offered excellent power sites. Faithful Myron Kinsley was sent to Niagara Falls to supervise the project, and Jessie his young wife had to run a huge household that included not only her husband and three children but a miscellaneous group of relatives, in-laws, and company employees.

From 1880 to 1895 Oneida Community, Limited stumbled along, making a little money in good years, barely keeping afloat in poor. The company was badly shaken by the panic of 1893 and its aftermath. During these years the management was in the hands of older men, more notable for piety than for business acumen. Preoccupation with otherworldly affairs reached a critical point when a group of spiritualists gained control and claimed to be in communication with John Humphrey Noyes from beyond the grave.

The company was rescued from these faltering hands by Pierrepont Burt Noyes, son of the founder and Harriet Worden. Born in 1870 in the earliest crop of stirpicult babies, Pierre—as Jessie Kinsley and other Community people called him—went to Colgate University for two years and was planning to transfer to Harvard when his education was interrupted by the serious illness of his mother. He took care of her until she died in 1891 and then went to work for the company in the Niagara Falls plant. Becoming discouraged with his prospects, he went off to New York City in the company of his half-brother, Holton Noyes, another of the founder's stirpicult offspring. They formed a partnership under the name of Noyes Brothers and went into the business of selling silverware and novelties. Holton presently dropped out and operated a restaurant, but Pierre was soon making a good income as a salesman.

Although Pierre's activities were at first in competition with Oneida's, he soon re-established contacts with his old Community friends, especially with some of the younger men still working for the company but discouraged by its bumbling management. Step by step Pierre moved back into the company. First he added the Oneida line to those that he was selling; next he seized an unexpected opportunity to obtain a place on the company's board of directors. More convinced than ever than new business methods were necessary, young Noyes organized a campaign to elect a reform majority on the board of directors. By tireless activity his party won five members on the nine-member board in the election of January 1895. Dr. Theodore Noyes, the founder's eldest son, became the new president. In this fight so crucial to the future of the company, Pierre had the strong support of the Kinsley brothers. Martin felt a fatherly interest in the situation because Pierre's wife was Corinna Ackley, daughter of Alice Ackley and Victor Cragin. After the breakup Alice had married Martin Kinsley so Martin was a step-father-in-law of the rising star of the company.

The new management sent Pierrepont to Niagara Falls to manage the plants there, and he took speedy steps to improve their efficiency. Leaving the day by day direction of operations to his subordinates, he spent much of his time developing new markets for the company products. During the late 1890s the company enjoyed an unprecedented prosperity, and Pierrepont rose rapidly to the top of the hierarchy. He was brought back to Kenwood and in 1899 made general manager, a new post created for him. For another decade other men still bore the title of president, but Noyes received that designation in 1910.

Noyes found faithful lieutenants in the Kinsley family. Myron was sent to Chicago, where his honesty and energy helped to create goodwill for the Oneida line. Martin's and Myron's generation, however, was growing old, and the two men retired and died a few years after Noyes assumed command. But by this time a younger generation of Kinsleys was working for the company. Martin's son who bore his father's name and who had married his first cousin Edith Kinsley, Myron's and Jessie's daughter, in 1903, climbed up the ladder with assignments in New York City, Niagara Falls, and Chicago, as well as Kenwood. For more than twenty years after her husband's death Jessie Kinsley lived in Mart's household. Mart's cousin, Dr. Burton Dunn, was another important company executive. Dunn, the son of Leonard Dunn and Sara Kinsley, gave up his practice as an eye doctor to work for the company. As advertising manager, he was able to erase the older rather stodgy image of Oneida silverware and make a successful sales pitch to the sophisticated younger set. Perhaps the most dynamic of all this hard-driving family was Albert M. Kinsley, Myron's and Jessie's son. Refusing to go to college, Albert became a "salesman in training" for the company at the age of seventeen. Three years later Pierrepont Noyes appointed him superintendent of the chain factory, where he doubled the business in three years. "Ab," as he was called, introduced scientific principles of management and orderly budget processes, but his most unusual skill was in handling personnel. He gained the reputation of being the most beloved and popular executive in the company. All these skills were required when Oneida closed its Niagara Falls plant and transferred its operations to Sherrill, a new town developed near Kenwood. Not content simply to relocate the physical plant, Kinsley followed a compassionate policy of helping employees at every level to move from one community to the other.

In his consideration for the feelings of the workers, Albert Kinsley was an excellent exemplar of the attitudes that Pierrepont Noyes was trying to cultivate in the company. Pierre was a much better businessman than his father had been, but he resembled the old leader in his idealism. He came back to Oneida to work for a salary much smaller than he could have made elsewhere; he stuck with the company on later occasions when he was receiving tempting offers. More remarkable than his own sacrifice was the sacrifice that he induced other men to make. In comparison with other companies, Oneida's executives were paid modest salaries, but Noyes convinced a very talented group of young men, most of them with roots in the old Community, to devote their lives to Oneida Community, Limited.

Noyes's most striking achievement was to instill the same loyalty in the Oneida factories that he did in the offices. Only once did his workers strike. This was in 1899 when the silverware hands at Niagara Falls attempted to unionize. Noyes rejected their demands, not because he was opposed to unions on principle, but because he had other plans for his workers. When the strikers returned to work after being out for ten weeks Noyes reconciled them to their defeat by generous treatment. Oneida reduced its work day from the prevailing ten hours to nine and established a wage scale higher than that in most establishments of the day. It instituted a form of health insurance and paid half the premium. As it transferred more and more of its operations to Sherrill, it tried hard to make this new city an attractive place to work and live. Its factories were cleaner and less forbidding than most others of that period; employees were aided in buying or building their own homes on individual lots; the new city boasted of its fine schools, its baseball field and golf course.

In explaining his philosophy of labor relations, Pierrepont Noyes said, "Make no welfare moves from fear, but always and only because you believe that company success should add to the comfort and happiness of every member of the working group."[3] And Jessie Kinsley, who remembered the old Community so well, was happy to see the idealism of the new generation of managers. They were, she wrote, "pressing toward an *ideal* not all of *commercialism,* nor yet of *communism,* but with the creed of character-building, toleration and brotherly love."[4]

For the years of her marriage, 1880–1907, only a handful of Jessie's letters survive, a few written in the early years to Lily Bailey Hutchins Cragin, her classmate in the old Community days; and a larger number

3. Walter D. Edmonds, *The First Hundred Years: 1848–1948* (Sherrill, N.Y.: Oneida Ltd., 1948), p. 8.

4. See p. 68.

written mostly to Jane Kinsley, her sister-in-law, telling of family experiences in Chicago between 1899 and 1902. Fortunately Edith Kinsley, Jessie's talented daughter, has left an affectionate memoir of Myron, her father. This provides not only a vivid impression of this long-bearded, robust, and competent husband and father, but of Jessie, the wife and mother, who loved books, pictures, and good talk, but uncomplainingly accepted her years of toil as a conscientious homemaker. Jane Kinsley Rich, Albert's daughter and Jessie's granddaughter, rounds out the domestic picture with her description of the spacious house built for Martin and Edith Kinsley a few years after Myron's death. This is the house where Jane, her brother Myron, and their friends visited Jessie and spent many happy hours listening to her read aloud, give a tea party, look at photograph albums, and see the braidings develop.

LETTERS TO LILY CRAGIN, 1880-1884

Soon after the termination of complex marriage there were a large number of weddings. One of these, taking place in the Mansion House on January 1, 1880, united Lily Bailey Hutchins, member of the same class of girls as Jessie, with John Cragin, a brother of Charles Cragin, whose tragic death in 1878 was described in Jessie's memoir. Jessie's marriage to Myron Kinsley followed on February 8, 1880.

Wallingford, March 14, 1880

Dear Lily,

How was it you were ignorant so long of that great event? Why, I'm a married woman of a fortnight. . . . We had a nice quiet little wedding at New Haven. T'was all so suitable and quite to my mind that I really wanted to go over the whole ceremony again.

I like my homey life here, the quiet, the pleasant company, but I do miss the music and the dramatic culture going on at the O. C. You must be in the very vortex of all that. Isabelle [Brooks] wrote me some weeks ago giving details of *Pinafore* mishaps and drawbacks. It was amusing and sounded quite natural.

George has gone for Annie Miller who has already reached Wallingford station. Such an arrival is, next to the coming of the mail, the event of the day.

Suspension Bridge, April 5th, 1882

Dear Lily,
Your pleasant letter has lain long unanswered.
Edith is a mischievous little chick, very active, but not yet walking. As for talking she will try to say every word she is told to and every sound she hears to the ringing of the church bells. She has nine teeth and weighs twenty lbs.
We shall soon move to the Falls, occupying our new house which will be comfortable. . . . Mother will come out then I expect.
Annie Miller's girl, named Violet, is three months old and almost as large as my Edith.
Our fire might have been terrible. It occurred on St. Patrick's Day in the morning. It started in a two-story addition west of the main building and was arrested before doing further damage. . . . Not even a gentle breeze was out that morning. The perfect calm was all that saved our great shop.[1]
My dear other half says he shall now call on you if he journeys to New York.
Do you remember the old time criticism of our class (of girls) for being too much together? Have we not at last taken it and gone asunder to the four winds! I do not think the old love and clinging to a few of you at least, has gone out of me. I could never ignore it if any ill came to you or Carrie, or Nora, Mabel or Marion. I am keeping a bundle of old letters written years ago for you and me to read together when we get to be grandmothers.

Niagara Falls, January 29th, 1884

Dear Lily,
Your rare note is at hand and receives immediate attention.
Do come. I want to see you. It is long since I have been with any of our old sisterhood. It was a strong cord that bound us together. Do you remember how the hackings of criticism failed to sever it and it has not yet ceased to vibrate though stretched from New York to Oneida to Niagara Falls to Boston. If you come you will have all you can stand of the enfants.[2]
I have always plenty of work to do and sometimes think I ought

1. The silver plate works at Niagara Falls, N.Y.
2. Edith Kinsley was born February 19, 1881, and Albert Kinsley April 19, 1883.

not to spare a moment to writings and like recreations, but I put everything aside now and devote myself to you.

Do come. If you do and choose a house just far enough away to make it easy for me to call, you will have company often.

LETTERS FROM CHICAGO, 1899–1902

Myron Kinsley represented Oneida Community, Limited in Chicago from 1899 to 1902. Living in this bustling city was an exhilerating experience for Jessie, which she described in a number of letters. Most of them were written to Jane Kinsley, Myron's sister, who never married and lived in the Mansion House. Although Jane was twenty-seven years older than Jessie, the two women had a very close relationship.

Chicago, March 12th, 1899

Dear Sister Jane [Kinsley],

We haven't a girl yet and have had such a busy week. All our boxes by freight came and were unpacked. Carpenters came and put up a partition. Expressmen came with our bookcase and a folding bed. . . . All these things with constant dings at the doorbell from butcher or baker or milkman, iceman or tramp. We keep our doors most sedulously locked on account of tramps who are numerous and of evil reputation among the neighbors here about. I usually speak to them through the window.

Jessie[3] is enjoying her school and has given you a good idea of it in her letter.

Albert begins going tomorrow to a business college in the heart of the city. . . . We shall have to have breakfast on time for him and Myron. Myron gets a five or ten cent lunch so we have quite a hearty breakfast. Oatmeal first, salt pork, potatoes and gravy and doughnuts. Jessie, Grandma and I have the simplest of lunches, a banana sliced with milk and sugar with bread and butter. At six o'clock (Myron usually gets home on the 5:25 train) we have another hearty meal. Sunday we have breakfast late and dinner about two. We imagine that will suffice for the day, but seven o'clock finds one or another in the kitchen lunching.

Grandma does all the dishes and lots besides. She has just finished making Edith a new summer dress. She does not seem homesick.

3. Jessie Janet, born March 18, 1887, was enrolled in the sixth grade of a "normal school for young ladies," taught by practice teachers.

This house is most conveniently arranged and fitted up. Work is more easily done than in our house at the Falls.

Chicago, March 17th, 1899

My dear Sister,

Another week has gone of this new life in Chicago. . . . Having no girl Grandma and I are kept very busy. Jessie and Albert have something new to tell us every day about their schools.

Thursday Grandma and I took the train at our little Eggleston Station (a few steps from the house). In twenty minutes we were in the midst of a great bustle and crowd. We set out in quest of Myron's office, found the Unity Building, took the elevator to the 12th floor, wandered about the marble-floored corridors 'till we found "M. H. Kinsley—representing Oneida Community" on a glazed door. We took Myron by surprise. Such a pleasant office. Two broad windows look out over the housetops. Most of these are way below. Far across and beyond these is the lake. We could see the dash of white caps on its gray surface. . . . Looking down, down, down we see a bit of State Street, I believe. The stream of passing people look small indeed. Many seem to be going in or out of a great doorway. Myron says this is the entrance to the Masonic Temple.

After Grandma and I had rested a bit, we started out with Myron to see the "Tissot Pictures" now on exhibition at the Museum. Myron and Grandma were a little disappointed in them. They had thought of them as being large oils. In fact they are small and nearly all watercolors, beautiful to me, each one a gem in color, composition and drawing. And what an imagination the man has.

Saturday was Jessie's twelfth birthday. Her papa invited her and me to go to a matinee with him. This was her first trip downtown. She is equal to finding her way anywhere. Myron having told her the objective points, let her lead the way which she did with dexterity. We saw Maud Adams in "The Little Minister." No wonder the play has had such a run. How we did enjoy it.

Chicago, April 8th, 1899

My dear Jane,

We had a joyful evening on Thursday when Pierre[4] came and

---

4. In 1899, at the age of twenty-nine, Pierrepont Noyes became general manager of Oneida Community, Limited and began a campaign to invigorate the company.

took supper with us. At ten o'clock P.M. he took the train at Englewood for California. He was our first O. C. visitor and you may be sure he was more than welcome. . . . We all felt as though the window into our beautiful Kenwood friendships had been opened wide for three or four hours. Our hearts were glad.

Will you believe it, this last girl was as Huck Finnish as all the rest. The others had set a day and told me to rely on them — then vanished forever. This last girl came and saw me, afterward wrote a postal . . . said she would be here Tuesday, even called to be sure I had received her postal. Tuesday morning — no girl. The veil of mystery fell. Rose H. had vanished forever, too. I can only account for all this happening by imagining that these girls belong to a society that amuses itself by making dupes of unsuspecting families and each one vies with the other to make the biggest dupe!

This was a windy day. Clouds of dust blew through the streets and the tumble-weed and newspapers climbed our fence and littered the yard. When I went down to Myron's office in the afternoon, this same wind had blown away the smoky atmosphere that dims the distant view from his lofty windows.

There are wonderful displays of millinery and dresses and all manner of fan-dangles in the shops. But I bought nothing. One window was curiously gotten up. A broad black background, all surounding it black and weird. In the midst stood the Devil clothed in red, bowing and scraping and beckoning us to come in. Finally he fixed his eyes on a short fat man in the crowd and began to draw a sketch of him on the black background. This background was charged with electricity and as he drew his pencil would emit terrific sparks. How quickly the crowd recognized the fat man and a shout went up as it came out so cleverly. All this to advertise a store where suits are made to order and every suit at 15 dollars "No more — no less."

Chicago, May 6th, 1899

Dear Jane,

This is a cold rainy Sunday. Shut in by ourselves we read, write, play backgammon and just now as our girl has gone out we are going to get our own supper. We had strawberry shortcake for dinner. Strawberries are 10 cents a quart and fresh asparagus is 3 cents a big bunch.

We have had great goings on all week. The landlord is having the house painted. Carpenters have been here putting in a new cellar door, and new boards in the porch. In the attic they have built a partition and closet making us another bedroom. In the kitchen the old coal stove has given place to a new gas stove. Gas men came to install it and stove men came to put the old coal stove to operating in the cellar. Then Myron has had a load of fresh, rich earth brought for the flower bed. A carpenter came to put a board around it, to bank it in while a gardener came to put the bed in shape and set out a honeysuckle. Two trees have been set out in front of the house. I have painted the water-closet floor and part of the bathroom.

Albert and his father always sieze upon my letters and read each sheet as I write. Albert criticizes my writing such small details as I have in this letter; says I am "the funniest woman to write such stuff that nobody will be interested in." Well, I'm not afraid about you people but don't show to the general public who might be of A's opinion.

Chicago, May 17th, 1899

My dear Mr. [John] Gragin,

You were ever so kind to write me about the suit and how well it fitted Johnny. We all appreciated so much getting letters from you and Lily.

We often speak of the brave fight you have made[5] and the courage you have shown—the faith given to you. It seems wonderful.

Myron has had good business until lately when there is a little slackening. He hasn't interested himself one bit in real estate here which is due, I think, to his feeling sure of going back after a few years to Kenwood. He also is very busy at the office and on the street.

If your plan for a sanitorium is practicable perhaps you will find it nearer at hand than in this far away city. You have no idea how dense and heavy the air seems here on some days. The smoke hangs low and the white dust of the streets fills every place. When the rains fall as they have for several days now, one can draw a long breath and feel it worthwhile since the rain has cleared away the mists and washed the atmosphere.

With love and kindest regards to you from,

Myron, Grandma and your friend
Jessie

Chicago, July, 1899

My Dear Lily,

I feel almost condemned when I think how long a time I have let

5. John H. Cragin was dying of cancer.

fly by without sending you an answer to your dear letter and thanking you for the little picture of Johnny and Lotta.[6]

Dear old friend, you don't know how my heart goes out to you in the warmest love and sympathy in this your time of long suffering. How brave you and John both are. Well, I can only admire, wonder and sympathize. If the time comes when John feels that the Lord's will is that his body shall no longer suffer, how brave he will be to say "Thy will be done." I am sure the greatest peace and blessing will come after the long struggle. When I think I might lose Myron then I realize what you are facing . . . [and] am so glad you are there at Kenwood surrounded by our friends.

Chicago, November, 1899

My dear Sister [Jane Kinsley],

I must tell you about the burglary next door. Bessie had gone up to bed and as she pulled down her shade saw two men in the neighbor's yard but didn't think much about it. At ten o'clock the people returned home as the robbers bolted out the back door. In the house they found things in such a state. Every drawer pulled out and dumped, every closet empty, mattresses pulled upon the floor, trunks empty, jewelry and a loaded revolver gone.

We don't any of us seem to feel especially nervous over it.

Yesterday's paper told of 2,000 cases of diptheria and scarlet fever.

Albert has a fine report from school this month and Edith had an honor mark on one of her sketches which means that it will be exhibited in the spring.

This week Myron, Jessie, Edith and I went to hear Richard Mansfield in "Cyrano De Bergerac." Oh, the play and the players were fine.

Chicago, November 20th, 1899

My dear Jane,

We are going to lose Bessie. She is to be married and goes to her sister's home in Michigan this week. We have been quite desolate over it,

---

6. Carlotta Cragin, daughter of John and Lily, who later married Jessie's son Albert.

but the grocer who takes our daily order thinks his wife's cousin would like to come to us. She is a German girl. If only she will, how glad we will be.

Last evening we went down to the Sunday Night Concert at the Studebaker and had a rare treat. The orchestra was good and Signor Campanari's solos were fine and then we had the pleasure of hearing Miss Nellie Hyde sing. We met her at the door for a moment as she left the theater afterward and she said she never forgot her Kenwood friends — time spent at K. was the happiest of her life. She has much of the society manner and a slow sort of sweet drawl in speaking.

Edith was invited to go over to the College Settlement on the southwest side. While there the manager asked Edith to teach a class of young men in art one night a week. Edith didn't feel very competent but said she would consult us at home. We advise her to take it up on trial.

Chicago, January 15th, 1900

Dearest Jane,

Has anyone heard yet from Gertrude?[7] It seems almost a nightmare to think of her so far away and so alone as far as relatives are concerned. And the bubonic plague in Manila too.

You know how often we spoke of the time when Mrs. H. should know about our Community life. Last night her son, Ray, was over here and in the course of the evening's conversation (without real prevarication) we could not get by the point where the OC was mentioned and talked about. So he was told of our living there and shown pictures of the lawns and buildings. I suppose he has told his mother and the time will come when she will "at" me about it. If only she was a reasonable woman I should have been glad to have had her know long ago. I will be glad to be on the right footing, nothing concealed, as it were.

Jessie sits here getting her homework done while Edith is in the kitchen reading German with Katie who is a fine German scholar with good pronunciation. They are reading a German storybook together, Edith reading, Katie correcting. Albert is up at his desk doing his Latin. Grandma is reading in her room. She has just finished a new gray flannel princess dress for herself. It is nicely fitted and becoming.

Last week I attended a meeting of the New Century Club. The

7. Gertrude H. Noyes was the stirpicult daughter of J. H. Noyes and Harriet N. Olds. She married Major Charles R. Noyes, the son of Horatio S. Noyes, J. H. Noyes's brother. Horatio was not a convert to his brother's creed and settled in Chicago.

meeting was taken up with the reading of interesting papers on Provence and Brittany and other French topics. Some very bright women were present.

Edith is getting along well with work at the Art School, painting from life now. Before this in the life class it was drawing in charcoal.

Chicago, January 28th, 1900

My dear Lily,

Last night we had free tickets given us to Central Music Hall to hear some prominent men speak in favor of the Boers. The audience was composed of all sorts and conditions of men and women, many very earnest and refined, some very anarchistic and vociferous. The speaking was good. I enjoyed hearing Rabbi Hirsch and Miss Jane Addams (she of Hull House) best of all.

Here we have very, very cold weather with wind that blows right through you . . . we must keep a brick fire going. The children are keeping well as are the rest of us.

LETTERS FROM KENWOOD, 1905-1912

In 1902 Myron Kinsley retired, and the family moved back to the Mansion House in Kenwood. Here Edith, aged 22, married her cousin Martin Kinsley in 1903. Two years later in a quiet ceremony in Syracuse, New York, Albert, aged 22, married Carlotta Cragin, the seventeen-year-old daughter of John and Lily Cragin. Myron was the only witness. Jessie Janet, aged 20, married Chester Burnham, member of an old Community family, in August 1907.

In November 1907 Myron died after a short illness. Following the old Community custom, his friends, led by William D. Hinds and Pierrepont Noyes, paid tribute to him in a service at the Mansion House. Less than a year later Pierrepont Noyes was the principal speaker at a much sadder occasion—the funeral of Jessie Kinsley Burnham, who was only twenty-one years old and carrying her first child when she succumbed to acute appendicitis on September 3, 1908.

During this period of grief when she herself was seriously ill, Jessie found comfort in corresponding with her friends, particularly with Gertrude Noyes, then living in the Philippines where her husband Major Charles Noyes, was stationed.

Carlotta Cragin Kinsley

Kenwood, 1905

Dear Lotta [Carlotta Kinsley],[8]
       You looked sweet and pretty that morning you went away and I felt like congratulating Albert again on his choice of a wife. Truly it has made me very happy that he has married you.
       Edith made me a mother-in-law first and now again I have become one through Albert. Mothers-in-law are thought to be such dreadful persons. Alack a day, I shall try to be good!

Kenwood, January 9th, 1908

My dear Gertrude [Noyes],
       It is several days since I received your letter [of sympathy] with its accompanying gifts of handkerchief and picture of baby Margaret. I cannot begin to tell you how touched and happy they made me. I am so glad you have a dear little girl.
       Miriam's baby, Virginia, has been a delight and comfort to me

       8. Written to Carlotta ("Lotta"), in October 1905, when Lotta and Edith went to the Adirondacks for a week.

Myron H. Kinsley

through Mr. Kinsley's illness. I could relax more by going to see the baby than in any other way; could then be strong again to help him for he depended very much on me. His death has been a great blow to our family and to me but I have kept well and have been able to take up Mr. Kinsley's duties as postmaster and carry on until such time as a new postmaster shall be appointed. I loved Mr. Kinsley so much that had I lived with him only ONE year, I think I should have been thankful. We lived together twenty-eight years and the fruit of those years (beside daily happiness) was three good children. So I must not ask too much of God but count my blessings with a thankful heart.

We are having much snow and typical wintry weather. Very few people are sick, the scarlet fever has disappeared; the agents have come and gone and the household (the Mansion House) has settled into a quiet, pleasant groove. The financial crisis has affected our sales seriously. The whole tone of the sales meetings and at the banquet was of serious and strong determination to meet changed conditions in the spirit of self-sacrifice and cheerfulness. As usual Pierre struck the dominant note at the banquet. He is so virile, but others, too, spoke exceedingly well.[9]

New York, September 11th, 1908

My dear Hope [Allen],[10]

Your beautiful letter has found me here.

I know how well you loved Jessie, and your mother loved her so that our sorrow is your sorrow too. It is everyone's sorrow who knew her.

She wanted us to be brave and she was very brave herself, tho' so young. Chester too. Oh, how noble he was and both physically and spiritually stood by Jessie to the end.

We all feel as a family that we owe Chester the love of a life-time and want to help him bear this blow which falls perhaps most crushingly on him.

It is something to thank God for having had such a dear child for 21 years. I have a darling treasure left in Edith, another in Albert and in Lotta, and Chester, in Mart and Josephine—in all my dear family and our big Community family too.

Aunt Jane is here with us in the city. She has lost Sara, Martin and Myron, and now Jessie who was like a real daughter to her. Does she grieve in a crushed way? Never. She seems to have none of that self-pity which is so weakening (sometimes it overwhelms me in spite of faith and determination). All Aunt Jane's thought is for others.

I thank you so much for your letter and send my love to your mother.

New York City, September 18th, 1908

My dear Gertrude,

I imagine you packing up and gradually getting ready for your long journey.[11]

---

9. One of Pierrepont Noyes's successful innovations as general manager was the annual convention at which salesmen, especially of silverware and traps, were brought back to the Mansion House for meetings and a banquet.

10. .Hope Emily Allen was the daughter of Henry G. and Portia Underhill Allen. See also p. 181.

11. Major Charles Noyes's family was being sent to Fort Sam Houston in Texas.

Jessie Janet Kinsley, 1906

Sunday I am going to the hospital for a small operation and after three weeks will be home again. I am afraid you will be gone when I get home so I want to write you goodby.

Dear Gertrude, a great deal of love for you is in my heart. You will be gone, Mrs. Marks will be gone, Jessie will be gone when I get home. From you and Mrs. Marks I shall be separated by miles and space, from Jessie by the mystery of death. I wish I could feel one no more dreadful a separation than the other. I can only trust God hour by hour.

Dorothy Leonard[12] wrote this poem about Jessie Janet, titled:

"DAPHNE–

The Indian plums are dim with bloom,
Bloomy their purple and crimson moons,
Falling in clusters and thick festoons,
Like wreaths adorning an old Greek tomb.

Dim are the hills in enchanted haze,
Blue with the bloom of the Indian plums,
When Daphne, sweet Daphne, the young bride comes
To the long, lone house of her bridal days.

Daphne, the girl of the beech-brown hair
And cheek like the bridal autumn lily,
Faintly freckled and burnished and stilly,
Stilly as windless September air

Or that we called but at last even her breath
Vanished like smoke from last even's fire,
For Daphne, sweet Daphne, the heart of desire
Denying her suitors, has wedded with death!

12. Dorothy Leonard, daughter of J. H. Noyes and Beulah Hendee, was the wife of Stephen R. Leonard, Jr., member of an old Community family and an executive for Oneida Community, Limited.

Kenwood, December 20th, 1908

My dear Gertrude,

Your letter has left a very clear mental picture of your present life. You cannot know how much your life has meant to me all this fall. When I have had battles of depression to fight I have thought of you and Major Noyes. I have prayed for the soldier spirit and thought how Major Noyes ever put the word *cannot* behind him, and went on bearing these hard tests without thought of giving in though sick and wearied beyond measure. . . . I have prayed God to give me that courage.

I have grown quite well and have been doing my library[13] work for some time. I walk a mile or more a day, paint too, and feel quite my old self physically. I think some of my negative thoughts are temptations born of self-pity. I am sure I can be better perhaps for having been through fire.

We are having flurries of snow today, one of those tempestuous days when the skies are blue one hour and the next dark as night 'till the snow has spilled down.

Chester is going to New York tomorrow to be with Burt and Rhoda [Dunn][14] at Christmas. I am so glad he is going. He is wonderfully brave, but lives on nerve.

R. L. S. [Robert Louis Stevenson] said our history could be written in the kindnesses of friends. Mine could be I'm sure. So many kind things come into my life—so much love, too. I am sure I ought to be thankful and trust God to keep me so.

Our reading club will soon be finishing *The Odyssey* and then are planning to read either *The Illiad* or the *Bible*.

Everyone is full busy today. This afternoon there is taking place a revival of that little pantomine "When I was a Bachelor." There are to be other children's performances tomorrow; Christmas afternoon, too. These are under the inspiring guidance of Mr. Herrick who has a genius for getting, with little drill, so much spontaneous pleasure for us all, out of the children. And they enjoy it too.

I am reading Matthew Arnold's letters to his wife, mother, sisters, and friends. It is like living with him and his family almost, and to my surprise he is the most genial man. (Surprise because I had always thought of him as a critic. Perhaps because of Robert Louis Stevenson's remark about him when he heard of his death, "I am afraid he won't like God.") His great ambition was to write poetry. In one letter he says "The

13. Jessie was serving as librarian in the Mansion House.

14. Burton L. Dunn was the son of Leonard F. Dunn and Sara Kinsley Dunn, Myron's sister.

gray hairs on my head are becoming more and more numerous. I sometimes grow impatient of getting old amidst a press of occupation for which after all I was not born. The work I do like is not very compatible with any other."

Christmas Day I was up at seven to see Edith and Mart untie their packages . . . then the three of us came down to my room finding there many beautiful gifts for me. We went on to Albert and Lotta's room to see their presents and so on to breakfast. Breakfast was a merry meal, the children's Christmas dolls and soldiers accompanying them and MERRY CHRISTMAS!! flying from one person to another.

Albert and Edith, Mart and Lotta carried holly to the graveyard to put sprays on many of the graves, thinking tenderly of their sister and fathers and other friends.

There is to be a masquerade ball on January 4th.

Dear Gertrude, I never shall forget your sweet sisterly kindness — shall always love you. I am looking forward to seeing the picture you spoke of sending of the three children.

Kenwood, February 23rd, 1909

My dear Gertrude,

I went to New York to see Dr. West. I had not felt too well and was glad to go. He said my operation was a success. I am feeling better again now and am not down-hearted.

I believe there is to be a new printer for the Quadrangle.[15] This one is troubled by intemperance toward spiritous liquors.

We had an interesting 20th of February meeting.[16] George W. gave a talk on the development of religious beliefs beginning back of the Christian era and showing the gradual changes through Judaism to Christianity, to Calvinism and the later revivals. How J. H. N.'s religious beliefs were a natural evolution and progression beyond these. Mr. Hinds, Mr. Herrick and Mr. Wayland-Smith also spoke and we had wine and cake.

I delight in the pictures of the children that you have sent me.

15. The *Quadrangle* was a post-Community, family periodical subsidized by Oneida Community, Limited.

16. On February 20, 1834, at New Haven, Connecticut, John Humphrey Noyes proclaimed his conviction that he was free of sin. Each year the Oneida Community celebrated the anniversary of this "High Tide of the Spirit" (see p. 10). The speakers referred to were George Wallingford Noyes, a nephew of J. H. Noyes, William A. Hinds, president of Oneida Community, Limited, James B. Herrick and Francis Wayland-Smith, long time members of the Community.

Kenwood, June 25th, 1909

My dear Gertrude,

I want to tell you what a good time I had with Miriam in Montreal. It has served as the best possible preparation for another operation I am to have next week or the week after. I have seen four doctors who agree there is a large fast growing tumor on the intestines or the kidney. The operation will be here at Dr. Carpenter's hospital in Oneida with Dr. West in charge. . . . I do not sit down under this in a hopeless spirit. There is much in life for me and I mean to make the most of every chance. . . . We can find places to put our sorrows where they lie quite outside our real life or if in sight, put on rosier color than we might expect.

Broad Street Hospital, Oneida, July 20th, 1909

My dear Gertrude,

I hope someone wrote to you ere this that there was no tumor only a bad appendix with adhesions to a muscle and a kidney so that altogether I deceived every one. . . . I have had a light heart. A little pain has seemed nothing. It's almost like being born again, isn't it?

I was so interested in all you told me of your experiences in camp. I have been braver always for the thought of you and Major Noyes — "The soldier spirit," I have thought, "the soldier spirit! — unafraid! undismayed!"

Kenwood, December 18th, 1911

My dear Gertrude,

I write this letter with much love in my heart for you hoping it will reach you for Christmas.

The open winter has been very favorable so far for the building of Christine and Grosvenor's and Mart and Edith's houses.[17] In Mart's I shall have three rooms of my own; a sitting room, bedroom and bath with the use of the great upper porch. And besides that shall live with Mart and Edith and the dear baby, Rhoda.[18] She is a round jolly baby with black

17. In Kenwood close by the Mansion House, key personnel of Oneida Community, Limited were now able to build private residences. The company leased them the land, but the executives had to pay for construction. One such house was being built for Grosvenor and Christine Allen; another by Martin and Edith Kinsley.

18. Jessie's second grandchild, Rhoda, was born to Mart and Edith in April 1911.

eyes like Edith's but rather better features than Edith used to have. She is happy all day long, is just being weaned. Edith has had good help. She is a devoted mother. . . . My other little grandchild [Myron] is nearly two. He is a very dear child to me.

This is a letter full of home items but I remember such used to interest me when we lived in Chicago.

I have another letter to write and must not make this one too long.

I could talk to you about painting which is as much as ever my enthusiasm but must desist. I have bought a lovely painting of Kenneth's. He seems happy, is teaching at the Art Student's League in New York and working hard at home. I found Helen[19] a lovable girl, very practical, devoted and unselfish.

MEMOIRS BY EDITH KINSLEY AND JANE KINSLEY RICH

After Myron's death, Jessie made her home with Edith and Martin Kinsley. Sharing the same interests in literature and art, mother and daughter were the closest of companions. Edith captures the stalwart character of her father and the gentle loving nature of her mother in the following memoir.

Jane Kinsley Rich was the daughter of Albert and Carlotta Kinsley. She has contributed a description of the spacious Kenwood house in which she used to visit her Uncle Mart, her Aunt Edith, her grandmother Jessie and play with her cousin Rhoda.

Father was born in 1836 on a stony Vermont farm, the youngest of four children, Sarah, Jane, Martin and Myron, born to Albert Kinsley and his wife, Maria Ellsworth. His less immediate ancestors were early colonists who settled in Massachusetts and later in Vermont. In the early 1840's, Father's parents had become convinced Perfectionists, and in 1848 they decided to risk all, selling lands and possessions and journeying with their four children to Central New York State to join a communistic experiment lately established under the leadership of J. H. Noyes, called Oneida Community. Father was twelve years old when he became a mem-

19. Kenneth Hayes Miller, son of George and Annie Kelly Miller, was an artist in New York City. He gave lessons summers in Kenwood, which Jessie and Edith attended. Helen Pendleton Miller was his second wife.

ber of that strange and adventurous society. In spite of the changes which Oneida Community underwent, I think I can say that he remained a member of the society for the rest of his life.

In 1879, by the common consent of its members, Oneida Community abandoned the practice of communism and the system of Complex Marriage. Shortly afterward, in 1880, Father and Mother were married. She was then twenty-two years old, and he was forty-four, just twice her age. They were married while living in Wallingford, Connecticut, where a second Community home and a silver factory had been established. Mr. Charles Cragin was the first superintendent of that business, Oneida Community's youngest industry. A period of transition followed, called "the breakup." It was decided to move the silverware factory to Niagara Falls, New York. At this point Mother temporarily returned to Oneida, and there I was born in the Mansion House where she had been born. In the meantime, Father was busily engaged in factory-moving as well as acting as John Noyes's emissary between Canada and Oneida Community, for difficult negotiations were in progress to turn the socialist experiment into an individually owned joint-stock company. Beyond these activities, Father was building a home for us on the American side of the Niagara River—a home that was to house our family for the next ten years.

The house and barns that Father built were of brick and were spacious. He used brick, I fancy, because he wished them to seem like adjuncts of the Big House [Mansion House] at Kenwood, which was our real home, where each year we spent a summer month or two; and spacious, because of the size of the extended family which they were designed to hold. Their size was, indeed, fortunate, for they were soon filled to capacity: the house crowded with human beings, and the barns with an assortment of animals.

Living with us at Niagara Falls were Grandfather and Grandmother Kinsley, Grandmother Baker (Mother's mother), Aunt Mary Baker (Mother's sister), Aunt Annie Hatch (a Community friend), and for part of each year, Josephine, our elder half-sister. Besides Father, Mother and I, there soon came the birth of Albert, and then Jessie Janet, our little sister. This group was called the "second story family." On the third story lived two Community men who worked at the factory. Added to the above were two maids and two men-servants. It therefore became necessary for us to copy the Mansion House in more than one respect; our dining room could not possibly seat the whole family at once, and first and second tables were always laid.

Dogs and cats, puppies and kittens, hens and chicks, cows and horses were all a part of our family, although they lived in the barns.

Father was fond of animals, particularly of horses. We had a handsome pair of black horses that drew the large carriage in which we took Sunday drives. Father had a horse and trap of his own in which he drove to work. He rode this horse, a spirited bay, and soon ponies and horses began to appear for Josephine, Albert and me to ride. Mother was not attracted to animals and she was even acutely afraid of horses. I think Jessie shared Mother's timidity, for neither of them rode.

It may be imagined that Mother's life was a strenuous one. It was also one unsuited to her temperament, for she was an intellectual, yet she was wholly engulfed by domestic duties. Young and inexperienced, she was obliged to provide for and run smoothly a large family, to keep careful accounts, and at the same time bear and rear three children. She was most successful in happy homemaking, however, save in one particular which was beyond her control: the two grandmothers were uncongenial and their coldness could not be dissipated. Grandfather's first wife, Maria Ellsworth, had died years earlier. He was nearly eighty when he married a Community widow named Olive Conant who was in her sixties. At the time of Grandfather's second marriage, my Father wrote Olive Conant a letter thanking her for making his father happy, saying he should always love her as a second mother and offering both her and Grandfather a home with him as long as they lived. Olive treasured this letter. She was childless and now, by her second marriage, had gained a son. Widowed Grandmother Baker was physically dependent on Father and Mother for love and protection. So, the two Grandmothers, doomed to be housemates, did not openly quarrel but neither did they speak to each other.

When Grandfather Albert died in 1883, Mother was pregnant with Albert and overwhelmed with household duties, so she turned the care of me over to Grandmother Olive Kinsley. It was at a period of cruel bereavement for Grandmother, and perhaps it was for that reason she transferred to me the fierce, passionate and possessive love that was in her nature to bestow upon some single human being. I verily became her child. She did not attempt often to interfere with my parents' authority, nor was she jealous of the love I felt for them and theirs for me.

The only unpleasant domestic scene I ever witnessed centered on me. I was perhaps six when I was taken by Mother and Aunt Mary on a shopping expedition to Buffalo. We missed the afternoon train we had intended to take home, so, delightfully, as far as I was concerned, we dined in the city and went to a theater — my first theater. We did not arrive in Niagara Falls until nearly midnight and found the family collected in the hall alarmed by our long absence. As soon as the door opened, Grandmother Kinsley snatched me from Mother and said, "What do you mean,

Jessie, by keeping the child out to such an unearthly hour?" Then, sobbing, she rushed me upstairs and locked us into her bedroom. Soon Mother tapped at the door and said, "Please let me have Edith. I wish to put her to bed." Grandmother did not answer. A moment later Father knocked loudly and said in a stern voice, "Open the door." I was frightened, and Grandmother looked frightened, too. Father told me to go at once to Mother. Then he said to Grandmother, "Never again let me hear you speak to Jessie in such a tone of voice. Remember, Edith is her child. You should apologize." So far as I know, the incident ended there. No rift was visible between Mother and Grandmother. They truly loved one another, and, no doubt, Community training helped to prevent explosions and preserve family harmony. In that respect I must regret that I did not know Grandmother Baker better. She remained almost a stranger to me through the twelve years she lived in our family.

I have said before that I do not possess a complete picture of Father's appearance. Separately, point by point, I can hear his deep voice, his hearty laugh, and see his quick, familiar gestures. Further memory tells me he had very black hair, a long black beard (later silvered), and deep-set, piercing dark eyes under level brows. He was of medium height, stoutly and strongly built, very masculine, athletic, never sick, and a lovely playmate with children.

Father was strongly opinionated in politics — a dyed-in-the-wool Republican like his Vermont forefathers. Harrison and Cleveland were the nominees in one presidential election, I remember, and Harrison was, of course, Father's choice. Cleveland he considered an unpardonable blunderhead. Nevertheless, one day Albert and I proclaimed that we were Democrats and should vote for Cleveland. Mother was shocked; it was sacrilege. Father was delighted. He had rebel blood himself and rejoiced to find young rebels in his flock — all the more, because he was soon able to crow over us unmercifully, for Harrison won the election.

I think Father must have reacted strongly against the religious fanaticism, the system of personal criticism and institutional restrictions under which he was reared. And certainly he was born an individualist and was probably an agnostic. On the other hand, he deeply respected and was deeply marked by certain Oneida Community tenets. "The brotherhood of man" was a principle in which he believed and had retained. He desired to share what he possessed with others and frequently did so. When we were somewhat older he undertook to explain to Albert and [me] some of the maternal and paternal puzzles that existed at Oneida Community, particularly the relationship between Josephine and us. Josephine was Father's eldest child. She only spent half a year with us and had at Kenwood a mother who was not our mother. Josephine's mother we called Auntie Smith. She had a husband, Mr. Edson Smith; and also a son, Deming Smith, Josephine's older brother, who was unrelated to us. Father told us that there were two systems of marriage; he had lived in both. One was called Complex Marriage which was practiced by Oneida Community and had now been given up. The other was called monogamous marriage, or legal marriage, and was in common usage. Josephine was born under the system of Complex Marriage, which had been a noble and unselfish system. We were born under the other, and while he would have wished us to be just the same and to have had the same mother, he was sorry we had not had the privilege of being born in Oneida Community. We accepted Father's opinion: we were sorry we had been born too late for Oneida Community.

A chief characteristic of Father's was the desire to give gifts — to surprise his family with pleasure: dresses for Mother, toys, skates and pets for us — and one day, a piano suddenly was delivered for the entire family. The gifts must be surprises in order to provide the giver with a satisfying joy.

Once, when Father went to New York, he brought home a fur jacket for Mother. Fur coats were then uncommon. It was an undyed golden seal jacket, a suit of the same shade in pale wool, and a little hat with a golden-brown plume. Mother spoke of this costume as the loveliest and most fashionable one she ever possessed.

Father liked also to bring home gadgets, not as surprises, but because he liked them. We had, among our novelties, Wanzer lamps that wound with a key and burned steadily and brilliantly without glass chimneys. We had a coal-grate fireplace in our sitting room. Fireplaces were unusual in the houses about us, and coal grates unheard of. We had one of the first telephones in Niagara Falls. Father, too, had a dream of an invention: a tunnel that one day might be built to harness the Falls and create electric power for commercial purposes. The idea took shape in his mind, and he drew diagrams and then called together a group of influential citizens to discuss the project. In the end the dream became reality, and Father received $10,000.00 for initiating it. There were only two inventions in his day that Father looked at askance — the bicycle and the automobile. They threatened his favorite mode of transportation — the horse. I do not know if he resented trains when they first appeared, or street-cars when they ceased to be horse-drawn, but certainly he reluctantly tolerated bicycles and gave them to Albert and Jessie and me — not as joyful surprises but as conveniences. As for automobiles, he utterly mistrusted them, never entered one and called them "devil wagons."

Father also instituted the custom of serving wine at Thanksgiving and Christmas dinners. At first we were allowed sips, but in our teens, at the same time that we graduated to cups of coffee or tea, if we chose to drink these beverages, we were given full glasses of champagne.

Back at Kenwood the Mansion House library was ours, and on its shelves were rows of poets. Mother and I gorged together. I well remember the day she brought Chatterton[20] to our rooms. She forgot that I was a child and should go to bed at a reasonable time. We sat up till dawn reading him from cover to cover.

Life at the Big House, aside from contemporary friendships, had let me come into my heritage from the past and a multiplication of parents, men and women, a unique reinforcement of childish security. Auntie Smith was beautifully maternal to Father's children; Mrs. George Miller and I rode horseback together; she also confided in me and seemed almost a contemporary. Mrs. Beulah taught books and Aunt Annie Hatch taught music. I loved them all. Mr. Hinds taught me the game of chess, while Mr. Freeman and I read aloud the New Testament—a critical study, for we drew maps, compared styles, noted discrepancies and discussed the graphic movement and vocabulary. We finished by reading the two apocryphal books.

More important, there was Doctor Theodore Noyes, a man of great learning who came to take the kindest interest in my studies. He joined our five o'clock reading class and by his membership transformed its character and personnel.

Among my list of adult parents I must not forget Mr. Miller,[21] who was one of the nicest. Gentle, humorous and naive, he had something of Mother's innocence of mind and Charles Lamb's quiet gaiety. During the two latter summers we read together, largely French literature—Montaigne's essays, for which we both had a passion. We also read Balzac, Flaubert and a novel of Tolstoy's.

Mr. Miller once said that if he was thrown upon a desert island and was allowed but two books, he would choose *The Bible* and *Pickwick Papers*. Why? I asked myself; in order to save beautiful words and images and to laugh. These were his talents. What a gift he had for story-telling, for anecdote at the right moment in the right manner, and with the most subtle selection of vocabulary. Kenneth [Miller] inherited the gift. To write that statement makes me recall instantly certain maxims Kenneth had uttered on appropriate occasions. Two are quotations and two Ken's own inventions. "Everything God has made has a crack in it" by Emerson. "The right word and the almost right word are as different from one

---

20. Thomas Chatterton (1752–1770), precocious English poet who committed suicide at the age of seventeen.

21. George Miller, J. H. Noyes's nephew.

another as lightning and lightning bugs" by Mark Twain. "Of ourselves we know as much as the seagull knows of the floating iceberg" and "Everything that happens in a life-time is written down beforehand in the contract" by Kenneth.

Looking back to early memories of Mother, I knew then that every thought, word and deed of hers was actuated by loving kindness. Later, as we became friends as well as mother and daughter, I understood her better. I realized she had a faun-like timidity. She was eager to learn, to praise, to admire, but disliked to blame, and even more to condemn. She spread a tent of love, not simply over her family and friends, but over every human being, extending it even to cover inanimate creation. If we assailed the weather she would rush to its defense. "No, no, children. You must not complain because it rains; change is natural, to be expected. You must not blame nature."

For a long period in her life Mother was willing to be ruled by the opinions of others — opinions not her own, and even opinions she did not actually respect.

It is difficult, of course, to see objectively someone who is profoundly loved, but I should say that Mother had a rare combination of qualities: greatness of mind united with a childlike and sensitive simplicity, imaginative and intuitive talents, spontaneous perception of truth and beauty, while at the same time retaining a timidity of opinion. She was creative rather than a critic. She never attempted to analyze intuition any more than she attempted to analyze opinion. Some instinct seemed to make her wish to leave knowledge unformulated rather than defined — probably a wise instinct in relation to her work, but in other ways sometimes uncomfortably inhibiting.

To persons deeply revered, she found difficulty in expressing herself. She became a child, too humble, and sometimes, she insisted, a gauche child, saying the wrong things of which she was acutely aware. It made her self-distrustful.

Mother received direct inspiration from such artists as Blake, Ryder, Rembrandt, the mystics and some primitive arts, rather than from masters like Leonardo, Michelangelo, Titian, Rubens, in whom the critical faculties operated in unison with the creative.

In 1902 Grandmother Olive died, and the same year Father retired, returning from Chicago to Kenwood. Father lived to see all of his children married. I had a large Big Hall wedding. Father marched down the aisle and gave me away. Two years later, when Albert was quietly married to Lotta, Father was their sole confidant and the only witness present. Then later still, Mother, Father and I arranged Jessie's quiet church wedding to Chester.

Father died in 1907 after a two weeks' illness. He had once prophesied that maternal Jessie Janet would beat both Albert and me in the production of offspring. This prophecy might have been fulfilled, for Jessie was pregnant when she died a year later of acute appendicitis. I have been glad that Father did not live to suffer that tragedy. It would have broken his heart.

After Father's death, Mother lived with Mart and me, first in Chicago and later in Kenwood where we had built a house. It was my ambition to set Mother free, to let her enjoy a liberty she had never had but had certainly earned through her years of service to others. She now had rooms of her own in our house in which to work.[22] She was an artist, I told her, and that being so, art must come first, everything else second. Henceforth, she was to do what she liked, not what she ought to do. She was never to sacrifice herself again to household duties, to Mart or me or our child. Her health had become frail. She had undergone a number of serious operations. I'm glad to say that under a new regime she improved and didn't suffer another serious illness until the age of seventy-nine when she died of a thrombosis. In the meantime, during her last twenty-five years, she turned out a large and very fine body of work.

Mart and Edith's House in Kenwood

Mart and Edith built their house across the road from the Mansion House. It was modified Georgian in style.

A long straight path led to the house. Cheery trees lined either side. An old willow tree stood before the house. On the north side the land dipped a little and here J. C. K. made a perennial garden with brick lined paths and circling clumps of forget-me-nots. A grape arbor and vegetable garden lay behind a circular driveway at the back of the house. During the year that Mart and Edith moved in, their daughter, Rhoda, was born. Later on a swing and sandbed were added in back. A row of poplars was planted along the south edge of the property.

There was a settle on each side of the front door. From a spacious hall, a winding stairway led up to a landing off which french doors opened onto a long glassed-in, screened-in porch. A corresponding open porch the length of the house was downstairs.

---

22. Jessie described this in a letter to one of her nieces: "We moved into the new house in July. My own small sitting room is beautiful with its grey wall hanging and Chinese rug, its casement windows and book shelving . . . the old easel before the north window companioned by the familiar old chair."

Mart and Edith Kinsley's house, rear view, 1911

As you entered the house, the dining room was on the left. A butler's pantry separated it from a kitchen with a flagstone floor. Under the stairwell was a tiny sitting room for the maid.

The living room on the right was large with french doors at the back leading onto the porch, a grand piano sat across from the fireplace which was flanked by twin mahogany glassed-in bookcases reaching almost to the ceiling.

Upstairs were J. C. K.'s sitting room, bedroom, and bath on the north side looking down on a cheery tree at the edge of her garden. Three other bedrooms and a bath completed that floor while on the third floor were two rooms for household help and on the north side a large, pleasant studio room for Edith.

A Wider World, 1913-1919

IN MAY 1913 JESSIE KINSLEY, then a fifty-five-year-old widow, sat down in a gold chair in the Doria Palace in Rome to rest for a few minutes. Writing later to Jane Kinsley, her sister-in-law, Jessie described her feelings: "Suddenly, I could imagine myself a little girl again looking into the old stereopticon in the Reception Room at one of those illuminated palace rooms. Do you remember them—the mirrors and chandeliers, golden chairs and tables, red velvet, etc.? Here they all were in reality."[1]

Countless American travelers have toured Europe, but few of them have articulated the experience as much as Jessie Kinsley. The little girl who had gazed in wonder at pictures of Old World art treasures was now journeying from one cultural center to another—Naples, Rome, Florence, Geneva, Paris, London, Edinburgh, Bath—seeing all these wonderful things for herself. Travelers' enthusiasm is sometimes synthetic, but Jessie's was not. All her life she had been a great reader; all her life she had loved to look at works of art—at first only in pictures, but later in the museums of New York and Chicago. She was thoroughly prepared for this new chapter in her life.

The fact that she was able to afford such a six-month excursion testifies to the growing prosperity of Oneida Community, Limited. Under Pierrepont Noyes's leadership, the company now depended less on its old line of products—canned fruits, silk thread, traps, and chains—and more on the silverware business. At first the tableware reached the public through plebeian outlets: William Wrigley gave Oneida spoons away as premiums with his gum; the American Cereal Company donated Oneida spoons with boxes of Quaker Oats; Sears Roebuck sold Oneida ware to its

1. See p. 114.

101

mail order customers. But Noyes and the young men he had recruited were able to make a radical change in the company image. Grosvenor Allen cooperated with artists in developing graceful designs for a new high quality line of silverware called Community Plate; Burton Dunn organized the advertising campaign that would appeal to fashionable customers. Full page advertisements in leading magazines associated the silver with beautiful women and lace tableclothes. Oneida commissioned Coles Phillips, one of the most popular artists of the day, to do a series. A little later Irene Castle, at the height of her fame as a ballroom dancer, was shown endorsing Community Plate, as was Mrs. O. H. P. Belmont, a granddame of high society. The market for Community Plate was growing very rapidly. Salesmen for Oneida were exploring foreign markets. One of them visited Argentina and Australia in 1905 and 1906; Martin Kinsley, Jessie's son-in-law, made a trip to Europe in 1913.

Jessie had a congenial companion on her tour of Europe. Annie Miller had begun life as Annie Kelly, one of the Kelly family who had joined the Oneida Community in the early days. At the time of the break-up she had married George Miller, who belonged to one of the most influential families. His mother was Charlotte Noyes Miller, sister and early convert of the founder; his father was John Miller, another Vermont convert. John Miller had been a leader in developing the old Community enterprises, and George Miller carried on his father's work, first in the Community, then in the company. In the struggle to control the board of directors, George — now one of the older men — provided strong support to Pierrepont Noyes. George had died shortly before Annie and Jessie made their European tour.

Kenneth Hayes Miller, George's and Annie's son, was an important person in the lives of both Jessie and Edith Kinsley. Kenneth had passed his early years in Kenwood with his parents but later moved to New York City where he became a well-known painter and a teacher at the Art Students' League. Still retaining a strong affection for Kenwood, Kenneth had spent summers there, giving lessons in drawing and painting. Both Jessie and Edith had taken his courses.

Even before they took classes with Kenneth, Jessie and Edith had begun to study art. As a girl in the old Community, Jessie had loved to draw and paint; later when her husband was working in Chicago she had taken courses at the Art Institute. Edith had displayed similar interests. As a girl of eighteen, she had spent several months in New York City studying art; later she studied in Chicago. Jessie and Edith both worked diligently under Kenneth Miller's guidance. Edith became a good painter and sculptor. For her part, Jessie found a much needed therapy in Kenneth's lessons. During the tortured years marked by Myron's and Jessie Janet's deaths and her own serious illness, Jessie devoted more and more of her energy to drawing and painting. The trip to Europe meant an opportunity not only to see for herself the beautiful work of the master artists, but to fill her sketch books with drawings of buildings and landscapes.

Jessie Kinsley was an excellent letter writer, eager to share her experiences with her relatives and friends. She was less successful as a diary keeper. Like most of us, she was full of good resolutions and good beginnings. She would start a journal, keep it faithfully for a few weeks, then neglect it or let it lapse. Fortunately she did better than usual for the period 1914 through 1918. These were the years when Europe slid into the terrible war that killed and maimed so many of its most promising young men, consumed so much of its wealth, and disrupted its civilization. Jessie's journal records her dismay at these sad events, but also shows how idealistic Americans finally accepted the necessity of American participation. Her journal conveys a fine record of the excitement, the anxieties, the hopes, and the fears of the months when the nation was at war. Although Jessie Kinsley did not always approve of Woodrow Wilson's policies, she shared his faith in the possibility of a better world, a peaceful world made safe for democracy.

Oneida Community, Limited received a variety of war contracts. Half of its production was now devoted to making trench knives, Bolo knife handles, cartridge cases, magazine tubes, periscopes, Browning gun parts, and surgical instruments. Responsibility for organizing this complex operation lay in the hands of Albert Kinsley, Jessie's son. In January 1917, even before the U.S. declaration of war, Pierrepont Noyes had given up the post of general manager and chosen Kinsley, then thirty-three years old, to succeed him, a choice the directors were glad to ratify. Noyes was only about forty-seven years old himself, but he believed that executives should not wait until they were old men before turning the reins over to younger drivers.

Just before he left his position, Noyes instituted a new policy that he called the High-Cost-of-Living Wage. Besides his regular pay check, each worker was to receive an additional payment tied to the Bradstreet Index, supposed to measure changes in the general price structure. Kinsley, no less committed to the workers' welfare than Noyes, stuck with the High-Cost-of-Living bonus throughout the period of wartime and postwar inflation. Oneida also instituted a Wage Service Wage to make up the wages lost by its employees who entered the armed services.

Meanwhile Pierrepont Noyes was playing his own important role in the war effort. For one and a half years he served in Washington as Assistant Fuel Administrator; for the next year and a half he was stationed in Europe as the American member of the Rhineland Commission, the interallied agency that supervised the occupation of the western part of Germany.

It was a period of excitement for the nation and for the Kenwood community, but in Jessie Kinsley's own life it was more than that. It was the time when she found something unique on which she could focus her energies. In a letter to a niece she described how it all began. The immediate challenge was the new house that Mart and Edith built in 1912, the house where Jessie now made her home. "Well then," Jessie wrote, "the beginning was a new round rug braided for my new bed. An 87¢ grey cotton blanket made fine long strips, and black print an edge. The rug was simple and charming. Then I made a hit-and-miss wool rug for Edith and found myself adept. My old easel chair needed a seat and braid would suit its antiquity — but it must be lovely, too. Thereupon, for the first time — of this mundane stuff — I began to conceive worthily, to think of pattern, to believe rags called to higher uses, higher destinies than had been assigned to them hitherto." And in another account Jessie described how she graduated to more exotic material and more ambitious scale. "So gradually, I found the fascination of this medium to my mind and fingers, and began the making of pictures in a wholly original way from my own designs . . . and unlike my painted pictures, *braided pictures* grew into satisfactory proportions and some large tapestries came with the years."[2]

By 1917 Jessie's braidings were attracting attention. Edith arranged an exhibition of her mother's work at Kenwood and then sent the pieces on to New York to be shown at the Craftsmen's Gallery. From there they went to the Carnegie Institute at Pittsburgh, Pa. Never able to paint as well as she aspired, Jessie was pleased to have her braidings thus recognized. She was even happier to learn from Annie Miller that the raffling off of one of her small pieces had raised $104 for the Red Cross. Jessie was expressing herself as an artist and at the same time doing her bit for the war effort.

Having come through the war in excellent condition, Oneida Community, Limited was eager to expand its overseas markets. To head up the London office, the company appointed Martin Kinsley, and Mart took with him to England his wife Edith, his seven-year-old daughter Rhoda, and his mother-in-law Jessie Kinsley.

Jessie's residence in England lasted only about seven months, from late March to late November 1919. She found London a far different city from the sedate and orderly world capital she had visited in 1913. This was a sugarless and butterless London, a "cabbage and potato" London, a London where taxis were scarce, the tube was unsafe, and buses would not stop long enough for one to board. Walking had become a fine art. There was "a sense of the unusual, of tension." Everyone felt unsettled.

This first impression of a country in turmoil continued through-

2. Beverly Sanders, "A Scrap Bag Palette," *American Craft* (April–May 1981), p. 17.

out the Americans' stay. Even to find lodging was difficult. Mart had to move his family from hotel to hotel and from one rented house to another. Prices kept going up; getting anything repaired was difficult; soldiers and workers took to the streets in protest. There was a succession of serious strikes by miners, policemen, and railroad workers.

Despite all these inconveniences Jessie was thrilled by her life abroad. Because of her Oneida Community background she took a lively interest in the social ferment. Trained in the virtues of hard work and thrift, she disapproved of demonstrators who seemed to want to loaf and wait for government handouts. Yet she sympathized with the plight of the poor, disapproved the heartlessness of the wealthy, and hoped that a better society might be born out of this postwar travail. English intellectuals knew enough about Oneida history to be curious about these Americans who had their roots in one of the great communal experiments of the nineteenth century. H. G. Wells, then at the height of his fame, invited Pierrepont Noyes to his home on one occasion and Martin and Edith Kinsley on another.

In other ways, too, Jessie made the most of her opportunities. She and Edith visited the National Museum together and attended the Russian ballet. Jessie took long walks by herself through the several London neighborhoods in which the family had its temporary residences. She particularly enjoyed the several weeks that they spent at Lynton on the Devon coast, a region rich in literary associations. She loved to walk through the countryside, sit by the sea, and bathe in the surf.

Above all, this was a period when she enjoyed the companionship of little Rhoda. With Mart and Edith often busy with social engagements, grandmother and granddaughter had to shift for themselves. They took walks together, told each other stories, and found secret benches to sit on. Rhoda was a bright and loving child; Jessie was a warm-hearted woman with a special talent for entertaining children. Three thousand miles away from their home in Kenwood each needed the other.

TRAVELS WITH ANNIE IN EUROPE

The Crossing

Hamburg-American Line—S.S.Moltke, Monday, April 22nd, 1913

Dearest Edith,[1]
    I think of you constantly during these days of seasickness and try

---

1. All letters are addressed to Edith Kinsley unless otherwise indicated.

to carry out your practice in Chicago—to eat in spite of it—and really am gaining ground. Almost thought I was quite out of the woods yesterday until we rode into a storm, and then away I went again. It has rained all day today, but I have mostly stayed out on deck until now. I have come in to try the music room and write to you, although on the verge of flight, so my letter may be short. At noon I went to table for the first time. We sit with a Dr. Robinson and family of Chicago. Dr. Robinson is very blunt and plain, Mrs. Robinson is very charmingly western, and their two nieces are with them. Mrs. Miller [Annie Kelly Miller] has already been useful to them, as they are to go to Spain, and she, having been there, can give them ideas. Well, I must fly . . .

Here in my stateroom the morning and evening stars are the steward and stewardess and the sun is Mrs. Miller. Here, too, a little drama has gone on for me—the stewardess being the one actor. It began, this drama, when I gave her a good tip and told her I should need many extras. She was voluable in very broken English of which I could understand only, "I do for you everyding you want." Well, she has done, and I have reciprocated by being thankful. This thankfulness has made her confidential, and her confidences have stirred my wrath, inwardly, towards this Hamburg-American Company. Imagine in these modern times, this frail little woman working without rest from four-thirty in the morning until eleven-thirty at night, nineteen hours steadily? And without very good food either, I imagine. Perhaps she takes advantage of me, too, for she brings me more than I can eat and then asks if she may have it, saying, "I am so hungry." She goes to eat behind the curtain and does not gobble which is most fortunate when I am sick, and I am so glad for the chance to succor her in any way.

Wednesday

You see I have skipped a day. That was the storm, and I was quite flabbergasted all day Tuesday. This morning I have bobbed up serenely and hope to keep well. The skies are blue, and the water a deeper blue—very beautiful. Mrs. Miller thinks that we are in the Gulf Stream. You remember Winslow Homer's painting called *The Gulf Stream*? This water is wild and beautiful, but, alas, this fashionable throng with its chatter and high heels are as out of keeping with Winslow Homer's gaunt castaway as with the water. Art was more beautiful than nature, in this instance.

There is a Welshman on board who speaks forty-five languages and has been around the world five times and seen all its crowned heads. Mrs. Miller says that she heard him tell someone this. Another character, and one who is in evidence, like the Welshman, all over the boat, is a short man of large mouth. He endeavors to be gallant to all the ladies, and yesterday attracted great attention by setting up a canvas behind the smoking room on the deck, painting a bright blue sky with clouds and some mountains with swamps for foreground. This pleased the crowd, and one of our young ladies, Dr. Robinson's niece, said it was "really very nice, too." These girls are charming to look at, very much like other western girls in quick wit, spontaneity and open-heartedness. They are bewitched with the looks of the young Italian doctor; he is goodlooking, and, oh, they so want to be introduced, but their uncle has put his foot down strongly against it, and we do think that is hard.

Last evening, looking across the waters so wild and deeply blue, the eye was arrested by a square bank of clouds, then again lost in the unmarked sky. Those cloud banks are all our world, until you turn again to the fashionable little world on our steamer, which is not particularly attractive. I was never more impressed by open space. I've never seen the desert, you know. This is a desert of water. We pass a few steamers on this route, but this morning, far to the north, was a sail.

April 30th

We have now left both Madeira and Gibraltar far behind and are on the old Moltke, pumping along toward Algiers — our next stop. We have certainly had a fine voyage: beautiful weather most of the time and calm seas. Even the storm of the first few days was nothing compared to what it might have been. I shall not dread the voyage home. Madeira was more beautiful than Gibraltar. I wonder if we shall see anything more lovely. The lack of dust in the streets there was unique, although they were not clean in one sense. At Gibraltar all was dust — white limestone dust. Every kind of vehicle flying down the narrow streets, from automobiles to donkey carts and hundreds of donkeys kicked up the dust. In the little Spanish village of La Linea we saw again the dark-visaged people and some beautiful women, but the costumes were sober and dirty, not exquisite in color as at Madeira — perhaps because this was a weekday, while we were in Madeira on Sunday.

It was curious to have a French steamer pass us at near range, and see that the passengers on both forward and after decks were Arabs heavily turbanned.

I cannot tell you how much we enjoyed a cup of tea and some little sweetened cakes in the Spanish tea house at Gibraltar, where we sent you postal cards. Also, at Gibraltar, our table friends, Dr. and Mrs. Robinson and Jeanette and Belle, beautiful, tall girls, left us. They were on tour through Spain.

One day we happened to speak of magazine covers, and Belle said, "Oh, I just love Coles Phillips' colors, and, oh, you must have seen

those Community silver ads of his! I'm crazy about them!" Mrs. Miller
said her nephew was acquainted with Coles Phillips, and I said I had seen
him. It was as though we had said we were living in a king's palace. What
does he look like? Is he married? And then Mrs. Miller gave Burton's
[Burton Dunn] little story about the baby and the change in the Coles
Phillips family. Belle heaved a sigh and said, "Oh, it's so good to know
something about the people whose work you admire so much. I'm crazy
over those ads."

In place of the Robinsons are four non-English-speaking boisterous Germans. That makes eight Germans at our table. The other people
are New England women: four school teachers — nice, too.

The steward is coming with those afternoon teas and cakes. I'll
write more tomorrow. Hereafter, I shall write to you and Albert together
which must do for the whole family. I do not imagine there will be anything worthwhile for the *Quadrangle,* but if you do let them use any,
please edit my grammar and spelling.

Friday, May 2nd

Our forenoon in Algiers yesterday was the climax of my excitement. For Mrs. Miller, it was not as new: one plastered house built against
another — almost a solid mass with only loopholes for windows. This is in
the native, not the French section; only little climbing, winding, slippery
alleyways filled with humanity. The men were clothed in flowing robes
and turbans, or burnoose, or the red fez on the head, while the women
were all in white with only the eyes uncovered. Such smells, such wonderful faces and forms and vistas up the winding stairways! Such color — oh,
the color seemed too beautiful to be true. The postal cards are most un-
true as to color. I never climbed so many stairs in my life.

We were taken into what was said to be an old Moorish palace
now empty. There we saw the carved marble filigree and mosaic in beautiful confusion. The French section was interesting and beautiful as only a
tropical place can be: salmon-tinted walls, red-tiled roofs and flowers in
profusion. We lunched at a little table on the street and wrote postcards.
Being a festival day, the post office was closed, but a very charming
young Frenchman asked to be of assistance to us and piloted us to a cigar
store where stamps were sold. This was after we had left the Cook's party
and guide. I can see we are going to get on all right by ourselves.

The festival was Ascension Day, so we had here, as we had at Madeira, the best possible opportunity to see the people. By noon the crowds
were tremendous; and how cosmopolitan: there are in Algiers, 80,000
French and 70,000 Arabs, Turks and Jews. The harbor was crowded, full
of boats, but no beautiful naked divers came out, and there were no gulls.

We are now south of Sardinia and can see its rocky coast. We have almost finished our packing. We rise early tomorrow to see the Bay of Naples.

Italy

The Pension Tinto, Naples, May 3rd or 4th, 1913

I know you will want to hear from me here. I sent off a cablegram and postal and am rather swimming from the motion of the boat yet and seem tired tonight, too. But unless I do write at these odd times, you will get nothing, and I do not expect this letter will be worth a cent.

Oh, Naples is just beautiful! We went down this afternoon to Cook's to send you a cable. I inquired about a cable from you but none has come. I think constantly of dear Lotta[2] and you can scarcely imagine what a cable from you will mean to me. Tonight the thought of darling Myron and little Rhoda swept over me like a storm.

Oh, Albert. Just as I was writing, your cablegram was brought to our room. We left word for it to be sent here from Thomas Cook's. My, I'm so excited that I can hardly write. It reads, "Girls all well. How are you?" signed Albert. My first thought was twins! I waved the telegram in the air and danced all over and said, "Twins, twins! I can never stay away until September." But a second reading has made me think you meant the baby and Lotta. You surely would have said "twin girls" if anything as tremendous as that had happened. But you may have twin girls after all; oh, what a thought that is. One is grand – a darling little girl.[3] I love her already, but two! Why I would boil over just as I almost am now at the thought of it. I'm thinking I will send you another cable of congratulation tomorrow.

What will you make of this letter – a crazy, glad old grandma gadding away from the home that holds the dearest treasures in the world. I cannot help being excited over such news way off here in Italy.

Naples, Monday, May 5th, 1913

Dearest Edith, Albert and Lotta:

My first waking thought this morning was of dear Lotta and your dear baby. Nothing in the world will seem better than a letter from home.

---

2. Lotta and Albert were expecting their second child.
3. Jane, who in later life became Jane Kinsley Rich.

I dreamed about you, dear Edith, so I was back home for a little while. Do not imagine by all this that I am homesick. We are having a great time.

You will have two cablegrams from me, as I could not withstand the desire to respond at once to the news about my new granddaughter (granddaughters?) Which, oh, which? We are taking things very easy and we are well pleased with our situation. Italian cooking is very delicious so far. I am beginning to get rid of the ship's motion which has been so persistent. The weather has been a trifle patchy — sunshine and rain alternating. Yesterday, Sunday, we went to the Museum of Fine Arts. In getting there we took a tram that carried us on a wide detour around by the bay and through a very interesting Italian section. Returning, we came uphill where the tramway spurts for a portion of the journey along the heights overlooking the lower part of the city, so that we made almost a complete circuit about.

We found where the beauties, at least some of them, are in the museum and will go there again, and yet again, if we can. Tomorrow, weather permitting, we go to Pompeii. But even Naples alone without Pompeii would be enough to thrill and fill me to the brim. Imagine looking out of the windows at the most enchanting house-tops where wild snapdragons grow in every niche and cranny among the tiles. Every balcony is full of flowers. Domes and minarets appear among the quaint roofs that cover homes, and the homes are open by casement windows to the, shall I say inquisitive — no, interested, excited eyes that are in my head. Then imagine walking down to Cook's and seeing at your left, between great marble and plastered walls, a street terminate in an almost never ending flight of steps topped by cypress trees far above. And at the foot of these steps, backed by the white marble, two superb oxen, white, too. One ox rises and stands beside its mate, and yet the drivers lie where they have thrown themselves down — the whole seems too beautiful to be true. This is only one strange picture among a thousand. I cannot find anything here that is not beautiful in its own way except perhaps the dirt, and we have not had that assail us badly. And we have had no fleas. Italian people seem delightful. I feel as though I could love them.

Here in our pension we sit at a long table in the dining room on the fourth floor where windows look up, up, into a great green-covered cliff. There are all sorts of people here: English, German, American. The waiters are pretty Italian girls. There is one man across from us who is a perfect Cyrano de Bergerac — almost too perfect — though he seems a nice gentleman. Then there is a little wizened English woman who is living here and is very deaf and inquisitive. Fortunately she sits next to Mrs. Miller.[4] Well, I need not describe more of our tablemates. We ourselves

4. Jessie was growing deaf.

are perfect specimens in our own way of the very types that haunt these pensions.

Naples, May 7th

We are planning to take the funicular railway to the heights above the city this morning and again to go to the museum in the afternoon. Our excursion to Pompeii was as nearly perfect as possible; a gray day that was not trying to the eyes, a most intelligent, courteous guide and the pleasant company of intelligent people—all were good factors. We left for the Cook train and our car was luxurious so to speak: an observation car with big windows. Our little screaming engine presently had us started. Then for the first time I saw the country, not the city, in this land. Well, I had heard and read of its being beautiful, but I cannot give you an idea of how much more beautiful it is for me than I had ever dreamed. Just one house, one common little house out of this countryside would be a place to go and see for its strange beauty if it were in Kenwood. Arched doorways, outside stairs of stone, rambling outhouses, all under one never-conventionalized roof of tile. Every foot of land is cultivated, up and down the sides of deep gullies, under every tree. Grape vines are trained for miles under and on to poplar trees which are like gaunt, rugged poles. These trees have great nubs on them and only a scant amount of leaves. And everywhere white and red poppies. There are groves and single great trees of a pine variety.

We were near enough to Vesuvius to see where the torrent of lava flowed down from the mountain into the valley in 1906 and at the latter place killed 100 and covered fields and houses and part of the village. It swept, too, across the railroad track but, of course, had been dug out and lay piled up, a chocolate-colored rubble, for acres about us. It is cheap building material, and we saw it being carted off and used with cement for that purpose and for fencing. When we reached Pompeii we had gone almost around Vesuvius. I'm not going to describe Pompeii. You know better than I can tell you about it. Of course we saw the Forum, the Baths and the basilica and everything! We walked miles over the rounded stone paving worn into grooves by the chariots of the ancients, and hopped across the stepping-stones at the street corners. I am sending you postals of the interior decorations found at Pompeii, so that you may see how beautiful they are, and really, here again, it's the color that impresses me most. (Color that was buried so long and now has been uncovered for many, many years and is exquisite beyond words.)

After our guide had given us this delightful time in Pompeii, he conveyed us to a restaurant where we had lunch. On the way home we stopped once where I had time to just scribble the island of Capri and an old monastery on a hill with grape vineyards everywhere, below and around. These sketches seem hardly worthwhile sending to you, but if you would keep them for me, they will be little reminders of my journey for my refreshment later on.

Rome, May 10th

We arrived here in Rome in due time and found a courier from Santa Katarina Pension awaiting us with a note for us from the landlady saying we could have a room there but she had no very good rooms empty for a week. Well, we went over there and stayed all night and slept well but did not quite like the room, so today we are out looking for something better. Have stopped in at Cook's to rest a little. We have found two of Mrs. Miller's pension addresses and may go back to Santa Katarina Pension yet, hoping within a week to get a better room. The food there was excellent.

The journey from Naples was interesting indeed. Our little screaming engine went uphill and then downhill through valley after valley, into tunnels, and on every hand were mountains or very high fantastic hills, many crowned with old ruins or monasteries. The foothills were covered by grape vineyards and olive trees, and again, the Italians had everywhere used to advantage every foot of available, tillable land. Timothy was headed out and barley and rye. Olive trees are bluish-green like sage brush. I imagine the villages often began by clustering around monasteries, for they, too, were most frequent at the crown of an eminence, seldom in the valleys, though one or two were so situated. We saw white oxen, donkeys, goats and a few horses. The beautiful poplar trees were used as supports for grapevines in all the vineyards until we neared Rome when poles stuck in the ground took their place.

The plains, the compagna, on which the hills of Rome look down, at last came into sight—a glorious sight—and far in the distance we could see the dome of St. Peter's.

When we reached Rome what a turmoil ensued over this baggage. All eight of us arose and pulled suitcases down upon each other. As soon as we had our baggage down and at the door, the porters shouldered it, and we made off for cabs.

Well, we are back here at the Santa Katarina in our little room which, after a day of hunting for others only to find them all full, seems a haven indeed. We are blessed with two great east windows and two good beds. We were disappointed not to get mail here. We left word at Naples to have mail forwarded. We shall be here in Rome until June 6; then in Florence for perhaps a week; then to Venice for two weeks; then short stops at

Milan, Bellagio, Lugano and Lucerne; and then a round-trip excursion in Switzerland: Interlaken, Lusanne, Montreux and Chamonix, and then back to Lucerne. We will go to Paris for a week and then to London.

Rome, May 10th

I have not given you a hint of the impression made on my mind and spirit by the paintings I have seen in Italy. So many crowding impressions are poured one upon another like hot lava, that sometimes I feel one thing blocks out another. While I can retain but a thin memory of the many madonnas and holy families, I shall remember the ones I like if I see reproduced in print and tell you about them.

In Naples was a copy of the Velasquez bacchanalian festival (I cannot remember the name). You have the detail from it — the three heads of men. That was said to be a fine copy and, oh, it was very beautiful. The blue of the sky was an old blue and it entered into the earth and men in perfect harmony with soft gray and brown and a little red. I never liked that detail but I adore the painting. A Claude Lorraine was opposite it in the same room. It was too blue and brown with bright colors only in the figures. These two with Titian's "Diana" and some drawings are all that hold fast in my mind from the museum in Naples.

Here in Rome I have seen that tremendous Titian, "Sacred and Profane Love." It is one of the greatest paintings I have yet seen.

In St. Peter's we stopped before the statue of Michelangelo's "The Pieta." At first, behind the lattice, I did not recognize it, but as I looked, I remembered it and felt how wonderful it was. Because this was St. Peter's, and the wonder and beauty pulled my mind hither and yon, and all made a stunning, almost a numbing sensation, I shall go again to see just the Pieta, and drink again of what is to me a most tender impression.

Do not expect me to write you much about these things. I am not young enough now, nor clear-headed enough as you would be, to formulate — to know — but I do enjoy. I think, too, of the things ahead of me in Florence and Venice and Paris. Good-bye, my dearest child. You might almost pity me, for a surfeit of wonder and beauty surrounds me that is overwhelming. I come back to life only at mealtimes, sitting by school teachers and travellers who discuss diets and trains and lace and shops. Mrs. Miller is splendid.

Rome, May 16th

Your letter came this morning. Such a feast! Also came a dear letter from Albert written the 5th. I could hardly eat breakfast or contain myself.

We are still in our first room at St. Katarina which has come to seem like home with its casement windows, cool and airy. But, though we almost wish to stay in it, we may yet move; for we only gain access to our room through another entrance! This other room has been occupied by two darling little children and their sweet Italian nurse, so we were free night and day to go through and not afraid of disturbing them. They go away tomorrow. These children's mother is a writer, Mary Harding Force. Did you ever hear of her? Her husband's name is O'Brien. I imagine they would hardly enjoy the usual pension element, those who discuss daily the linen shops, the lace shops, the coral shops, the sights they have seen or expect to see, the car they should take or did not take, etc. Not that they, the O'Briens, are any better perhaps, but I long sometimes for more general conversation although I have not much to offer in that line, I admit. It is the babbling little brook you used to tell about at Oak Park, Edith.

This morning we saw some exquisite Claude Lorraines at the Doria Palace, a glorious Titian and Velasquez's wonderful painting of Pope Innocent X. I am not disappointed by the Claude Lorraines, though some are different in point of color than I had anticipated, but most of them are very beautiful and are given the finest place and light in the gallery in which they are hung. The Titian I shall ever remember. A long, brown, twisted tree trunk carries only a little foliage to shelter a slightly crouching, shrinking figure—Minerva, I think. She has thrown off her garments—some of them look war-like—and she quails before the pointed finger of a god-like creature and her sister who are at the left. A sea, out of which are coming horses is in the background, and a wonderful sky above all.

Tired by walking and looking for the few beautiful things we wished to see in rooms full of dark and dismal ancients, I sat down in a gold chair at the end of a long corridor or gallery. Suddenly, I could imagine myself a little girl again looking into the old stereopticon in the Reception Room at one of those illuminated palace rooms. Do you remember them—the mirrors and chandeliers, golden chairs and tables, red velvet, etc.? Here they all were in reality. I'm going out now for a few minutes into the Borghese Gardens which are just a step away, while Annie goes farther down to the shop. We have stayed in all afternoon since lunch to write. Give my love to all who inquire about me.

[No date]

Dearest Albert,

I am so glad Lotta got along well and that you have Miss Smith to help out. How does Myron feel about a baby sister coming into the family? Tell me about him if you write again.

This is a very busy city, but I notice no great department stores. All are little shops. Some are wonderfully fine. The street cars are very often crowded but never in the aisles between seats, as no one is allowed inside except as many as the seats will hold. But there are large platforms front and back and these are jammed. We frequently take cabs. I believe it is in the cabs and street cars that I get fleas. I began to get them in Naples after the first day or two, but there they were not as vicious as they are here in Rome. Oh! how they bite here. I have three bites now on one cheek and one on the other. And streaks of them up and down my neck, and in my hair, and my body is just a mosaic. I do not see how I stand them but, really, I am just so tremendously interested in my surroundings and usually so sleepy at night that I do get along. Annie is hardly touched by them. They all fly to me.

If you share this letter with Edith, I would like to add a little more. Tell Rhoda the same kind of birdies—English sparrows—awaken Grandma in Rome, but here, after October first, the natives snare them for pies so they do not become quite as rampant. Also, tell Edith that her words of love to me, and what she says about going to Jessie's grave with flowers, made me cry but not with pain. Oh, I'm so glad she thinks to do that, for though it cannot perhaps touch her, it deeply touches me. I think the great pleasure and beauty of the day at Keats' and Shelley's resting place, which will be a life-long memory to me, was accented by the thought that I was turning away from sightseeing to inward feelings and dwelling in thought, not only with these illustrious dead, but with my own dear ones and with nature.

How calm and silent and strange it was. I read, "Bards of passion and of mirth, ye have left your souls on earth" while we were seated on the "Elysian lawns"; and nearby were "bluebells tented" and "daisies seemed rosescented," and "the rose herself has got perfume which on earth is not."[5] And then the nightingale sang. "The same that ofttimes hath charmed magic casements, opening on the foam of perilous seas, in fairy-lands forlorn."[6]

While I read again, sitting by Keats' stone, from his *Ode to a Nightingale:* "Still wouldst thou sing, and I have ears in vain—To thy high requiem become a sod."—you know all these things so well; I, only a lit-

---

5. From John Keats, "Ode on the Poets" in *The Golden Treasury of the Best Songs and Lyrical Poets in the English Language,* selected and arranged by Francis Turner Palgrave (New York and London: Houghton and Stroughton, n.d.), p. 232. Jessie took a copy of this popular anthology on her travels.

6. From Keats, "Ode to a Nightingale," ibid., p. 344.

tle, but—you can imagine better than I can tell you what that place and hour meant. If only you could've been there, too. Rome is such a mixture: business and ruins, tourists and villas, beggars and flowers, but the most interesting place in the world. We are going to spend the rest of our time in the galleries and in the Vatican and the Sistine Chapel. We have seen a lot of Rome, but I am only beginning to feel the city a concrete thing. As we have gone day after day among wonderful ruins, I have had fragments of these lines in my head—I brought Shelley along, you know, but I never remember anything very well, so only fragments floated around with me—

> My father time is hoar and grey
> with waiting for a better day.
> See how idiot-like he stands
> fumbling with his palsied hands!
> He has child after child,
> and the dust of death is piled
> over everyone but me:
> misery—oh, misery!

The misery I have left out; I'm having too good a time. Oh, and by the way, I have pasted into your little copy of Shelley, between the flyleaves, a little acanthus leaf picked near the wall behind Shelley's grave, and, over Adonis, a bit of the abundant box-hedge that encloses Keats' and Severn's[7] stones.

I think Mart and Albert would feel I was very sentimental. Perhaps I am, but, if sentiment is in our circumstances, we'll bring it out—and so they have here in Rome. I'm so glad I brought Shelley and the *Golden Treasury*. It has been a great outlet for over-abundance of feeling to read them. I wish I could go about expressing myself in their beautiful lines all the time. I believe you will not get tired by so many letters, for I know yours bring me joy, and that mine will be just as welcome at home.

Rome, May 27th

A girl goes from our dining table in this pension today who has been reminding me during all our days here of Jessie: her teeth, her mouth, her color. I have so loved to look at these features and have almost loved her because of them, though she is unaware of having given me, with her beauty, one added loveliness in this country.

---

7. Keats's devoted friend, Joseph Severn, was an English landscape painter and consul to Rome.

Yesterday, Sunday, when I rested, I re-read *Adonis.* Do you re-member that one of the last stanzas speaks of "one keen pyramid with wedge sublime pavillioning the dust"? I sent you a postal of the pyramid Turino, but had forgotten it was spoken of by Shelley.

I am promising myself to write you of our going to the Sistine Chapel because I think you will want to hear of it through me: Mother. It really does seem a miracle that I have been there just as all these days seem dreams. I cannot thank Annie enough for her planning which brought me here to Rome.

We entered the chapel by a wee little door near the altar so that the great end wall covered by the painting, *The Last Judgment,* was the wall the little door pierced, and this great painting was not at first visible. We looked down the long room lighted by windows set deep in stucco or carved marble frames. High up there was a golden light over and in and a part of everything. When we were halfway down the room we turned from whence we came to look at the great wall behind us, and blue had taken the place of gold. This was not from any change in the light, but the impressions made as a whole by the masses of paintings.

The backgrounds in the painting where there is sky, and all the framing or bands which separate the different scenes in the ceiling which you know so well, might once have been white; age has made them creamy-golden, and with the reds and browns in the paintings, they made for me this first impression of color. The background of *The Last Judg-ment:* blue, deep, serious blue, sometimes almost black, only occasionally bright blue. When you sit or stand where that dominates, the blue comes out in all the other paintings, and the impression changes. Of course I be-gan to look at the paintings one by one — the mass of *The Last Judgment* first because I couldn't help it. The central figure there is forever holding the eye, but little by little, I recognized in the ceiling all the familiar figures so many times studied, yet now wholly different except in form.

Only as it was time to leave the room had I found time to glance at the Botticellis, Rossinis and Ghirlandaios. They were on the side walls under the windows — there are really no windows at either end. Of course, *The Last Judgment* occupies the whole of the altar end, thirty-two feet down; it is sixty-four feet wide, but windows are painted in the opposite end to carry out the effect. If I could not go again I should bring away the impression of a new heaven and earth, as I wrote on one of the postal cards, but I shall go tomorrow and many days more, I hope.

All the seeing of Rome is over, I believe; now it remains to see these mighty fruits of the Renaissance to leave in our minds a Rome be-yond words. We have seen the grave, the city and the wilderness; this is to me perhaps paradise. You see I am quoting *Adonis* again; it is because my words are so few and poor, and Shelley's do express what I want to and cannot. I went back to the little door once more and again saw the great, high room: golden.

Annie has other things she wants to do tomorrow, and I shall go down alone. I have tried not to write very many descriptions, dates, figures and so forth in my letters — this comes nearest to description perhaps.

Florence, June 7th

Time has seemed to go faster than ever here in Florence. We go about here among the churches and museums finding each one has its own glory, either in some grand piece of statuary or wonderful pictures or, as for instance, in old San Marco, from both pictures and association; for there the pictures were painted onto the walls of the monks' little cells by Fra Angelico, and in one of the cells was the furniture and chair of Savonarola, that daring old monk who was first loved and then burned here in Florence. A funny old print showed that the burning was done in a sort-of pit led out to by a tressle in the public square, through which we pass every day. We stopped in crossing the square one afternoon at a brass slab which marks the spot of the burning. How foreign this seems to the present.

Venice, June 24th

Lying awake this morning I thought as I do always of my dearest ones and of Jessie. Oh, how I wanted you all — most of all, Jessie. I thought of what it would mean to me to get a letter from her, knowing so well what your letters coming across these many miles mean. What a glow and thrill and love-warmth they give. "A letter, only a little letter from her!" my heart cried. Then came the thought that I would write my want out to her as though she were living. And up I started to give aching memory that relief. Yet before I had pen and paper ready, I realized that I would be writing only to myself, wasting on myself what I might give to you, dearest. Oh, yes, you are everything to me. I will write to you and forget heartache in heart-joy, because I have you and Albert — my own, dear Albert — and Myron and Rhoda and Jane. But the tears will flow over Jessie.

Wouldn't she be glad I am having such a good time? Wouldn't she miss me, too? And be glad of letters? Wouldn't she be full of her own busy, joyful, helpful life, mothering her little girl or boy, perhaps building a home as you have built one? How I wish the hours could be turned back, and knowledge swift as lightning come to save her precious life before too late. Too late. Too late. Too late. But this is not a happy letter for you, and I'm not heartsick and will not let myself cry out for the impossible.

Venice, July 2nd

Dear Mrs. Smith and Sister Jane:

I wish I could give you some idea of Venice that would be vivid enough to make it seem as beautiful as it really is. It must be the situation and the water and the canals that make it lovely, and then the architecture for another. Why, even way out here where we are on the Giudecca, I can, by turning my head to look out of the window, see little chimneys that are not plain like ours, but all delicately built with indentations and projections and carving. The windows are arched with leaded glass, and the casings are white marble. Across from us is one window which is ornamented above the arch by a carved head. It has a little white balcony to step out on. We look into a large garden where there is a magnolia tree all in blossom, a banana tree, wisteria climbing to the roof full of purple blossoms, oleander of several colors trained in masses to cover the house wall and the garden wall, and a marble court. It seems as though the people who built these old houses in Venice must have all been artisans and never in a hurry.

We went over to the Lido yesterday. That is a long island like Coney Island with a fine beach; and here, the modern Venetians have put up a mass of summer homes that are not beautiful at all — almost ugly.

And then it is so restful here; nobody seems in a hurry, and there is not much noise. The Giudecca is a canal wider than The Grand Canal, twice as wide and full of ships. It is a harbor.

On Monday we hired a gondola for the day, from nine in the morning to seven in the evening, and it cost us only a dollar-twenty each. There were three of us.

We visited palaces first and then wandered here and there among the watery streets, finally out into the lagoons and across to Murano where they make Venetian glass. We saw them making glass chandeliers and bottles and all sorts of things. We ate our lunch out beyond Murano, sitting under a canopy in the cushioned gondola. We visited an old church or two and came back to Venice and crossed the Giudecca to San Maggiore. Here a thunderstorm came up, and, for shelter, we went into a church, and our gondolier and gondola went under a bridge.

Venice, July 5th

I shall have a sense of gratitude to Annie forever; for not alone did she plan our trip, but she manages everything so well and easily and is mother and sister to me. I hope she feels I am daughter and sister to her.

Journal—July fourth: rained hard all day. We sewed, mended, I sketched a little and wrote up in this journal—wondered what might be going on at home. I thought of Albert and all his energy and hoped he was well. At dinner we had my little silk [American] flag laid on the table—the flag Mr. Sattig sent me.

July fifth: Annie off to see more churches, and I out to sketch. I made several small quick sketches in pastel. The sun was high. Difficult to find shade—wherever I sit down fleas assail me unmercifully. I will try going in gondola tomorrow as the day is fine. Our active artist, Miss W., makes me almost jealous by her smell of paint and the lovely sketches she brings in, but I dare not work as hard as she works. She comes in "tired to death" but gay and festive. It would be running too much risk for me to work hard so far from home. Tomorrow is our last day here. We had our picture taken in San Marco.

July fifth—afternoon: a little shopping still left undone. We receive our penny-postcard-photos of Mrs. Lecks and Mrs. Aleshine feeding pigeons.[8] Annie has a touch of toothache. The sunset was fine. I went out and stood long by the parapet, my back to the Campo. A young man, taking my back for the back of youth, was about to accost me, and when I turned, he was aghast at age and made off very quickly, laughed at by his fellows. 'Hah-hah!' quotes Age, 'Got the better of the devil that time.'

While Annie was at Academy I took the gondola and had a famous ride away round the island of Giudecca. I made one sketch. Am getting more independence and self-confidence here, though I think the gondolier took too much money when I paid him.

We leave for Milan in the morning, so we are packing this afternoon.

Bellagio, July 10th

I saw Rembrandt's pen and ink drawings: a whole case-full of them laid out, not piled up, marked "Rembrandt"—so many lovely ones I had never seen in books—all this at Ambrosiana in Milan. We saw miles of galleries in Milan, and I made some notes of a few things that I have pasted into my notebook for you to see when I get home. But the too numerous religious pictures, madonnas, assumptions, and so forth make just one drawing or a bit of Greek sculpture like a glass of wine. How I shall enjoy for a change French modern art. I don't know though; we

8. Frank R. Stockton, *The Casting Away of Mrs. Lecks and Mrs. Aleshine,* was an amusing story about two ship-wrecked women.

"Mrs. Lecks and Mrs. Aleshine," Annie Miller and Jessie Catherine Kinsley, feeding the pigeons in the Piazza San Marco, Venice, July 5, 1913

have really been seeing heavenly things. If only I can remember any details out of all the mass to tell you. I will send some postals along, but be sure to save them up for me—won't you?

July 17

We start out on our roundabout tour of Switzerland today. This will take us a week or ten days — it depends on the weather. Leisurely touring will cut a little from our stay in England, but I think that is all right. We shall have six weeks in England, and I tell Annie it will be much easier for me to go again to England possibly than to Italy or Switzerland. We are enjoying ourselves and keeping well. Later the same day at six, p.m., Interlacken: we arrived here after a fine journey over a pass 3000 or more feet high, and the latter part of our journey was by boat. Our room is on the third floor of the Eden Hotel. There is a lift, and we have a balcony. I'm sitting on it, and the Jungfrau is straight before me. We left all unnecessary baggage at Lucerne until our return.

We are still having ups and downs with the weather; our feather-bed covering is excellent for this temperature. Annie has gone down to dinner. I had a mid-afternoon lunch and am not hungry, so decided to leave out dinner for once. The rain has begun to fall again, and the clouds obscure all the mountains. We were fortunate to have bright skies as we made our journey this afternoon.

Annie saw so many interesting flowers as we were among the mountains. What a storehouse of knowledge she is: flowers, birds, beasts, humans — she knows them all. Across the lake at Lucerne, early this morning, she heard the lions roar. They were in the zoo and were being fed. The city was still, so what a wierd sound it made, so unaccustomed and so inhuman. That zoo from our window at night is a fairy place. I shall not forget the night view from our window in Lucerne.

Switzerland

Geneva, July 22nd

All this long journey among the mountains has been a delightful change from the days of visiting ruins and churches and picture galleries. Now we begin to feel keenly the opportunity we shall soon have to again see art in Paris. Jean Jaques Rousseau lived here in Geneva on a little island. I see his monument. Did he write about his native city? We have enjoyed our ride and feel the city full of modern ideas, although we see touches of the old. There are immense power plants here as at Niagara Falls.

July 25th

I write as we drive along at breakneck speed through the French country. We have had lunch in the dining car, an unusual luxury and an excellent repast.

We have left the mountains far behind us. This is flowing and rolling land with wooded hills on the horizons. We pass little towns, one very like another: small red-roofed houses, a church with square tower tucked generally into a crotch in the hills — probably where some stream runs down. There are no fences, no rocks, no hedges, but the "harp of the winds" plays everywhere over the landscape and is the principle feature: the straight, trimmed, quivering poplar — not the lombardy poplar — follows for miles the edges of canals that cut winding ways from town to town.

A curious thing is the emptiness of life in all the countryside. We go miles and see no man or ox or dog or child; perhaps it is a festal day, and everyone is in the town. We have just seen a large company mowing and raking; perhaps they do their work in groups. There are highly cultivated fields of beets and potatoes, and all kinds of cereals, but no one in them.

Paris

12 Rue de la Grande Chaumiere, Paris, Sunday

We drove yesterday afternoon for a general view all about and now we shall revisit many places. We have only a step to go to an omnibus line. Just think of it. We are going to the Louvre today! I shall probably come back here at noon as dazed as a bee by the many things I have seen and not have an idea in my head, but now I am full of excited anticipation. If only I had keener wits, better insight, more knowledge! I'm going to tell you what the secret of classic art has seemed to me to be: serenity. I do not know perhaps what I mean by classic, but I think of a Greek temple as I write the word, and of much sculpture and painting in Italy. Perhaps a classic has perfect proportion, too, but as to that there is much serenity in some things out of proportion. I'm going to withdraw the word "classic." It is too far beyond me. I'll say that that which has satisfied me as most beautiful has seemed both strong and serene. Then always — most always — I have found what Kenneth said once to me: that the sense of the perpendicular gives strength and it also gives serenity. In the old mosaics and the later mosaics in St. Mark's, the strength and beauty of the perpendicular, though there not proportioned, was most vividly exampled and contrasted. The old were so serene, the new all wavy and swooping lines with perfect proportion but maybe yet lacking in that beauty which satisfies. Does modern art seek to disturb, to provoke emotion and have such a spirit of adventure in this that all serenity and strength is lost? I have the modern spirit and like adventure, too, so now that I have been seeing all these old serene things, I'm looking forward to the new with keenest expectation.

Afternoon: well, we have been to the Louvre and, as it happened, have seen nothing but a gorgeous recapitulation of the old masters. Just happened to get started through the rooms that way. We need not have gone to Italian galleries at all! I am most pleased just now with the Watteau, for I had before seen only one little one. Today I saw the *Embarkment for Cythera;* it is wonderfully beautiful. Puissant is great too, but not quite equal in my mind to Claude Lorraine. You might think quite the other way. I'm no judge. If I only had your powers, Edith, what wouldn't I give; but my mind just hobbles along on all fours—doesn't stand up straight. Of course we shall go again and again to the Louvre and to the other places. How we shall ever do all we want to do in one week is a puzzle. I begin to want a month here. But there is England, too, and we shall not prolong our going home, you may be sure of that.

Louvre

A Mary Cassatt, one Legros and several Monets you will know I enjoyed, and also a Whistler. There was only one Gauguin there to my great disappointment: a little still life with oranges and a bottle—really exquisite. I was prepared for something much more radical and surprising than I found in Cezanne, Pissaro, Sisley—they are lovely! I was proud of a Winslow Homer. I have seen his work before and thought some of it harsh. But this one is a gem—a beauty. Two women are dancing beside a floodtide sea that sparkles in the moonlight, and other black figures silhouetted against the sea and rocks. The women are graceful, and the colors have an inner radiance like Ryder's.

Then there were Degases, all interiors, very vivid. There were landscapes by Renoir in the Monet manner, only small and with even bigger feeling for me than the Monets.

My love for the older masters seems stronger now. They seem to give greater gifts to me than before I began this journey. I used to be so fascinated by La Touche and La Sidinier—copies of their work—and I saw them in reality today. They are charming but not what I really like. Have I, in another letter, written to you about seeing the Watteaus? You know I looked forward to them with great eagerness. They are not disappointing, they are beautiful. How I wish for you, Edith, to be here with me.

England and Scotland

London, August 5th

The cliffs of Dover and all of England we passed so swiftly through on our passage here from Dover were as beautiful and charming as I had expected, perhaps more so. We draw a long breath to hear our own language spoken freely all about us and realize a vast sort of content. The sun shines here in London this morning.

London is a great city but not to me at first impression what Paris seemed or many another city. So far I have not fallen head over heels in love as with many another city. Annie loves it. She does not like Paris. I tell you here the gasoline smell is so strong it has given me a headache. All the terrible buses are gasoline users. In Paris they are electric buses. Gasoline fumes so strong leave a horrible memory, like a bad dream. Well, I'll probably get used to it. Up here at Miss Lugg's the air is clear and better. What a silly impression this is of London. Look for a letter later when I haven't a headache.

London, August 10th

At Miss Lugg's, 13 Gordon St., Gordon Square: when I lay wakeful this morning I thought of you and Jessie. Six years ago in Utica; you and Jessie lying in bed and talking on that most eventful morning for Jessie;[9] and of your father and I getting up very early and pretending to go to the lake. Perhaps you were thinking of Jessie, too; no doubt you were, dear. I must concentrate all thought on you and Albert this month—try not to think of Jessie, for the pain of that, without you near, is too terrible. Really, I'm not unthankful but somehow go about with a heavy heart and not much spring. I hope you will let me hear from you.

Yesterday we went to Westminster Abbey. We dropped in just at the right time to hear a long service. The boys' voices were exquisite, and the multitude was reverent, and the organ notes swelled and echoed among the arches. Afterward we found Poets' Corner and wandered up and down, up and down, looking at familiar names. Far away from Poets' Corner, on a stone slab in the floor, I saw written, "Rare Ben Johnson." We finished our day by having tea at the inn Samuel Johnson frequented, The Old Cheshire Cheese, and I bought my tea cup and saucer as a souvenir for you.

Today we have been over to the British Museum, not a very long

9. Jessie Janet's wedding day. August was the month of Jessie Janet's marriage in 1907 and her death in 1908.

walk from here. I found there some beautiful Japanese paintings and shall look for more at South Kensington Museum. We saw the Elgin Marbles and miles of interesting things: Egyptian, Persian, Indian. Not the least interesting were drawings by Rodin and Millet. I long for some of the interesting things at the British Museum to be photographed; or if they have been already, to find them. I have quite a budget of photos to bring home.

Glasgow

We have had quite a wonderful day getting down here from Edinburgh; just wonderful to me, I suppose, for everyone travels over the same route who comes to Scotland. Nevertheless, it was grand. The alternate coaching and travel by rail and boat, through the Burn's country and Rob Roy's, Carlyle's and Livingstone's and Stephenson's and Scott's, is exciting to the imagination. Such an amount of reading as it makes me want to do.

The day was a glorious one, too: Cloud shadows and brilliant sunshine on the heather and basalt rocks, though there was a mist while we were high up among the clouds, driving with four-in-hand and a red-coated coachman down to Loch Katrine from Aberfoyle, Loch Lomond, Ben Lomond and Ben Venne—each has a charm, though no greater than the charm of Switzerland and the Italian lakes. I have come into Glasgow full of that excited, interested feeling that you have when a curtain has gone down on a magnificent play. I have been at the theater all day. Really, I am at the theater still, for where I sit to write I glance down at a brilliantly lighted street upon a thronging Saturday evening crowd of Scotch people. So dense a crowd that I should imagine some special occasion had called them all out did I not know better.

Lynton, August 26th

We have found nice rooms and have settled down here at Lynton as we have hardly done since before leaving Italy. It does seem good.

We have had gorgeous weather, but today a storm is brewing, and a fog has settled down over the sea. I sit on the edge of a cliff, four hundred feet above the sea: the headland looms dull and gray.

I sent some postals of Lynton and Lynmouth yesterday and I hope I shall see the waves come beating up on the old lighthouse as one postal showed them.

There is no real harbor here, but when the tide is right, steamers anchor behind the headland, and passengers are carried to and from the shore and steamer by small boat. We make, perhaps, an excursion to Clovelly by steamer from here next week. I shall let Annie go alone if there is any sea, as I would be sure to be seasick. We are both of us quite ragged and dirty, and a rainy day will be hailed as a chance to mend up dresses and wash collars and so forth.

I went down the hill to Lynmouth yesterday, tucked under the arm of a big, talkative Englishwoman whom I had told I was deaf and who immediately took charge of me. I am beginning to find the English not as forbidding and cold as they had first appeared. But how much alike they all are. And their faces: how all of one type—short upper lip, slightly showing the teeth, and much curved and cupid-like; small nose, finely shaped with good nostrils; often a small chin; often, too, a narrow forehead. I told Annie I thought the women had a look of greater placidity than we Americans. They do not scowl or have lines as heavy above the mouth. Their dreadfully quick, highvoiced way of talking with no movement of the lips perceptible—no expression or change in the face— must keep the lines out.

I have been sketching, too—just little scrawls that greatly disgust me, for they are such perfect specimens of how such work should not be done. I cannot feel that all my observation has practically helped me, but I am sure of having gained something to think about.

Lynton, August 30th

My dear Mrs. Smith,

We shall stay here until next Wednesday and then we go to Wells, and from there to Bath and Oxford, and to Windsor, and back again to London. Mrs. Miller loves London. Perhaps I shall this time. I expect to. We are going to have a better room when we go back. London seemed so proper. We had a mean little room designed for a servant with iron bars across the window, and not very good light in the evening. Unless you were out sightseeing, you felt like a prisoner. Miss Lugg has promised Annie a room in her own house next time. In the other countries like Italy and France, from which we had just arrived when we went to London, the self-conscious, proper feeling was not so tremendous as in this little London lodging street. The iron bars, Annie said, were to keep the servants from hanging out the window. Why, in Paris, on our street, everyone hung out of the window. In Naples the whole family next door came to bow to me from the balcony. The baby was held up for my pleasure; the blind grandmother made a deep curtsy. In Switzerland every window in Bern had a balcony with outside cushions of crimson and was the living room.

Annie said Miss Lugg ran up to her room when she and Violet were there years before to tell them to pull down their curtain, for every curtain on the street must be down if a funeral was passing. I think that was rather thoughtful and kind of the street, but how much more self-conscious than even we are.

Well, I need not criticize London any more after a very one-sided view of it.

September 1st

We have a smart manufacturer of velvet from Manchester at our table now. How I long for good hearing to catch his every word. Quite often we introduce some political subject, like the situation in Mexico, or the way Lord Grey has managed the Balkan matters, or the subject of the tariff, mentioning that in December we in the United States are to have free rule. Then the judge and the manufacturer begin a discussion. Annie hears and joins in. I have to sit tight and get what I can. I heard the judge ask the manufacturer what would happen should the idea arrive and there be no tariff? "Our manufacturers would control the world." "Why?" said I. "Because," said he, "We make everything better than you do; we take your bright ideas and then we go ahead of you in carrying them out." He mentioned the shoe trade; said the English shoe did not have a good reputation at one time, but now the English have taken American patterns and ideas and are putting out the finest, cheapest shoe in the world — much better made than the American shoe, yet with all its advantage in fit and style. He thinks President Wilson has done a smart thing in the way he has dealt with Mexico. He thinks Lord Grey has been keen and strong and admirable, but the situation now is very awkward.

Bath, September 5th

Here we are about to leave Bath where we have spent the night. I have not been disappointed in Bath; Duke Street, the North Parade, The Avon and the houses all fell into line with the previous imagination. We drank a goodbye glass of the hot water which bubbled up behind the bar and found it good. We gazed with interest at the baths of hot, yellow-green water at the old Roman Baths and so forth.

Now we go on to Oxford.

We duly arrived in this interesting town, lunched, and had a two hour ride up and down and around, stopping occasionally to take a peep into one place and then another. Annie says she is satisfied, but we are not due in London until Sunday, so I shall have time to make a closer acquaintance with a place so full of the romance of history for me: the history of people who have shown the beginnings of their genius here and have gone on then to make beauty and glory for us all.

September 8th

Dear Mrs. Smith,
Here we are back in London after a very fine trip which took us not quite a month and gave us great pleasure. And I want to qualify my criticism of London boarding houses very decidedly, for having come back to Miss Lugg, we have this time a charming room as fine as we could wish: French windows opening onto a balcony, electric lights instead of candle, and we do feel very much pleased and at home for our two weeks here before sailing. These two weeks will go fast, and then only nine days and we reach New York.

We made nice friends everywhere on our journey who seemed to find something in us to love, and whom we leave with real regret, having drawn quite close to them. In Oxford, a Boston girl full of enthusiasm; also, the sweet little English daughter of our landlady who is afflicted as I was and has a tumor in her breast. She had been advised to have the knife used but was hesitating. I encouraged her greatly, and we parted with a promise on her part to write to me and I to her.

London, September 14th

London has come to seem as fine as Paris to me now: full of human interest, and I cease to criticize but learn to love. How much better even this little street looks from this side and from our sunny balcony.

Annie's new suit is a beauty, and with her fine velvet bonnet she looks a queen. I felt very proud of her when we went to lunch in a fashionable restaurant in Colburn today — today the anniversary she keeps, for it is George Miller's birthday. I wish that George could see her, too. We finished the afternoon by a ride in a taxi in Regents Park, and by going to Madame Tussaud's, where Annie and George tried to go twenty-nine years ago but found it then closed. What a charming thing to do to celebrate the birthday of someone gone from life yet living in the heart. Let us invite our friends for Jessie's birthday, shall we?

In the Kensington Museum I found a room full of Constables — oh, beauties! And in the Ionides Collection were paintings and drawings by Legros. The drawings were impressive enough. They filled me with excited delight much more than did his paintings. Almost beyond all were drawings by Daumier, though you will think this strange and exaggerated

View from the window at 19 Marlborough Road, St. John's Wood, sketch by Jessie Catherine Kinsley

when I tell you that etchings by Millet and Rodin and Whistler were there, too. Perhaps because I saw the Daumiers last they gave more. I do not know. And, oh, beautiful and satisfying Chinese and Japanese things, too. You will like London, I am sure.

I think I have taken all this journey in the right way. It has been easy so to do, and now the last thing seems almost the best. Every place and experience has had its own charm and has not seemed comparable with anything else; and I have not wished anything changed or different (except only the first week in London when, within myself with pain, you were suffering over Rhoda; but, though I did not know it, I was in a gulf of depression which I laid upon our room and no letters which I longed for).

I'm glad I can travel in such an ecstasy and hope I may go through life with as few ups and downs of spirit. But perhaps that will be impossible. It will certainly be the height of bliss to get home again to you all. You cannot imagine how much I owe to Annie. If I were to get the give-and-take spirit, I should be in despair over my debt to her. You will help me perhaps to give good things to her later. She sends you love. Your ever affectionate mother.

London, September 19th

Just one more letter. Five months ago today we sailed out of New York at just about this hour. I draw a long breath when I think of it. Oh, dearest, are you and Rhoda well? All these fourteen days in London I have hoped to hear just one more word from you, or from home some word more, but no, yet the *Quadrangle* came. We sat down, and while Annie sewed, I read it aloud straight through. So much for home yearnings.

WARTIME JOURNALS AND LETTERS

April 1st, 1914

April 1st, 1914—This little book [diary] is taken up again, this time in hope of greater continuance. My pen is such a dullard that a re-reading of October and November entries made herein sickened me, and I put the book away. Now I shall keep it beside my bed at night and morning, whenever the wish comes to use it, less perhaps as a diary—no, as a diary but also as a practice in writing. Not that I expect to attain grace or beauty or any perfection. With my bad habits of slip-shod expressions, too many "ands" and "buts" distorting my sentences will make that impossible.

On this All Fools Day our family is broken by Mart's absence. He went to England in February. Edith saw him leave the harbor in New York for what proved a most tempestuous voyage. He writes of his work in opening an office in London.

Edith brought from New York a gift to me of two plays: *Medea,* and *Bacchae,* by Euripides, translated by Gilbert Murray of Cambridge. I presume the translation is of the best, for the plays are wonderfully haunting with a sort of beauty that makes all other men's efforts shrink.

I have finished the first volume of *George Meredith's Letters.* This reading has followed closely upon a volume of *Leslie Stephens' Letters,* and two of Edward Fitzgerald's. Like the people themselves, these letters have flavor. All are choice reading. Yet I would again and again read the first volume of Fitzgerald where I would not again read Stephens or Meredith with like pleasure. I'm quite sure the opposite of the above expression would be Edith's. She would prefer the richness, humor and touch of genius in Meredith's letters, and a lesser but allied quality in Stephens, to the quite nothingness of which many of Fitzgerald's seem a part. I did not quite enjoy the growing-old letters in the book, where, one by one, friends dropped out of life until ripe age saw the letter writer brave but pensive. That part I have not yet reached with Meredith, though I suppose such letters will come in his *Volume Two.* They have already shown depression in *Volume One.*

Later: never were there braver letters than Meredith's, as I have gone on with them. Stephens mourned in his epistles over every departing friend; Meredith said little of such events but sometimes sent brave words out of his own experience to others. He scarce mentioned his growing old or the many physical ills he suffered.

Our United States is on the point of having war with Mexico. There is an incident of an insult to our flag and a refusal from the Mexican government to make reparation by a salute to the flag. Congress had voted to give President Wilson the power to coerce Mexico in any way that he sees fit. War seems unavoidable and truly awful.[10]

April 22nd, 1914 — The Franklands are here in Kenwood. It is most interesting to have Mr. Frankland[11] as a guest and talker in our house, for perhaps never have we had with us at Kenwood, since Doctor Noyes and Mr. Noyes died, an intellect like Mr. Frankland's. Indeed, I am sure he even surpasses these men in intellectual power. And with intense mental development, Mr. Frankland combines perhaps as spiritual and high-minded character and habit of thought as there is in the world.

10. The so-called Tampico incident involved the arrest of some American sailors and a refusal of the Mexican authorities to accompany an apology with a salute to the American flag. President Woodrow Wilson ordered U. S. marines to occupy the port of Vera Cruz. Full scale war seemed likely but was averted when the United States and Mexico accepted mediation by Argentina, Brazil, and Chile.

11. Though never a member of the Oneida Community, Frederick W. Frankland was an ardent propagandist for its ideals and published many pamphlets written by former Community members. He wished a headstone in the Community cemetery, and though he is buried elsewhere, his wish was fulfilled.

Grandma Jessie surrounded by, from left, Rhoda, Edith, Myron, Albert, and Jane Kinsley

May 1st, 1914 — Baby Jane's first birthday. Jane is, first of all, a darling. And she is individual, not one of a type; in fact, very unlike most babies in appearance. Really, the distinctive attribute of Jane though, is not her features, but the expression her face wears. It is never dull, placid, unthinking. Rather it is always alert, filled with inquiry, ready to find the least thing of interest and call it good fun. She is small for her age—weighs not quite fifteen pounds. But quite up to the average in other ways of development. Myron loves her, and I was glad to hear Lotta's mother telling Edith that Myron had never been unkind to Jane. Lotta said that Myron was instinctively loving and gentle to Jane from the day of her birth.

[Date unclear]—Long before Christmas I began planning various gifts. One for Gertrude Noyes was quite elaborate: a braided mat of silk for a tray.[12] The pattern: cocks fighting. This proved of such interest in the making that I became ambitious and made another for myself. This rag-rug making and sewing filled hours of time.

Mr. and Mrs. Bate came to live with us before Christmas.[13] They are fine, lovable people, and we are still quite awestruck at the marvel of our good fortune in getting such splendid help. Mr. Bate works in the shop.

Myron came down to stay with us a week or two. And Annie Miller made us a visit shortly before Edith's return, which lenghtened a few days beyond Edith's coming and was a great delight. Myron slept in Rhoda's room, and the two were very happy together. It was a great pleasure to me to live so near Myron. He was extremely good, large-hearted and chivalric. Once he preached to Rhoda quite seriously, saying to her over a fit of crying, occasioned by a fall, "If you are patient and brave now, you will be patient and brave when you grow up."

Rhoda is a keen, bright child but not given to remarkable sayings. Her mother says Rhoda enquired one day about the Holy Ghost: "What was the Holy Ghost?" Told that it was the spirit of beauty—a beautiful, good spirit—she said, "Oh, yes, I saw it once when it was flying through our house and it was blue."

In March I went south for several weeks with Hope and Mr. Allen.[14] We stopped off in New York, also in Washington and Philadelphia and Baltimore, then went down to Virginia to Old Point Comfort. We heard Paderewski[15] with the Philharmonic Orchestra in New York: a very wonderful concert and a memorable afternoon, for the human aspect of the great player was almost as impressive as his music. The tragedy of his native Poland seemed written in his changed gaunt appearance.

We went twice to Hampton to hear the singing, and Hope strangely met there a young Bobby Betts, a Negro lad who attended

---

12. Jessie's first venture in braiding.
13. Mr. and Mrs. Bate immigrated from England.
14. Henry G. Allen, Hope's father.
15. Ignace Jan Paderewski, then at the height of his fame as a piano virtuoso.

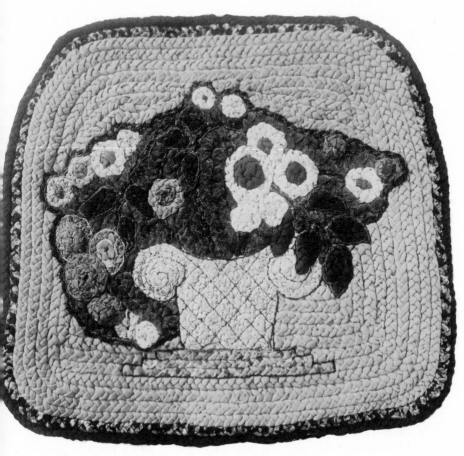

An early work, a chair mat, 1915

school with her once in Canada, now educated as a musician and teaching at Hampton. We found interest in watching some ultra-fashionable and yet charming women near us in the dining room — McNoughtons — and how dull the dining room was without them. We walked on the ramparts of Fortress Monroe; we haunted the docks, we talked of the past and the present and had rides across the harbor and to Newport News. We saw that romantic British vessel, the *Appain,* captured by the German raider, the *Moewie,* still anchored off Newport News in charge of a German prize crew. We haunted the library, a strange, military library. We continually were reminded of Conrad's stories, and of Dana's *Two Years Before the*

Mast, by the great five-masted sailing vessels that came into the harbor with all sails set, and there remained for days waiting for a headwind to take them out again.

I could not sketch at Old Point, for it is a military post, and the European War has made Uncle Sam a trifle wary of those who use the pen and draftsman's tools, even cameras. I felt there was hardly caution enough used against possible ill-disposed people at some points.

Letters to Aunt Jane

July 13th, 1914

Dear Sister Jane,[16]

I expect you are in your Cozicot[17] by now and perhaps getting rested. I have awakened early and sit where I can look out from my porch bed into the top of our butternut tree, and then across the fields into the early morning sky. Always the clouds in the morning sky are long, drawn out, I notice, as though without the sun they chase the horizon. At the other end of the porch Edith and Mart are peacefully snoring.

I am making sketches in pen and ink daily for practice, and, because my paper is thin and absorbent, I can never erase, which makes the work intensely interesting and fine practice, for every line must be sort of an inspiration and mean all that can be put into it. I saw one of Daumier's drawings in Paris in which four people and a dog sat wearily waiting for a train, and only four lines made a spirited landscape as you looked through the door of their trainshed. Well, I shall not attain to any such art — he was a great master in his line — but I wish to strive. Kenneth [Miller] is pleased with my work.

The Fruit Department[18] has begun picking cherries. Our trees are so beautiful, and the fruit so luscious to nibble on as we pass to and fro, that I wish it might hang even longer. But now it seems finally ripe. The robins come in flocks to pick the upper branches, and this morning I saw a father and mother Oriole and four young ones partaking.

Annie Miller came down later to see me. Our upper porch at my

16. Jane A. Kinsley was for some years purchasing agent for the Community household.

17. Cozicot was the company-owned cottage on the Connecticut coast. Jessie had spent some time there during the old Community days.

18. Oneida Community, Limited still preserved fruit. This had been one of the first industries established in the Oneida Community.

Annie Miller, 1913

end is our meeting place. She brought her sewing, and I read aloud. My bag of mending was nearby, but I feel that I am well off when I can read to dear Annie, for she enjoys it, and I do, too, and I am happy to be adding any small happiness into the days of a friend who has crowded such great happiness into my life. Without her I could not have had last summer. Annie and I read one of Lady Gregory's plays. It's very quaint and poetic.

Kenwood, July 17th

Mr. Levy[19] came down after supper, and we talked about the storm which had not yet ceased, and he played some Bach music and explained its beauty and meaning and seriousness, going over and over one refrain and talking about it most interestingly. But, alas, I am getting so that I miss most conversation not directed exactly at me. I must be getting me a hearing machine of some sort.

Mr. Levy played at Albert's, too, the other night, and from where we sat on the lawn, I never felt music more beautiful. And at Pierrepont's several evenings before, where many were gathered to hear him play, there arose a discussion that was even more interesting than the music. Edith, who has the power of a quick mind to draw the best out of her associates, drew from George W. (Noyes)[20] a really remarkable talk. I can only give you the gist of it and wish it could be better told than I shall tell it. It was fine enough to make the world seem a greater world to me, so that my imagination flew out and on, and I was thankful to have been born and to have my children born.

George said history showed him how development of spiritual growth had come in great cycles. For instance, Abraham, if we want to begin there, was the first to say there should be no human sacrifice. That was the negative word God gave to him; and the positive word was of the invincibility of God. Then for centuries that thought spread and worked like a slow leaven among the Jews. Then Moses brought out the negation: no other God but the one, the invincible; and the affirmative, positive word: good conduct! So again for centuries the world was digesting that God-given thought and gradually living up to it. Then came the greatest: the final word from Christ of negative: No sin; and positive: intent, that is, good conduct is all right but there must be perfection of intent. Then George went on to say how he thought that the early and really great

19. A musician-teacher and friend of Kenneth Miller, from New York City.

20. George Wallingford Noyes, J. H. Noyes's nephew and author of several works on the Oneida Community.

thoughts of Mr. Noyes were to emphasize Christ's message of no sin and intent—perfection of intent—and to seek and make the application of it altruism. George said the whole world is growing in that direction: all progress is toward some form of socialism, some form of altruism: suffrage for women, eugenics are discussed, and man's relation to his fellow man are ever being set on a higher plane by slow, slow degrees. We shall go on for century after century with Christ's great message of perfection of intent before us, and altruism as its application.

Do you know, dear Aunt Jane, and Miss Niles,[21] I think of you both as finely tuned into your cycle, our cycle, as altruists. How much Aunt Jane has done to forward the good of her fellow man, and how much dear Miss Niles is doing. I hope you will not be tired by this report. It seemed as though I wanted you, Aunt Jane, to be in your room where I could tell you about all this, and since you were not, I have written it. Miss Niles may not agree with George's thoughts that centuries hence, when the labor problem and the women problem and the sex problem have all been solved and ever-wider vision is reached, then perhaps, through that distance of time, what was undertaken by a handful of Perfectionists in the early days of the Community will be seen to have been prophetic. If that is true, you will be glad to have lived, dearest Aunt. And if it is only imagination, then you will still be able to feel that you have sincerely tried to live so that you have fitted into the need of your age. I do not think George thought the Oneida Community was alone in these things . . . —only trying them more radically.

Kenwood, July 29th

Here we are again. Sun just risen into a band of clouds, and a thousand little bands racing for life above. How soon these will all scatter. The clouds are thin and lean, as though they had raced all night like greyhounds.

I expect Aunty Smith has told you about Professor Loomis's visit. I asked Professor Loomis if he found his interest as greatly engaged at Scranton, where he has taught since leaving here. "No, no," he said. The situation for him here was most unusual, most absorbing, and never since has he had pupils like George and Pierrepont, Irene and Burton, Steven and others.[22]

21. Miss Niles was Jane Kinsley's nurse.

22. Professor Loomis taught the generation of children known in the Oneida Community as stirpicults from 1887 to 1891. The pupils referred to were George Wallingford Noyes, Pierrepont Noyes, Irene N. Newhouse, Burton L. Dunn, and Stephen R. Leonard.

Kenwood, August 2nd, 1914

On Friday night there was the big dance,[23] and as far as I can judge it was an enjoyable affair. I never saw so many dancers on the floor at once. The refreshments were served on the new porch and were very good. And that place was made delightful by green stuff and electric lights shaded in Japanese lanterns.

The morning has come clear and warm — so quiet — and with a sabbath feeling. I cannot imagine that in another part of the world on this very morning, thousands upon thousands of men are preparing for war. What horror it will be, and all because those nations are not content with their possessions and want more. Austria would never have started such a conflict had she not made a previous understanding with her ally, Germany. And of course the Serbians are a wholly different race; they are Slavs like the Russians, and race hatred runs high — and Russia will not see her blood brother overwhelmed, and so the excuses go. But what of the women and children? I do not believe that women are natural fighting animals as men are fighters. Perhaps as we progress, and women have equal voice in settling matters of dispute, they will hold back for more, and these horrors, which General Sherman called Hell, will be avoided. It is good to look forward with hope to a saner future, although I well know it must come slowly as all good comes.

As for our own country we shall not feel the weight of distress at first because our market will be good, but when the war is over there will be retrenchment everywhere, and a slump in our market, and probably such hard times as this country has not known for years.

I went home to find Rhoda in great distress because her doll, Elizabeth, was leaking sawdust. While she went to play, I fixed Elizabeth with a rag body, and then Edith returned and said there was to be a family picnic up on Snell's hill. So away I went. The arrangements were fine, and the view was magnificent.

Kenwood, August 4th

How does one stand the strain of this war in Europe? It comes home to us although we are so far away. Of course you have a paper every day. Are you not glad Annie and I are safe away from Paris? On this day, the fourth of August last year, we left Paris at eight in the morning, went to Bologne, rushed across that city and changed cars to go from Bologne

---

23. Salesmen, often referred to as "agents," were given a dance twice a year at sales meetings.

to Calais. I cannot imagine a greater nightmare than Paris would have been for us touring under present conditions, for we neither of us understood a word of the native language, nor did we have a male friend or acquaintance there, and only checks, no cash. Think of being in that little old pension in that narrow, winding street in the Latin Quarter with those excitable French people rioting! And a million Germans marching toward Paris! And a flock of warplanes overhead dropping bombs! All the boarders in our pension would have been looking out for themselves. I can only think that perhaps the Rhodes scholar might have tried to help us. Well, we are safe, but imagination pictures others just like us, even more helpless.

Gertrude tells me Colonel Noyes's letter of today to her says that almost every officer in the army has applied for the position of observer of foreign wars. Men are always sent on this duty by other governments when there is war. Colonel Noyes has not applied, yet he says he knows he is in a position to be very available for that duty. His not applying may mean he will be sent. Of course he hopes not to go on account of Gertrude.[24]

It is curious to see the trend of prejudice toward one side or another in this conflict. Mart does not like Russia, but likes England better than Germany, so he is rather divided about taking sides. Burton is quite on the German side, so Edith says, and so are John Humphrey and Clifton, but most of the other boys are anti-German. I think if the Germans had not wanted to fight, and backed up Austria to hit Serbia, then all this horrible carnage might have been avoided—so I do not want to see Germany successful.

Kenwood, August 7th

These momentous days go by with scarce a ripple of family thought, happening or excitement that is not colored by the great and pressing events outside us. How they crowd in upon our thoughts. Since England declared war on the fourth of August, Italy has been urged by Germany to enter the conflict as her ally, and Italy has determined not to, but is arming.

Later, [after tea in the garden], as Mr. Hatch[25] sat alone on his porch with a book, I went to chat with him. I asked him if he reminded himself of his father. He said he did—in tones of his voice and in his choice of words—often. Then he spoke of his mother, and of two in-

---

24. Gertrude Noyes was pregnant with her fourth child, Charles.

25. Cornelius C. Hatch was Jessie's half-brother, if Eleazer Hatch was her biological father.

stances when I, as a child, was quickly benefitted at her hands. Once, when I was wrongfully playing in the busy kitchen of the old Mansion House and ran into a bustling waiter and had pea soup poured over my chest, Mrs. Hatch, as quick as a flash, put me in the sink and poured cold water over me. Another time, when I had the croup, she tended me. And so Cornelius and I went on talking of the past.

We are all pained by the thought of Mrs. Wilson's death coming upon the President now. What a sad month this is, though seven years ago, now, Jessie was preparing for the greatest happiness of her life: her marriage to Chester, which came on the tenth of August, 1907, just three months before her father's death. I like to think how full of joy those months were.

Yesterday, Kenneth gave me the most interesting lecture on art, the way in which he works and sees it. This is so present to my mind and seems so full of really great interest and thought, that I imagine you, too, may find interest in it. If I set it down here for you, perhaps you will save this letter for me, and I shall be able then, when the memory of it has grown dim, to return to it in the very meager outline I can write out even now.

He said the significant thing about all visible things for the painter is the part they bear toward space: their movement, direction, diffusion. Everything is volume moving toward diffusion. Form is movement in direction. We are acquainted with the idea of a layer of space surrounding all objects; all painters, all artists and architects use that thought. For instance, the molding on the door or base-board breaks the sense of flatness of surface. What is flatness? It is an unbroken line where surface and space come together — break the line and you break the layer of space and make it conform to a curve which pleases the eye. Where that breaking into space goes forward in an intricate variety of ways in architecture — as in a cathedral — it gives the sense of something very grand. But Kenneth's thought was not only of breaking into space but of diffusion in space: volume moving toward diffusion, the earth and its very curvature, and its every object, even to the tiniest blade of grass, pressing forward into space, becoming a part of space in the inch where there is diffusion.

The ordinary way to think of a landscape in painting is to observe a tree, a house, a spot of bare ground or a grass plot, a man, or a group of trees as objects scattered about, bearing a certain relationship to one another. We study that relationship and we make above them all a sky.

But a greater way to think of these objects, of the earth itself, the trees, the grass, the house, the house the man has built, the man himself, is as movement: volume moving toward diffusion into space as a symphonic whole. We shall not then think of light as separate from shadow;

we shall see light in the shadow as well as in the mass—the sky, not off there, but here, everywhere, space pressing upon volume, a part of volume, as volume is pressing towards space.[26]

I do not know as you will find this very interesting, but if you could hear Kenneth's talk, with his painting at hand with its sense of light and movement and volume all showing so plainly how he puts his theories into concrete form upon his canvas, I'm sure you would be immensely interested. This is a poor outline. As to putting any of this thought into my own endeavors, it will never be possible I fear, however much I may work for it—though Kenneth says I have come near to doing good work in some of my pen and ink sketches this summer.

It does not matter whether I do or not, but I am glad to see Kenneth work, for I am sure, just as Chopin and Mozart brought into the world what was within them in the form of beauty, so Kenneth is bringing forth beauty in his way—and his thought about it is all interesting.

Journal, 1916–1918

April 18th, 1916—On May 8th of last year I wrote in this book of the sinking of the *Lusitania* by the German submarine. At the end of the page: "We are waiting for President Wilson's word about this event. He is preparing a note to be sent to Germany." Now, at the end of a year, with no satisfactory reply from Germany about the Lusitania, we are waiting for a reply to another note about another sinking of a vessel containing American passengers, the *Sussex*. We are in a much more serious frame of mind. For the year has brought us to the point where President Wilson's note is this time really an ultimatum. We may ourselves enter the war against Germany in defense of our rights and the rights of humanity upon the sea.

Alas, people in our country are so at variance. Wilson, our idol of a year ago, is now discredited for his appointment of weak men in important posts with an eye to politics. Then there are the pacifists who are forming a political party; and, of course, the pro-German element, full of plots for the undoing of the allies and of uncertain patriotic value as Americans.

There is a critical situation for us, too, in Mexico, where Pancho Villa, once trusted, is now being chased as a murderer and bandit by our U.S. soldiers.

---

26. The paintings of William C. Palmer, at one time a student of Hayes Miller, provide an example of this.

Months go by. We see the conflagration spread. We see [William Jennings] Bryan and [Henry] Ford try to put out the great fire with words; a few followers and one little boat. We see Serbia crushed. Turkey fighting in her last ditch. Russia victorious in the south, beaten in the north. Greece in deadly peril between the Bulgarians and Germans on one side, and allies on the other. England muddling along, often too late, withdrawing from Gallipoli, making tremendous effort and sacrifice, apparently secure upon the sea. And now are we to be swept up by the fire? With our fire engines not ready and water short!

Well, "preparedness" is the word of the hour, but, oh, how I long for peace.

May 18th, 1916 – The days are long. How easily we could add an hour in the morning as the Germans have.

The children showed aroused interest in our walks. Three or four, headed by Albert Noyes, come down early to get my promise to go out. They linger in Rhoda's sandbed, and their voices hurry me with my morning work. When at last we are off, it is, "Let us go to the stile." I do not quite know the lure of the stile unless it be story-telling. We have been this morning for clay to Parson's Gulch and ended by playing in the empty silo at the top of the hill behind the mill. We found the echo and the round, deep, hollow place inside the silo, open to the sun, grass grown but quite shut away from all the world, most exciting. We saw no snakes. Edith says there were snakes there last summer.

August, 1916 – June and July have slipped by, and I have been too occupied by painting to write in this journal. Kenneth is using my studio and giving my work occasional criticism. Again, he and Helen are up from New York and at the Elms[27] with little Louise.

August, 1916 – It is often torture to have a lesson with Kenneth, for while I gain as much from his words, his speech is hard to catch. I have to guess at things sometimes and I cannot continually say, "Louder, louder" to him. I do hear, too, at times, when the roar of my own head lets up for a moment, and I am getting to be a good guesser. I could laugh if I was not so busy guessing at the turn-about I make in a sentence, changing it by a quick thinking from its heard construction, sometimes most ridiculous, to what I am sure must have been said.

Kenneth has two canvases he works on. He draws often. And he

27. An adjunct of the Mansion House. The old Children's House in Community days.

has been painting on the picture I bought of him several years ago. He has made it splendidly radiant. I wish this painting had a name. If I could choose, I would call it, *The Sisters.* My own work seems without vision. It is great pleasure to work though, and Kenneth thinks I improve.

We have heard of the death of Mr. Frankland. A great blow to Edith, and a cause for sorrow and regret to us all. His death seems more than a personal loss, like a world loss. Moreover, Edith says the spirit of the old Oneida Community seems dead now without Mr. Frankland. It was kept alive in Mr. Herrick and Mr. Miller, but passionately alive in Mr. Frankland.

While Edith and Mart were away in Vermont, Rhoda was left with me.

Beginning in June, increasingly in July, an unwonted disease, poliomyelitis (infantile paralysis), has come as an epidemic to N.Y.C. There are long lists of new cases and of deaths each day in the paper, and like that scaly monster of William Blake's vision, this "pestilence" is now stalking across the country. It has reached Syracuse, Rome and Utica.

August 8th, 1916—We have had the annual field day with its sports. There was a fine parade, and the suffrage club marched in good form: a line of 40 or 50 women dressed in white bedecked with yellow. Lotta was everywhere present to guide and arrange. Then she worked hard and long in preparing competent committees for a suffrage booth in the park, and refreshments to be served in the booth. The field day was a great success. Every event went off with snap. There were crowds. In our suffrage booth alone, we cleared over $100.00. The airplane went buzzing overhead like a great bird, making several successful flights. We did not take Rhoda over to enjoy the games as we did last year, because of the dread of possible infection from infantile paralysis, though Mart took her about in the auto once or twice.

September 4th, 1916—All our walks are circumscribed now, and Rhoda and I go alone, for that plague, poliomyelitis, came to Kenwood! Peter was taken with a slight attack, followed by a serious illness for Barbara, and an attack of the dread disease for two of the Skinner children, Joseph and Prudence. It spite of immediate and stringent precaution, many have been exposed by these latter cases, for Dr. Carpenter had failed to call Peter's attack or the others poliomyelitis. And so, when Peter was better, before Barbara showed paralysis, there was an unfortunate picnic, and children were exposed then and later. From the first, Burton counseled separation for the children and he had disapproved the field day being held. He went to New York and talked to Mart's friend, a doctor, to gather knowledge for us all, and returned sure that segregation was the best and surest procedure.

Now the children play alone. Only brothers and sisters live and play together, so poor little Rhoda is quite alone.

My ears have been in a beaten water jar for many days. Every noise has a new sound and really a fearful sound, too: music is discord; the passing of a car is a blur of wildly unmeaning rattle. Mart's voice and conversation, or Albert's, even Edith's, seems a running together of words and echoes of words into a jumbled chaos. I am a little better now and less nervous. I had a happy ride with Marion Nolan one day to Syracuse to see a doctor about my ears. I am less depressed. I long to be just cheerful and thankful, but my ear trouble certainly does make me nervous, and the war and struggle and plague heap up things to weigh down an imaginative mind.

Pierrepont went abroad for our business interests. He saw no active sign of an England, France or Italy at war other than old cannon, many officers, many men in khaki, many wounded. He heard no sound of cannon, saw no zeppelins, nor heard of any raids while he was in London. But the spiritual atmosphere was penetrating, earnest and tense and sorrowful, though not depressing. Active signs of war for him were the troubles he had in getting about to do business. The Europe he went in to does not want travellers unless they have immediate and pressing business, and it has devised—especially the French—a perfect system for keeping strangers out. Fortunately, he had a complete set of Anglo-Saxon names for ancestors and wife's ancestors in the first place. Then he found a letter speaking of him as the President of the American Hardware Dealers' Association. That was a talisman better than his passport to open doors. In London he had to report at the police station each night. In every British or Scottish town, the police must be sought at once, and hours and hours were spent in satisfying their persistent curiosity about his movements, though all were courteous. Getting into France seemed almost impossible. He was held back for days on one excuse and another. Finally he was told that he must show a letter that someone in France had asked him to come to do actual business with them. Argument did not shake the French system. At last he bethought him to seek first from the Italian office a permit to travel in Italy. The Italian system was quite imperfect, moreover he did have one letter of the right sort from an Italian customer, and that, with high flung insistence, quite quickly brought the desired permit. With that permit, and his Italian letter and a bunch of new letters in English that the French examiner found difficult to wade through, he at last wore through the French preventative system and got to France. He was in Paris on the fourteenth of July, their great holiday.

Saw impressive parades and so forth. He spoke of seeing a field in France full of rusting automobiles, and another great field filled with rusting locomotives. These he could not explain. They might be refuse from Belgium. His route to Italy took him through the Pyrenees. In Italy he went first to Milan, then to Rome. His trip proved valuable financially.

War in Europe goes on and on with ever increasing fury. The long drive on Verdun has failed; the French defense has been marvelous. Now the English and French in their turn are beating back the German lines in the West little by little, and the loss of life on both sides is frightful. Rumania has waited for the tide of battle to sway to one side or the other as Bulgaria did last year. Bulgaria joined the Germans last year. Now Rumania has joined the allies when the central powers seem less victorious. Greece, too, may cease to be neutral and join the allies, for Bulgaria, her ancient enemy, has invaded her Macedonian territories, and the allies are able to coerce her by means of her situation in the sea. Moreover, the Russians are pressing the Austrian and German forces and making gains in the East. As for our place in this world of conflict, we succeeded in making Germany feel the necessity of curbing her slaughter of unwarned neutrals and merchantmen at sea by her submarines. And now, by act of Congress, we, too, are seeking redress and retaliation on England's policy at sea, her unwarranted conduct toward our commerce and mails, and the black list she has announced, in which some of our shippers are deprived by her proscription from their right to trade in Europe.

Because this is an unquiet year of presidential election at home, every move made by the Democratic Party and by President Wilson, is watched and criticized. Surely no President ever had more hard and new problems to meet than has President Wilson. Supreme Court Justice Hughes, a Republican, has left the bench and is running against Wilson. The Progressive Party has in great measure joined forces with Republicans for Hughes, since Roosevelt, not having received the united nomination of both Progressives and Republicans which he had hoped for in the summer, has given allegiance to Hughes. Edith is strongly against Wilson. I am glad, really, not to have a vote, for I am two-sided as usual. I can see so much to seem good and to seem doubtful on both sides. The Women's Suffrage Party, however, is showing power, and Hughes has publicly come out for suffrage by federal amendment, while in his own state, Wilson voted for suffrage.

September 30th — Now that the children are living apart, because of pestilence, life has changed for all of us. Most of the children have easily adapted themselves to the restrictions of segregation. Little Eugene Hulbert, in his big way, says he finds it rather interesting to get acquainted with his family. Here at home we have a cheerful and very careful household. We change our garments and air them after contact abroad. We wash, boil dishes and sterilize milk, etc. Edith devotes herself completely to Rhoda, who has no playmates, as great love, great pity and dread compel her. Constant association with the child is often fatiguing. Rhoda has a growing mind and intense pleasure in listening to reading. Presently she will be reading herself, and then her mother will have to be wide awake, for a gourmandiser of books becomes a person of sedentary habit, and then good health is apt to depart in some measure. We have many rides in the auto since quarantine. The fine clear days and full moon have drawn us to the highest hills. We shall not quickly forget the picnic we had last Sunday right up on the pinnacle, the expanse of horizon, the sunset, the moonrise, the gradual darkening of the tremendous space below us where twinkling lights came out, the plunges down as we came home. But, most of all, I shall remember the sensation of the climb upward as the car seemed to hesitate at the final desperate rise. It is not fear of existence, but of experience that makes me restless and nervous in adventurous places. I suppose there is a breaking down of high spirits with the breaking down of tissues. For old people, their ways should like quiet places. But then, I was always timid.

December, 1916 — Before Election Day really came, I had swung into the Progressive ranks. That is, I think they are progressive and I wanted Hughes elected, but there were not many voters here for Hughes, I believe. Perhaps Hughes would be no better — he is a lawyer, not a fighter. I do not think or suppose that either of these men could be a Lincoln. It's my very timidity that calls for the biggest man. I hate war, but it seems as though the cloud over Europe is almost appearing on our horizon, and an un-united nation needs a great leader. Even in England and France they needed great leaders that they did not find, although now Lloyd George seems capable. Sometimes I admire Wilson tremendously.

January, 1917 — Our troubles with poliomyelitis were over in November, though one or two scattering cases were noted in the papers as late as December.

Christmas was a happy time for us, though the war in Europe leaves its mark on every kind of experience, and I was not feeling well.

I made several more books for the children. Though I have not painted I have been doing some successful braiding: a funny thing I call "a futurist mat" given to Hope Allen for a tray; a Buddha tray for Edith; and I have plans for a round tray for Albert and Lotta; and an illuminated letter for Chester.

The finest experience, that is, perhaps one of the happiest, was the fact of Albert's advancement in business to the place of General Manager. In back of the actual change, in my mind, was the thought that he had grown into the place through qualities and powers of spirit and mind that made his choice unanimous. When Pierrepont spoke of Albert's qualifications for leadership and told of giving over his place to Albert, he said he thought the greatest and surest reason why Albert was chosen by everyone for the place was not alone his business acumen and power but his essential brotherliness.

I sat by Albert at the meeting. I did not want to make him feel ashamed but I could not help crying with joy. Years ago, many times, I held that little fellow in my arms and wondered what he would grow into — what would be his lot and his character. I never then dreamed this dream. I only wish his father had been beside me at the meeting. He dreamed bigger dreams for his children than I dared to. When Albert accepted his new position simply and modestly, I was proud of him and thanked God in my heart for all that seemed so good.

March 19th, 1917 — Rumania went headlong into the great war in the fall, and the hopefulness of the outlook against the central power seemed complete. Then Hindenberg was given the Teuton reins, and Mackensen made a brilliant defeat of the Rumanian forces after they had taken Transylvania. Peace offers came to the allies from Germany, and then our President intervened with letters to the combatants asking what they were fighting for. England scornfully gave her terms, and Germany declared these a menace to her very existence. She withdrew her offer to talk peace and made announcement of a ruthless submarine war. Ruthless in what she called a proscribed zone. This announcement was such a contravention of international law of the freedom of the seas and the rights of humanity and of a previous promise to us not to sink merchant vessels, that President Wilson went before Congress and declared his purpose to sever our diplomatic relations with Germany. He was upheld. Now seven American vessels have been sunk, and many American lives lost. Congress has been called into special session, and we are feverishly preparing to enter this worldwide conflict.

But even this prospect, at the moment, is blurred by two stupendous events in Europe. First, the retreat of the Germans from the long-held Western Front, and their pursuit by the French and English. Here the possible danger of a repetition of Von Hindenberg's masterly strategy lies. Once he lured the Russians by retreat onto ground they could not hold and then again last fall drew Rumania into a similar defeat, makes everyone wait and hold their breath, fearful of what may occur. Now the Germans seem to be standing for the moment on the line that runs through St. Quentin and La Ferc with a desert, a wilderness of wrecked territory behind them over which the French and English must come with their supplies. So the Spring Drive has been stopped or delayed, but there is desperate fighting going on, for the pursuit of the Germans has been swift and strong. Second, the revolution in Russia is such a stupendous thing, so secretly, so quietly begun, so successfully carried through without great excesses and seeming to spread by leaps and bounds to the provinces and to the army. The Czar abdicated in favor of his brother, Michael, on the twelfth of March, and then, after a day, Michael abdicated, and the people are now establishing a provisional government. All political prisoners have been liberated. Finland promises a liberal regime; reforms of all sorts announced. Like the French Revolution, danger will come in Russia to the new free government, from the fanatical radicals, and then perhaps the republican, democratic spirit will be crushed by civil conflict, and the situation is critical. It will be so for a long time. The prisons are full of princes and governors now: the former Royal Family is guarded. All this began about March 14th and now, on the 24th, it is still the greatest event in this wide, war-stricken world.

March 26th — My Birthday — Aunt Jane gave me a party. It was a fine supper at the Mansion. Rhoda gave me flowers; Mrs. Bate made a cake; while Hope gave me some silk to braid; Aunty Smith, a nice handkerchief. I enjoyed the day, and the party was lovely. I wore my new evening dress, and that made me look nice enough to receive many compliments about growing young instead of old. Moreover, the day was remarkably warm and spring-like: robins and bluebirds were fluttering about, too. I enjoyed a morning walk with Edith. She had stayed in bed late, and when her headache was getting better, she told me interesting things of her work, of her grasp of business and her ability to look all around a thing. It was more than interesting, and "my heart was like a singing bird," and so it sang all day, as it should on my birthday, in spite of war and rumors of war. I am ambitious for Edith and see so much of her talents that I am always hoping for her greater scope. I long to have her a sculptor, but she says that would not be her choice of work. Her choice would be writing. But living at Kenwood, she feels the office of historian gives her much that she desires. I think she sees a type of beauty in the practical work and energy about her, turning dreams into reality, so wholeheartedly a part of our time. She loves life — humanity more than anything else — and desires to know its present expression. She idealizes energy, love, courage and self-expression. Just now she is at the gate called "present moment" (she did not say this); she sees the long road stretching into eternity in either direction, but the crowds in the gateway, the things they are saying, the surge of their progress, these interest her and seem worthwhile. She could not say all these things to me this morning; part of this is my guess work. How differently she might have expressed her ideas.

Looking back over the last ten years, I began to paint under Kenneth when I was forty-nine. I think he has helped to open the springs of self-expression that were in me, and given me a chance to be my inward self more than my outer self. And so, I know a little more of reality. For reality is probably flame and fuel within us. I owe quite as much to Edith as to Kenneth, too. My unfolding is trivial in its manner, but I am thankful for it. And at this moment, home from Atlantic City, with the good the change has done me, raising my spirits, I feel as though my days of work are stretching out before me. The things I want to do surge and rise up in mental vision. When it comes to the doing, that is always a letting-go and claiming the happy accident.

Here at Kenwood I think we are hardly touched by the war cloud —that cloud that has come out of Europe and hangs dark about us.

April 6th—Spring is here. Hepaticas are in the woods. Snow heaps still fill the deep and shady places. Miss Salingre and Miss Terry have sent me two books by Tagore which I read quickly and with pleasure. The other, the third *Edinborough Lectures,* I could not read while in Atlantic City; not in the middle of new surroundings and events. Now I have read that, too, and taken some extracts from it.

More than once I have had experiences which put me in touch with this book though I have never used its phraseology. Its author would have said I rose out of secondary causes into first causes and touched the infinite at those times. Those experiences were great moments in my life and left their imprint on my character, I am sure. Perhaps William James would have said the balance between my subjective and objective self was complete momentarily. Yet often experiences have brought the reverse— not despair, discouragement and unthankfulness, but bewilderment: a sense of overpowering mystery. Such came when Jessie died. The mystery encompassed us both. I used to go to her grave and call out, "Jessie, accept! Accept what has come to you with thankfulness." I was fearful for her. She had so often relied on me. Then one day crossing the windy golf links, there swept into my soul—Peace. Peace for her, peace for myself, and I felt there could be no doubt that we should both meet all that came in life and death with courage, because, well, I called it God's love. But it really has no definition in my mind. It is not theology but feeling, a sense of partnership with something great. "First cause," "universal mind," "the infinite," "the universal livingness," "the center of life" or whatever it may be called. I wish to live strongly in this feeling always, although perhaps I do not do so.

April 7th — Both the Senate and the House voted that President Wilson's recommendation to Congress be made effective, and so we are now at war with Germany. I hate to think of this this morning. I will not write about it. Perhaps I should be eager to do so if the Russians, the French and the English were not getting some set-backs just now.

May 16th — Col. Noyes is busy with sudden orders at Fort Mc-Pherson to put up cantonments for thousands of troops. Twelve days are allowed to put up eighty-eight wooden buildings, furnish them with electric lights, plumbing and drains. Gertrude, who was with him, said, "But how can you do it?" Col. Noyes laughed and told her the story of the student at West Point who was asked by his instructor to erect a flag staff. "How would you erect a flag staff?" After the cadet proceeded with elaborate detail to tell how the job would be done, the instructor replied, "Incorrect. Order someone to do it." But of course the responsibility rested on Col. Noyes in the end. Gertrude said that in two days, nine-hundred men were at work on the job.

May 19th — Today, after six weeks of fussing, Congress has passed a bill for conscription. Pershing is to be sent with a division of regulars as soon as possible. Our fighting boats are in English waters now. Russia, awfully imperiled by her radical element, is again staggering to her feet. On the Western Front the English and French make slow gains. The lines sway back and forth in terrible battle. England, under Lloyd George, has great problems on her hands in Ireland, having again offered home rule with the exclusion of the Ulster Counties. There has been great enthusiasm here over the French and English commissions sent to us. Joffre has been the hero of the hour, and Vivani and Balfour have come next. If anarchy in Russia prevails as the Germans have striven to produce it, then the U.S. has the great war practically [on] her hands. England and France are hard pressed for men. Oh, for a consumate weapon to strike down the submarine terror.

April 27th, 1918 — It has been a long time since I have written in this journal! I have been much occupied with braiding.

When Edith and I speak together of Jessie, I am glad. It seems to bring her back from such a distance. But I cannot help feeling in these days of war, when thousands of young creatures are hurried out of life, and thousands at home are heartbroken, that Jessie and I are just a part of this experience — little threads in the fabric, forever broken and forever replaced.

It is strange to realize that we are a changed nation, because it has all come about so naturally. Conscription, before it came, seemed a thing much to be dreaded, but it has been a marvelous school, quietly and carefully administered throughout this great land, met by each quota of draftees with equanimity and willingness, and by those left behind with courage and patriotism. There have been many volunteers outside the draft. We are indeed united and uplifted by the need to fight the world's fight for democracy. Our men are going to France in great numbers, and already the lists of our dead and wounded are returned to us.

We have a scarcity of wheat and sugar, having to supply our allies. Many a cargo is swept out of existence by hostile submarines. Food is under government control and coal and railroads, too. Daylight saving has come. We have set our clocks ahead one hour.

There were heatless days during the winter when the factories, offices and stores were closed to save coal. New York City suffered, New England suffered, and western states, too. There was coal going constantly to England and France.

Now we are indeed at a critical period of the war. Russia has gone all to pieces. Her problems were too great for Kerensky. He disappeared, and the new leaders, Trotsky and Lenin, played a weak part, perhaps a treacherous one: they made a German peace, let all the western provinces fall into German clutches — and the seas also. Germany has, in consequence of this Russian collapse, been bringing her men and guns from Russia to France and begun a tremendous drive on the British, French and American forces. We are called on to hurry our men overseas.

I found voting a simple matter the other day, the polls a very decent place. There was an exhilerating feeling of taking the step forward long struggled for by just such missionaries as Lotta. Many women were voting; some looked timid, but most were bright-eyed and serious. One held a baby in her arms, others warmed their hands at a sheet-iron stove while waiting their turn to vote. I thought the farmers looked a little quizzical and still felt their superiority: voting was an old story to them. How would we women get through it? The one women-watcher, who was Christine Allen, was alert but principally bored, too, I thought. As the voters went into the booths, she ticked off their names.

In December Edith gave my braided pieces an exhibition here; then they went to New York to be shown at the Craftsmen's Gallery. From New York they went on to Pittsburg to the Carnegie Institute. The exhibition will close tomorrow, the 28th of April.

Mr. Bate has been feeling he must go to England to bear his part in the war. Mrs. Bate holds him. But now that our factory is full of government work — making knives, periscopes, surgical instruments and parts of the Browning gun — our workmen are to be exempt, I hear.

May 9th — Claude Marble has been here. I thought he had already left for France. He goes in a few days, his destination, Paris. He will have charge of a factory for making false arms and legs and all sorts of things for rehabilitating soldiers. All of this work being done in France has been turned over to the Red Cross, and Claude has been appointed head of it. He was the only one among all Red Cross helpers with factory experience, and, trusting him, they have insisted on his taking the job.

May 12th — I have just finished the Jonah mirror braiding[28] for Albert. I'm afraid it may prove a white elephant.

If it were not for the fact that my braiding pictures are a new idea in the world, I think it would be a wild thing to go about handing out my creations to friends, loading them down with white elephants they might come to loathe. It's the bulk, the bigness of my braidings that can hardly be made very small, which makes them seem all the more troublesome to give as gifts. I ought to stick to trays which can be used very practically.

My patriotic activity has included making three blankets, or rather putting the knitted blocks together. The school children knit the squares, and the blankets will be sent to hospitals. When I had finished the first one I put the following verse in red, blue and white letters, embroidering it onto the two blue and white blocks:

"Soldier's Question:"

Little quilt, who made thee
Made thy squares so brightly gay
Blue and pink, and green and grey
Made me happy, too, today?

"Quilt Answers:"

Soldier boy I'll tell thee
Soldier boy I'll tell thee
Loving thee who went to fight
Loving children with delight
Made these squares of color bright
Kenwood children made me.

28. A mirror bordered by the Jonah and the whale story in braid.

It seemed almost a sacrilege to parody Blake's *Little Lamb* but it was easy and might add a bit of interest to a passing moment for a soldier.

May 21st — Within a few days, Raoul Lufbery and James Norman Hall, two American fliers, have been shot down. Lufbery fell within our lines; Hall simply disappeared in Germany and may still be alive. These men have become even part of my personal consciousness from the tales of Hall's *High Adventures* in the *Atlantic*. My tears flowed out at reading they were lost and still come to my eyes when I think of them. They are a part of our army that is, most of all, a high romance — like the knights of old. Lufbery was a Wallingford, Conn. boy.

July 8th — Edith and I went to Syracuse. I left some of my braidings for framing. Edith shopped, while I went to a new doctor for ear treatment. I do not more than half believe what this doctor said of my ear difficulty — of nerve rather than catarrh. The origin matters little now. It has progressed so slowly for twenty-five years, that with all my anticipation I am not yet deaf. And though I may have to look forward to that affliction as a part of my later life, I do hope to work hard enough and long enough to cut short my days and not linger out a decrepit old age. But you never can tell, and I have awful longevity as an inheritance which is appalling.

I am really glad to be living in these days and seeing history made so mysteriously. If Germany is beaten we shall probably have seen the end of secret diplomacy. The end, perhaps, of militarism. Perhaps out of the Russian catastrophe, which seemed such a glorious hope a year and a half ago, but now a perilous condition, will come social betterment for all classes.

July 21st — Today in the Big Hall we had a memorial service for Elliot Hinds.[29] Impressive and simple it was. To me there seemed to be a relief from some of the dreadfulness of death's ceremonials in the fact that he did not lie sadly below in the reception room with flowers, but was far away in France. There was the lowering of the flag to half mast. A requiem was sung, followed by a chapter read by George [Noyes]. Then came the old Community custom of talking about the dead. Many talked of old times, youthful days and traits of Elliot's. But everyone who spoke

---

29. Elliot Hinds, son of William A. Hinds, president of Oneida Community, Limited from 1903 to 1910. He was commanding officer of the 12th Aero Squadron besides being the post athletic instructor and flight commander. He was forty-four years of age and one of the oldest fliers in the American Aviation Service.

mentioned his light-hearted adult life, his skill, justice and unselfish friendliness.

September 10th—Here is a letter from Annie Miller which delights me. Now I shall feel more at rest about doing my work in these restless warring days, when everything must contribute to the general need, not altogether to one's own development. I have overdone a bit, trying to do my work and the Red Cross work. But my! How much such people as Annie are doing! Annie's finger in the pie went a long way toward making the $104.00 possible, for she framed the piece in New York.

East River, Conn., September 10th

Dearest Jessie,
      Was it not a coincidence that your letter should have come about a half hour after the drawing for the tray?[30] And I received it at the Red Cross rooms. You will be immensely pleased to learn that $104.00 was raised by selling tickets at 50 cents each. Every penny of that goes to the Madison chapter. Mrs. Marsden who had the soliciting in charge came upstairs to the sewing room with the names of all those who had taken a chance face down on the tray saying, "Mrs. Miller, the women downstairs told me to come to you to decide this matter." While she held the tray, I partly turned my face away. Closing my eyes, I took out a slip and on it was written "Mrs. Fred Hollbrook." We are all happy, for she wanted it very much. She had said she might try to buy it from the person who would win it and she also took two chances. She is one of our faithful workers and a young woman. All glory to you, Jessie dear, for making it and presenting it. I feel proud for having had a finger in the pie. Every word of your letter is interesting, and so much news, too. Fondest love,

Annie

October 17th—A wonderful month this October. Germany almost brought to her knees. Bulgaria out. Two Turkish armies captured. Belgium is being cleared. Our armies are now near both Lisle and Ghent, while farther south Americans are fiercely fighting in the Argonne.
    My braidings in two lots have gone for exhibitions in response to invitations. One has gone to Chicago[31] and the other to Smith College in

---

30. A tray-braiding Jessie had sent Annie Miller to be raffled off for her Red Cross chapter.

31. The National Society of Craftsmen in New York City was contacted by a Mr. Block of the Chicago Art Institute, who was interested in Jessie's braidings.

Massachusetts. [The exhibition at Smith College brought Jessie the following letter from Northampton, Massachusetts.]

> My Dear Mrs. Kinsley,
>   I wonder if I can convey to you the degree of excitement and
> pleasure with which I greeted the arrival of your braidings and paintings.
> I made myself a nuisance to the art dept., dragging all my friends over
> before the exhibit was really open, and we were all enthusiastic together.
> I lecture in the room above the exhibit room, and every day I see a group
> of students examining your work. You have given us the greatest amount
> of pleasure.
>
> > Faithfully Yours,
> > Esther Lowenthal

November 2nd — Italy is now drawing up terms of capitulation
for Austria-Hungary. And in Germany there are said to be upheavals, a
possible abdication of the Kaiser. In France the terms for the allies of Germany are under discussion, and Germany, all through October, has been
asking Wilson to intervene — to bring about an armistice. There is the cry
of unconditional surrender hurled at Germany from all sides. Wilson has
turned the matter of terms for an armistice over into the hands of our
allies and military leaders in England and France. High commissions sit
in France. Unconditional surrender is in these last few days a political
watchword.

Here at home we are on the eve of an election which may seat a
new, changed Senate and House. I am glad I have a vote; and though I
hate both political parties, I shall make my vote stand behind the President, because it seems to me he is our greatest statesman.

November 6th — Voted yesterday at the middle cheese factory on
the West Road. I split my ticket, because I did not like the Tammany nominee for Governor, but I voted Democratic otherwise.

Spanish influenza has brought immeasurable distress and sorrow
into our country. The death lists have been long.

November 7th — I must put down a line or two about this
wonderful day. About ten, I went up to see little Jane who has the flu and
found her better. Then I went down to A.'s where Annie Miller is staying,
to invite them to tea here this afternoon. A. invited me to stay to lunch.
We lunched and then sat together by the south windows. Annie was knitting when suddenly she cried out, "I hear bells ringing!"; and looking at
her wristwatch, "What time is it, for I believe those bells ring out the sur-

render of Germany?" She saw it was three o'clock, and we all ran out-doors. We saw groups gathering, so I started home, promising to tele-phone the news back, but before I reached the store our red fire-cart with siren blowing came tearing by. A stranger ran out to his auto. I called to him, "What does this mean, Peace?" "Yes! Yes! Peace!" he called back. What a thrilling word. I waved joyfully back to A., and then ran toward home. A crowd was already in front of the Sales Office and store; chil-dren were running down the hill from the Mansion. Dorothy waved a flag from her window. I met little Rhoda: "Grama, the war is over! It is over! And the soldiers are to march in Oneida. I shall ask Father to take me to see them." Edith and I sighed great sighs of joy every other minute and talked of the wonderful changes to come, how hatred, Edith said, could now die out; and being victors we could learn to forgive even the Germans after a while.

I prepared for the tea, which dear Mrs. Bate was baking for, while she threw her dish cloth to the ceiling in exuberant joy. Then I went to the store for flags and carried one to sick Janie who lay on her porch alone—and one for Myron. The nice factory men paraded by carrying a huge flag. All the offices and shops closed. Everyone went off to Oneida to help celebrate. The air was filled with the noise of Oneida's sirens. An-nie and A. and V. came to tea. In two of the cakes were stuck tiny flags of special interest to Annie and me. They were ones I brought home from the Hamburg-American ship we sailed to Italy on in 1913.

We looked at a questionnaire made out a year ago at a gathering here when Anita was to be married. Mart had guessed the nearest to this welcome date of November 7th, 1918. He said then that peace would come November 11th, 1918. Oh, how we all hope Jim, Anita's husband, will come home safely to her now.[32] He has been, until this tremendous hour, in danger on the front lines.

I cannot sleep and have written this in the dead of night. Such wakeful hours as these have been colored by the thought of no man's land, of gunfire, of men killing and being killed, of cannon fire and star shells, of zeppelin raids, hospitals bombed and submarines—now silence —peace—or the sound of joy and weeping together where people celebrate.

November 8th—The tidings of peace were fraudulent. The cele-bration was premature. The Germans had not even arrived in France to hear the terms decided upon for an armistice.

November 11th—I woke this morning late to the sound of a con-

32. James Raynsford, Anita Kelly's husband, returned safely from the war.

tinuous blowing of whistles. I knew it must mean peace. I'm thrilled again. And here alone I am celebrating. For the first few moments I couldn't stay in bed and with all sorts of flannel draperies I got up and capered about in pink wool slippers, clapping my hands and squealing. But the twinges in my ear sent me back to bed. There's enough joy in my heart to fill this whole empty house.

Mart, a year ago, put November 11th, 1918, as the day on which the war would end. That was a great guess Mart made. The exact moment was the 11th hour of the 11th day of the 11th month of 1918.

I cannot take socialism as the panacea for governments as Lotta and Mr. F. do. Having seen one dream of heaven on earth and realized its limitations, I do not imagine utopia established by socialism or any fundamental change brought about quickly. But it is good to see people awake from bad dreams and tumble into what seems better dreams, though they may wake again and again and all hopes and actions prove to be but dreams. If the Germans do not pay the debt to France and Belgium, I hope it may be our dream to help pay it. Edith thinks England will now meet her fundamental changes peaceably, as she has done in history many times before. But she thinks America may struggle harder than before with her labor problems.

December 29th—There is a change coming to our family soon. Mart and Edith and Rhoda go to Europe to live, and I go, too.[33] Albert and Lotta will take our house, and dear Albert will help finance my trip. I am delighted with the prospect of this adventure.

LETTERS FROM ENGLAND

The Imperial Hotel, London[34]

This is our third day in London, and I am only beginning to find myself. Everything has motion. We were the last people able to leave the boat because we were going to live in England and therefore were immigrants, thus, red tape.

The rooms here present a great contrast to the usual first class hotel rooms. They were a shelter, and we have now come to be glad even for them. Even for them, I say, because Pierre and Mart have been look-

---

33. Martin Kinsley was to represent Oneida Community, Limited in England.

34. Unless otherwise indicated, all letters are to Jane Kinsley.

ing everywhere, and the answer is absolutely no room. Although we have dirt, unspeakable food and cramped quarters, with my room on the fourth floor as well as Mart's, with Edith's and Rhoda's on the second, and Bob and Pierre's on the sixth, still we meet at meal times, and our rooms are warmed by steam and have hot and cold water.

I wish I could give you a sense of the London we have come into. Surely a changed city since Annie and I were here in 1913. First of all, a soldiers' London, then a WMCA London, a Red Cross London, a butter and sugarless London, a cabbage and potato London, a place where it is almost impossible to get a bus because you have to jump on as they are moving. Taxis are scarce, and we are warned not to use the tube. Walking becomes a fine art. There is a sense of the unusual, of tension. Everyone feels unsettled.

Hope and Pierre say London has changed. The change is in the people, in the attitude of mind. They seem to be at the point where, having touched bottom after a terrible struggle they say, "What next?" They are self-conscious of the wonderful things they have been doing. I heard a maid say to a woman who was impatient because the lift was slow, "Oh, you would never make a soldier." Well, I suppose to be a soldier, unafraid, patient and "ready to do your damndest," as I heard a man say downstairs, is the righteousness brought out of war.

7 Langford, St. John's Wood, April 18th

We are nearly settled here. I have been floored by a cold and a fall on a visit to Rochester, but getting into this house where it is warm has cleared up ailments, and getting back to simple food is a help.

Our house is of gray stone set in a garden. It was a chapel once and reminds me of the stone cottage in Niagara Falls, only tiny. There are no end of queer levels. Two steps to enter my room, four steps in my room lead up to Rhoda's room, two down from her room to the lavatory and three down from it to the upper hall. One step up to Mart and Edith's room, two down into the drawing room. So, you see, it is a matter of watching your steps constantly. There are carvings and stained glass windows and timbered ceilings. This certainly is the house for a story book. I expect to see a ghostly nun come spooking into my room any night. So far, only the moon shines in the windows in the high peak of my ceiling. We're happy enough with it all. The furnishings are quaint, too. There are two trees in the garden, and a liburnum tree against the wall; a paved place for out-of-door dining, and all sorts of rockeries, and the whole garden enclosed by a high brick wall, with a battlement of broken glass and an arched gateway. Well, enough about our house, delightful is the word for it.

[No date]

Claude Marble took dinner with us night before last. He will soon start for home. He has recently returned from a trip through the Balkan states. He looks stout and is bronzed in color but he feels the long strain he has been under nervously. His auto-truck train has been over the road of the long German invasion into Rumania and Serbia; also into Montenegro and to Asia Minor, as well as other states. In all these places depots for supplying false limbs were established. Where he was led to believe four or five hundred would be needed, in Rumania he found five thousand were required! These must be fitted and made for each individual case. He told of one old man, run over and leg taken off, whom the doctors would not operate on and had given up as a hopeless case. But a girl, educated in the Massachusetts General Hospital, a Greek nurse, operated herself on the man and saved his life. She had only a razor, black thread, and a common needle. These she sterilized, and having very small fingers, she could reach in to find the arteries which she secured without other tools. The man was then sent to Cavallo, and the nurse told Claude he was almost well.

We have the nicest maid now and will soon have her young daughter to do upstairs work. This maid is both happy and executive; also neat and an excellent cook.[35]

I am finishing up a new braiding.

May 26th

Today, Rhoda, Edith and I went to lunch with the Willoughbys at Horsley. The day was perfect and it was our first glimpse of English country life on an intimate footing. There was first a pony's cart to convey us by long, hedged rows of hawthorn in blossom, through the tiny town and by the old Norman church to the manor house, home of the Willoughbys for forty or fifty years. It's an old rambling house of fourteen bedrooms, to say nothing of the other rooms. Gathered in the drawing room were the grandmother, stately and learned, eighty-four years old; her two daughters; a soldier son just returned from India; her older son, a farmer; young Mrs. Willoughby; her child, George, family heir and his grandmother's idol. So, you see, with Edith, Rhoda and me, it was a goodly party—on the English side, a typically novelish English sort of party. Out of doors the cuckoo was calling; cowslips and bluebells blossoming; and there was a garden as old and rambling as the house. A short walk ended in the woods. These people were warmly hospitable.

35. Sissy and her daughter, Evelyn.

I could go on writing about conversations; how Mrs. Weston's observations of America were based on the movies; how Grandmother Willoughby was interested to learn that my mother was a Hobart, for Willoughbys are related to Hobarts; that all of these people were interested in the flyer, Hawkins, being rescued (he is the English hero of the day); how the older brother discussed the evils of prohibition, while Edith had long and animated conversations with the two sisters. One thing that Mrs. Weston said was striking, I thought. She said that land values were going down tremendously. A few months ago, a large estate near her was offered at ten thousand pounds. Then it went down to eight, then to five and now may be bought for two. She says it is doubt, unrest and fear, fear that the government will take the property or something—a real panic about land and the future in regard to it.

On Monday Edith and I went down to the National Museum which is on Trafalgar Square on Oxford Street. On the bus we slowly passed a long procession of demobilized sailors and soldiers attended by a policeman or two on foot and followed by two on horses. Their banners bore such inscriptions as "We have done our best for you, now do your best for us," etc. They were a young crowd, not too serious, but they were ominous, too, in their numbers, and there were hard-looking faces among them that showed the strain of war, of drink, dissipation of city life and poverty. We thought, as we went into the museum, we would find them in the Square being addressed by some speaker when we came out, but the Square was more than unusually quiet, and we did not know until this morning's paper that they armed themselves with paving blocks as they approached the Parliament buildings, where there was rioting and an attempt to force the gates. The leaders were then allowed in to present their case to Parliament in the lobbies and committee rooms.

Now there is a more serious crisis that will culminate next Tuesday: the police union may strike. The police also apologized to the rioters whom they quelled on Monday. England will never go back to the old, dull acceptance of its lot by the laboring men and women.

Tuesday will be Rhoda's eighth birthday. It's the King's birthday, too. Rhoda is counting the days as she would till Christmas. George Willoughby and his mother are coming in so she will have a playmate.

19 Marlborough Rd., St. John's Wood, June 12th

Here we are and settled yesterday. It was a delight to go from the Imperial Hotel into Lady Lumb's quaint little house full of charm and warmth, but now it is a pleasure to get away to bigger spaces, where the furnishings are well selected and simpler. We have three apple trees besides many other trees set about near the high walls that enclose this large garden. There are flowers in profusion, and, best of all, a large grassy space and stone terrace. We can live a country life. We are on a hill and get more breeze here. One thing almost like home is in the evening breeze, a good, full breeze that does not fail.

Rhoda finds it hard to go to sleep, because day-light lingers so long. Not until ten o'clock does it really become dusk.

Prices of fruit, in fact, of everything, are exorbitant. Grapefruits sent over from the grocer were fifty cents each. We did not keep them. Eggs are a dollar a dozen. The worst of it is that the merchants and tradesmen cheat. They seem to need the closest watching and have no idea of a good relationship. We are not used to such systematic, uncanny dealing all around, added to extreme dilatory ways.

We went to see the Russian Ballet again yesterday with Mrs. Colenso and her daughter. She has lived in St. John's Wood many different times, once near Huxley, also near Herbert Spencer, and many other celebrities. On Grove End Rd., we passed Alma Tadema's house, said to be one of the interesting houses of London. George Eliot lived on Kilburn Priory Rd. and she and George Lewes, after a morning of writing, often walked in Regents Park. I wish I could now meet them there, "she with a certain weird sybiline air, he not unlike some unkempt Polish refugee of vivacious manners, swinging their arms as they hurried along at a pace as rapid and eager as their talk." Through George Eliot's garden now runs a railway. I could give you a list that would fill this sheet, if only I could remember all the historic, interesting names. Then something that adds to the charm are the names of the streets, such as Primrose Hill, North Bank, Greenberry Hill, Abbey Gardens, Pineapple Place, Violet Rd., etc.

June 22nd

Our life is very quiet. Mart has gone to France, and at such an interesting time, too. In a week he will be back with a thousand things to tell us.

Today we are agog at the news of the sinking of the fleet at Scapa Flow, and of the chance of the signing of the peace treaty tomorrow. By the time this reaches you, those events will be left behind, and we will be swinging down the current with the others. Here it will be the Irish question, the Indian and Afghan question, the nationalization of coal, the loan, etc. We cannot peer ahead very far by craning our necks but must keep in the stream even if we do not know its meaning or what is ahead. We must kick out and keep moving, have theories and opinions, not be just refuse, I suppose. So Edith and I discuss and read and look forward to Mart's return.

One must seek the post office here for sending messages. Our branch office on Queen's Road was closed, so I went to the general St. John's Wood one on Circus Rd. This road is a street of shops. I have become familiar and confident in getting about. I even go downtown by myself though Edith is inclined to distrust me. I found the Circus Rd. P.O. full of people. The room was no bigger than our P.O., and three lines were waiting to be served, the queues reaching to the street. If I'd been in a hurry I'd have been in a tew,[36] but I had time and enjoyed watching the people and procedures. I assure you there was no hustle. Some of the people were old ladies with upright, bedecked bonnets of the fashion of 1889. There were errand boys, maids wearing caps, and nurses with long veils. There were a few old men and one soldier, one man in a derby hat and several young women in raincoats. (Our long drought has ended.) I noticed teeth in the crowd. Fifty years from now teeth will look better — earlier than that in America, because we give more thought to them. It was shocking to see the teeth of youth so badly cared for. I have not noticed ears but I have noted noses and feet — fine noses as a rule, and large feet that seem to toe out a good deal.

Edith has an artist friend come up to draw with her sometimes. A model comes, and they use the nursery upstairs where Sissy makes a fire in the grate. I was invited to join their little class and I've learned something but I'm not very good with my pencil. The model is a lovely young woman who has learned to be natural with her hands and feet and body as well, in any pose. These drawings will help Edith in her class at the University.

July 5th

Rhoda and I have been on a walk and found a new street, Ellsworthy Rd. We visited Primrose Park and came home by our secret bench which is a favorite place. Much excited by our discovery of so much beauty, we urged Edith to go with us to all these places, and, after visiting our secret bench, we then came to our secret church (Rhoda has given it that name) and, lo and behold, we came upon a very pretty scene. It was a naval wedding, and the bride and groom were coming out of the church under the drawn swords of the groomsmen. It was an unexpected climax to our walk.

July 26th

I want to thank you for the Irish lace collar. It's just the perfect present for the moment and for time to come, too, of course, but I senti-

---

36. A state of great agitation.

mentally say "for the moment" because, about the time the collar came, I had been reading books by Yeats, and Lord Dunsany. The Irish collar seemed to fit into the mood brought by the beauty of Irish thought. Perhaps the girl or woman who wove the collar lived in a hillside cottage of Geesala or Carraroe or of Dingle Bay. Perhaps her eyes were "those eyes with a big, gay look out of them would bring folly to a great scholar," or "she would be telling you the finest story you'd be hearing from Dundalk to Ballinacree with great queens in it and they with shiny silks on them." Or maybe she's saying, "thou art the chief of the deer of the hill, the step of the horse of the plain, thou art the grace of the sun rising, thou art the lovliest of all lovely desires." I will believe she did sing that and echo the last line thinking of my present of lace.

It has added to the happiness of this life in London to have Hope with us, as she has been at invervals. She is now at Caldecot Rectory near Cambridge with Marietta, going daily to the Cambridge Library to do her work.

I cannot help finding this change of life a wonderful experience, and already my pulse beats a sort of English beat from intense interest in the things about us.

There are three new Whistlers and two Blake paintings in the new room at the National Gallery. The Blakes are wonderful: all symbolism and of a magical color, deep and penetrating, like his words, "spaces between the stars" or, "pillars in the deepest hell to reach the heavenly arches."

We have been having chilly weather all through July. I find walking a much better way to get warm than the fireplace and usually, after beginning to feel cool, I clap on my hat and raincoat, if it is raining, and sally forth. Every day, three or four times a day, sees me closing our pretty front gate and starting off. I am as familiar with this part of London as possible, from Maida Vale to Primrose and Regents Park; from Baker Street to Belsize Rd. Belsize Rd. begins the great climb to Hampstead Heath. I know all the prettiest places and have just discovered a house built like a Spanish or oriental house—all over filigree work.

The present outlook for the settlement of the miners' strike in Yorkshire looks brighter. Many factories have had to shut down for lack of coal, and transportation was threatened for lack of coal, too. In Germany and France the men are going back to work. Here the men do not want to work. Mart says they are a tired nation. Others say they did not like to work before the war. If that is true, it must be a fundamental defect of the class distinctions that makes the work not *their* work. The Englishmen we have in America are workers, and Mart says the men he has working for him are just splendid.

How it will all come out, no one knows. There are tremendous needs for changes. Child labor here is one of the horrible things. You see dreadful instances of it. But I feel England has a great leader in Lloyd George, and there is good sense in the nation, although the lordly and the wealthy, like the workers and the slackers, have much need to change their ways.

July 31st

The weeks fly along fast. There is certainly much unrest, and things do not seem to straighten out quickly. Prices soar higher and higher. I do not see how poor people live. I wish for their sake there were stores like Woolworths with set rates. Hairpins, for instance, that we pay ten cents a half dozen for at home are fifty cents over here, and other things in like ratio. There is much shoplifting.

I was reading in the *Times* this morning of race riots in Chicago and Washington. It is curious to see here white girls and negroes making nothing of walking out together as chummy as possible. And seeing a white mother and dark father taking a little brood of blacks on the buses. There is not the same feeling about negroes here or in France as in the U.S. But there have been some disturbances between the two races in the cities here.

August 19th

Mart and Edith started off to find a sea-side residence for us. They went by train to Barnstable, a quaint town, and thence south by auto to all sorts of coastal towns. But they found nothing available for a family our size until September. Again, from Barnstable on Sunday they did set forth and found one large room at Lynton in Devon for September 1st. So now it looks like ten days of getting this house in order, and putting our trunks in storage and packing the bags to take with us. Edith says we will overlook the sea and, after a few days, instead of all being in one room, we can move into a cottage next to the hotel and be very comfortable. We may stay there until the middle of October. It is really hard to plan, for Mart goes on the 6th of September to Italy, and our movements depend on him. Lynton is where Annie and I stayed a long time on our visit in 1913. It is a glorious place and will seem like home to me. It will be fine for us all to be out of London for a time before winter sets in.

Bob H. has returned from Germany. He says Belgium has gone to work. The people are not spent in spite of their hard, hard years of war, but in France, as here, there is not the same spirit of self-help; rather there is the tendency to stand by and wait to see what the government will do, or, in France, by charitable America. Well, the holidays will be over before long, and people will be more seriously turned to work.

Lynton, September

I wake in the morning, and the first realization is of a sense of smell. The night air is full of the scent of blackberries and bracken and the salt sea. I look from my window onto the massive hills and the sleeping village, as quiet and invisible as possible in the cup-like hollow below me. I realize that far, far below is another village with its harbor, just as quiet.

Later: here I am alone, down in Lee Bay. The sun has set, because the hills are so high. At four the carriage was to come for us. The girls waited an hour and then, as it did not come, they left me and the luggage here and walked home, a long walk of two and a half miles uphill. It is interesting to be here, for the tide is coming in. I never have seen it at this height, and it creeps over the rocks where we have been and dashes against the cliffs. Way over to the left is a natural gateway in the rocks, and when the tide was low, Mrs. M[axon], Edith and Rhoda climbed through it. Coming back, they had to climb from small rock to small rock at the base of the cliff. Now, not a stepping-place is left.

Lynton, September 14th

We have been here two weeks. Sea bathing has been delightful. We have been often to Lee Bay where there are rocky caves for dressing rooms and a fine beach at half tide. There are legends connected with Lee Bay above which are the castle and manor house called Lee Abbey where the Whichehalses of *Lorna Doone* once lived and where Janefreid jumped off Duty Point in sorrow over disappointed love. When Lynton was invaded by the King's troops after the battle of Landown, the last Whichehalse desperately put to sea in a storm and was drowned. Now the beautiful place is for sale, and on Saturday there was an auction of carriages, blooded stock, etc., for the late owner is dead, and his heir wishes to live elsewhere. Mrs. M., Rhoda and Edith went to the auction: in through the great gates with the good country folk, not to buy, but to see the place and the people. Edith was enthusiastic over the house, furnishings and grounds. When I went out to walk myself I met country people loaded down with purchases. One old man had a table, another a chair, two women had pictures; one man had bought tools: augers, planes, etc.; another a toilet stand; a woman carried a secretaire; and someone a mirror; each went his way by the little country lanes or the way I went, by the wider road. I somehow had the feeling that the old time of lordly country families was breaking up—that these ancient places had perhaps seen their most picturesque days.

Lynton, September 28th

We are feeling as though we were in a new and uncertain world—in a cast-away corner of this uncertain world. We knew a railroad strike was impending, but so many strikes have threatened and then been averted that we felt optimistic. Mr. Thomas had issued a grave warning that things look black. We woke yesterday to find the strike was on and no trains running. Simultaneously came two cables from Mart. The first was sent from Southampton, the second from Paris, having been delayed. The Paris one to Edith read, "Albert arrives in Coblenz Wednesday. Meet me London Sunday prepared for week in Coblenz. Wire in care Russell Hotel. I arrive London Saturday." The Southampton wire showed us Mart had arrived in England, but had there met the conditions and would know Edith could not go to London. That message read, "Expect to reach London by automobile. Will telephone."

No newspapers came to Lynton, only flying rumors. On the library window upstreet was pasted this message, "National Rail Strike commences, troops guarding railways, smaller rations for all, less butter, eggs, conditions serious."

All day Edith waited in the hotel, ready at any moment to go to the one and only telephone downstairs in the office. She finally put in a call to the Russell and waited up anxiously until eleven when the whole house went to sleep, and the office closed.

I may write and write on this letter, but there's no knowing when it will get off to you. Just now Edith has finally had a call from Mart. He said he had been sitting by the phone since yesterday afternoon. He said he would come down here within a day or two. The tubes are not running in London. There were a thousand questions Edith wanted to ask, but the connection was cut off. She says she feels almost more homesick about Mart than before he telephoned.

Monday morning: we hear that the miners and the dockers have also gone on strike. No newspapers, just rumors. That would mean labor putting all its strength against government. This morning a family living beyond London were to leave here but had car trouble, and, lo and behold, they found car repairmen on strike.

This is a brilliant morning, and going upstreet it seemed as though all the town were out idly waiting for something to happen. At the post office there is a crowd sending out telegrams. There is no shortage of food. There are vegetables and plenty of sheep on the hillside. A newspaper has come, the *Devon & Exeter Gazette*. It contains an appeal from Lloyd George to the country, calling on all citizens to hold firm and have patience and asks all skilled men, loyal to the country, to volunteer for service on the railways. Mr. Thomas on his side gives the railway men's reasons for striking once again.

I long for quick hearing, to catch remarks here and there, to know more of the human side at first in so great an occurrence. There is excitement in the air.

Lynton, October 3rd

Mart had a more or less adventurous trip down from London. He took one of those charabancs—cars seating twenty or more passengers. As he stood waiting to board it in London, Lloyd George walked by into Hyde Park, "a small man with a large head, somewhat stooped over and looking just like his picture"—so Mart described him. Tire and machine trouble came on the way down. The journey from London took two long days. The last of the second day dragged for us. Our thought ranged over Exmoor with its steep hills, and the wind roaring and the rain falling. Edith and I were sitting by the warm fire reading, when Rhoda's glad shout rang through the hallway and told us of Mart's coming. I have caught snatches of his travels in Spain and Italy but I cannot forever be asking, "What? What did you say?"

October 6th

Edith and Mart went on horseback to Brenden-Two-Gates up on the moors. Peter's nurse took Rhoda and him to a hockey game. I put on my hat and went up into the quarry. Here I was sheltered from the wind and had the southern sunshine alone. I could let my hair loose, having just washed it, so it quickly dried.

We all go to the Washington Hotel in London, I think, until we can turn around and know what next to do.

Hotel Washington, Curzon Street, October 12th

Here we are back in London. I feel the lack of nice fires and the change in climate, but, if I feel chilly, I put on wraps and go out for a walk, rain or shine.

We shall always look back to Lynton as a sort of refuge and paradise. We made friends there and really must tell you of our last compliment, for it was quite out of the commonplace. For the last two days of our stay, Mr. Jones ran up the American flag for our benefit. We saw it big and beautiful on the flag staff at the gates. We were puzzled the first morning as to the significance of the 7th of October to Americans and British and had no idea it was a personal compliment until one of the guests told us so. Mart, in his nice way, thanked Mr. Jones for the care and service they had given us.

When we go back to America, Sissy, our maid who has had an operation in our absence, would like to go back with us, if we can manage the matter. We are trying to find a few rooms with serviette which we can go into quickly and leave on short notice, where we can have Sissy with us. This hotel is expensive.

October 18th

We have had a London fog — new in our experience. It's a dense, yellow fog with a disagreeable odor. It penetrates through windows and fills rooms. If it lasts for days and gets to be an old experience, we will get to hate it.

We shall be coming home soon. Mart will be needed by Albert there during the meetings.[37] Then he will have to come back to his work here. If these were ordinary times we could stay here until his return, but with the coal so short, and uneasiness everywhere, they think we must not remain behind alone.

Later: 43 Claridges St: we made our move last evening. We simply put on wraps and walked over. Our rooms are up two floors. Breakfast is served in our rooms and also tea. We go out to lunch which will be our principal meal. All Sissy's meals will be served to her in the maid's room downstairs.

Claridges Street, November 2nd

Our little one-grate fire does not warm any bedrooms but keeps us quite comfortable. We have a large screen, and so, all four of us use the sitting room as a dressing room. Our landlady now furnishes us with a mid-day meal, so we no longer go out for it. She is a splendid cook. Bathing in an unwarmed bathroom certainly seemed at first to require nerve, but we are all quite used to it now. This part of town is of enormous interest. How I wish you were in my shoes. How you would enjoy the shopping streets. Now, before going home, I want to do a little shopping and

37. Sales meetings in Kenwood.

yet, I hate it, while you, like a divining rod, would find all the bargains and would make a success of this particular job. I know myself well enough to be sure to shy badly at the big prices and make bad decisions. Edith says it is remarkable to go about shopping with various people and note their different methods.

Claridges Street, November 14th

When Mart and Edith went away to the continent, I told Rhoda I would give her an annuity of six pence a day, so she feels enormously rich, and when she and Sissy go out for a walk, she looks about for certain purchases. Twice a week she has to get into the bathtub in the icy bathroom downstairs and have a washup. Sissy is a fine companion for R., who would otherwise find life in one room too confining.

On the 11th, Armistice Day, we were standing in the gateway of Green Park at that 11th hour when silence was to fall. "Boom, boom," went the maroons, the signal for silence. Everyman's hat went off; all heads were bowed, and the silence seemed to spread and spread. For once in all the century the roar of London was hushed; not a vehicle moved; the trains and tubes came to a halt; pedestrians stood in their tracks; many were silently weeping. Then the two minutes were up and the men began to put on their hats, and the crowd started to move reluctantly. I thought, as did all those in silence, I suppose, of those who had laid down their lives in this war and this war not yet ended, or the passions not yet stilled and the problems still unsettled.

Monday we saw President Poincaré, his wife, King George and wife, Churchill, Lloyd George and Prince Albert. They were going past the park from Victoria Station to Buckingham Palace. We stood very close to them as they passed by.

It is good to hear that the U.S. coal strike is over, and what has been a great burst of speculation in Wall St. has come to a crisis. In the old days, before the establishment of the reserve banks, this would have meant a panic, would it not?

English newspapers are extremely interesting, and we shall miss them when we go home. Lloyd George is continually having to defend the government's policy about Russia and to describe how difficult it is to have any policy at all under the given circumstances. *The Times* takes him to task in almost a yellow jouralistic manner, censoring his speeches under big headlines.

November 27th

Lately our time has been filled with all sorts of engagements:

people in for lunches and for teas, and we have been invited out. Today Edith and Mart are to visit Mr. H. G. Wells and wife.

Now there is the matter of getting the papers through the passport office for Sissy's daughter Evelyn. Evelyn has been living in Leeds and wants to come with her mother to work for us.

Sailing for home looms ahead. We leave for Liverpool a week from today. I am in a more or less phlegmatic state of mind at what will be ahead for me on shipboard. Sissy and I and Evelyn will be sharing a stateroom. I shall miss Hope's company. Beyond any discomfort is our dear home and the companions I long to see.

Aunt Jessie, 1920-1938

*D*URING THE LATER YEARS of her life almost everyone in Kenwood called Jessie Kinsley either "Aunt Jessie" or "Grandma Jessie." To some extent, this was a survival of old Community days when such terms as "Aunt," "Grandma," "Father," "Mother," and "Sister" were not reserved for blood relatives but were used much more widely, particularly by the young people to show respect for their elders. But in Jessie Kinsley's case the appellation had an appropriateness that everyone recognized. "Aunt Jessie is the most lovable, and the most loving person that I know," wrote George Raymond Noyes, the son of Dr. Theodore Noyes, "and I am sure that she has been a subtle influence upon the character and nature of all of us, individually and as a group."[1]

Aunt Jessie's love for children found many channels for expression. The illustrated booklets that Jessie made for Rhoda, Myron, Chester, and Jane are treasured. The first of these bearing the title "A Christmas Book for Jane from Grandma Jessie, 1914," could not have made much impression on a child less than eighteen months old, but within a year or two it must have brought delight because it told the story of Jane's birth while Jessie was on her European tour. "When Grandma sailed for It-a-lee Over the water," the booklet said, and the accompanying drawing showed a puffing little steamer approaching the bootline outline of "Italee." The story continued, "Mama's arms were empy-tee, No little daughter," and the picture showed "Poor Mama" waving good-bye. Next, "But on a wire, to It-a-lee, (Under the water) with a drawing instructing the child to "See the wire down under the water." "Papa sent a messagee 'Fine

---

1. Clipping from the *Quadrangle* (1932), a Community magazine, collection of Jane Rich.

little <u>daughter!</u>'" and a drawing showing Papa operating the telegraph instrument and reading "Papa has on his pajamas" — a legend sure to amuse a child, as would later drawings showing Grandma, waving a handkerchief, losing her hat, and dancing with joy, "Janee" walking alone, "Janee" talking into the telephone, and "Janee" being tucked into bed by her mother. In later years Jane and the other grandchildren received similar gay little books made specially for them. These fortunate youngsters had frequent opportunities to visit their grandmother, watch her at her work, walk with her, and sit in favorite spots while she told them stories.

For a woman who loved her grandchildren so deeply it was a painful blow to lose one of them — and all the more devastating when death took Rhoda, Edith's and Mart's only child, and Jessie's constant companion. In 1923 shortly before her twelfth birthday Rhoda was struck down by meningitis. To try to comfort the distraught household must have been very difficult, but Hope Allen wrote an inspired letter from England assuring Jessie that she had given Rhoda "treasures of happiness all her life through and helped to make her one of the most fortunate of children who have ever been." [2]

Edith said that "now she should love all children — more." And that must have been Jessie's resolution too, because she extended grandmotherly affection to all the Kenwood children. At the time of her death someone wrote of her: "When she went for walks with the children along High Bank or through the Larches, she made a story about it. It turned into a Dream Walk with people on clouds and talking cows, and apples of gold. She made friends with all children; made friends literally, for although she was universally 'Aunt Jessie' or 'Grandma Jessie,' she had a way of thinking contemporaneously and the children accepted her as the perfect companion." [3]

Jessie loved every aspect of life in the Kenwood-Sherrill community — the good talk, the fireworks, the concerts. In a sketch written in 1932, Ray Noyes said: "She has two pet diversions at present — she *must* go to the movies on Friday and to the band concert on Monday evenings, and she *must* have her ice cream cone on each occasion. It is conceivable that she really attends these functions for her ice cream cones, since they are her only vice." [4]

This emphasis on Jessie's love for children and ice cream cones, however, gives a somewhat distorted picture of her character. She may have been childlike in her innocence and her enthusiasms, but she was

2. See p. 191.
3. Manuscript account of Jessie Kinsley's funeral, collection of Jane Rich.
4. Clipping from the *Quadrangle* (1932), collection of Jane Rich.

thoroughly adult in her intellectual life. She continued to devour books, often reading to and being read to by Edith. She preferred books of substance, works by established authors or thoughtful contemporaries.

During the last fifteen years of her life, Jessie conserved her limited fund of energy by spending mornings in bed, where she wrote letters, made sketches, and read. As she lay there, she copied passages that pleased her into what she called her "Bedside Book." Edith and Albert had this privately printed and distributed to her friends after her death. The little anthology demonstrated the richness of Aunt Jessie's intellectual life. Her favorite quotations were drawn from every age and country: Euripides, Socrates, the Bible, Montaigne, Donne, Tennyson, William James, Einstein, Wordsworth, Shakespeare, Anatole France. She memorized especially appropriate bits of philosophy and poetry to repeat as she took her walks. It might be a bit from Chaucer:

> For to walken in the wodes wilde
> And se the fresshe flours, how they spring.[5]

Or from Emily Dickinson:

> To make a prairie, it takes a clover and one bee
> And revery;
> The revery alone will do
> If bees are few.[6]

But the anthology was not restricted to well-known authors. Jessie copied down also bits of verse written by Kenwood friends like Dorothy Leonard and members of the Kinsley family — several bits by her daughter Edith, one by Rhoda Dunn, wife of her nephew Burton Dunn, and two by her grandchildren Myron Kinsley and Rhoda Kinsley.

The *Bedside Book* discloses the intellectual springs that fed the stream of Jessie's life as an artist. To call her "Aunt Jessie" suggests that she was a kind of "Grandma Moses," a self-taught folk painter producing simple realistic pictures of landscapes and people, pictures that charm through their naïveté. But Jessie Kinsley was a well-trained and sophistiated artist. She had studied under Kenneth Miller and other teachers; she had seen the great masterpieces of European art; she had discussed art

---

5. *Bedside Book: An Anthology* (privately printed by Edith and Albert Kinsley, December 1938), p. 19.

6. Ibid., p. 20.

with her highly intellectual artist-daughter, Edith Kinsley. Jessie's specialization in braided tapestries was not evidence of her primitivism but her intelligent development of a new medium ideally adapted to her talents. In a section of the *Bedside Book* entitled "Poems for Braidings — or for Possible Braidings," she collected snatches of poetry that called up vivid images. For example, there was a bit from William Blake:

> Speak silence with thy glimmering eyes
> And wash the dusk with silver,
> Then the lion rages wild,
> And the tiger glares through the dun forest.[7]

From Walter De la Mare:

> Slowly silently now the moon
> Walks the night in her silver shoon.[8]

And from Shakespeare:

> Orpheus with his lute made trees
> And the mountain tops that freeze
> Bow themselves when he did sing . . .[9]

Braiding, the activity that Jessie had developed during World War I years, occupied more and more of her time during the last two decades of her life. The tapestries became larger and bolder in design. When magazine writers and reporters sought her out for interviews, she gave them a warm welcome and a stimulating discussion of how she did the work. She started with drawings that she "copied out" upon wrapping paper with ink and a soft brush or pen. Then she basted this pattern upon a piece of oilcloth to make it strong yet pliable. Next she assembled the braids and planned the color scheme. She then basted the braid upon the pattern "holding the wrong side of the braid uppermost, the right side against the pattern." Jessie would bend the braids to cover every part of the pattern and then sew them firmly into place. "You use your braids," she explained, "just as the painter does his brush — making braids take on

7. Ibid., p. 14.
8. Ibid., p. 15.
9. Ibid., p. 15.

movement— direction — perspective — design, by the way in which the lines of your drawing show you that the braid must be sewed together." The moment of revelation came later. "When the last stich has been taken in the overhandling of braids together, then the pattern and the oilcloth may be ripped away. . . . At last you will see the right side, which has lain so long against the paper pattern." [10]

In 1924 a reporter from the *Utica Press* described a visit to Jessie in the Kenwood home where she was living: "On the wall of the reception room a gorgeous piece of braiding illustrated her talk. In this one piece of work, which measures seven feet square, and is bordered in a soft, almost horizon blue, there are 11 landscapes representing the things man does not make. Winter, spring, summer, autumn; morning, noon and night; the sea, the vegetable kingdom, the animal kingdom and finally a triptych of birth, love and death are pictured there. A title, "Things Not of Man's Devising," is woven in the border." [11]

The Kenwood community took pride in Aunt Jessie's achievements. Among her cherished papers was a hand-written document headed "In Appreciation" and signed "R. H. N. 11/10-1932." Whoever wrote it paid tribute to Jessie's "gift of unique expression and unbelievable perfection in the treatment of colors, and color blending through the medium of blended silks. . . . The mind that conceived this medium, that stayed with it in its early development, is the mind of a vastly superior person — artistically and individually." [12]

In one of her letters Aunt Jessie tells of a little talk that she had had with her son Albert in November 1922. "Albert has liberalized me lately and I am getting sunshine and moonshine and all the beauty of heaven and earth in my bureau drawers in *new* silks. I had asked Albert in to talk about my finances, and his whole response was for me to spend more money. Especially after seeing my big braiding, he said I should buy new silk and never skimp on it. He is establishing a bank fund for me — for silk — so here I am, all free, though I still contrast these wonderful beauties falling to my lot with the distress of others and wonder how I am entitled to them." [13]

Jessie's freedom to buy new silk for her braidings testified to the excellent sales that Oneida Community, Limited was now enjoying. The company had experienced all the ups and downs of the general economy

10. Beverly Sanders, "A Scrap Bag Palette," *American Craft* (April/May 1981), p. 17.

11. Clipping in the collection of Jane Rich.

12. Manuscript in the collection of Jane Rich.

13. See p. 189.

during the postwar years. During 1919 and the first nine months of 1920, the company had made such big profits that in October 1920 it ended the High-Cost-Of-Living Wage, a supposedly temporary policy, and raised the regular pay scale by about 50 percent. Then came a devastating blow. A severe depression began to afflict the country in October 1920 and conditions worsened through most of 1921.

With the company losing so much money that it had to go on short time to prevent mass layoffs, Pierrepont Noyes resumed the leadership again. Calling the employees together in a general meeting, he explained the seriousness of the situation, announced that he was cutting his own salary to $5,000 a year and other management salaries proportionately. He asked the workers to accept a 33 percent wage cut in return for a promise that the company would share future profits with them. Still retaining their extraordinary faith in Noyes and the company, the employees rose to their feet and applauded.[14]

Pierre's boldness was rewarded. In 1922 the company pulled out of the doldrums and began earning a profit. True to its promise, the management set aside $300,000 for a so-called contingent wage, the workers' share of the profits. For the next eight years the company continued to do very well. Pierrepont Noyes felt able to relinquish the general management to other hands. This time he chose Miles Robertson, a man who had started to work for Oneida in 1913 at a salary of only $9 a week, but who had risen steadily through the ranks of management. By courting and marrying Pierrepont Noyes's daughter, Robertson had demonstrated that he had good judgment in love as well as business. A talented young woman, Constance Noyes Robertson eventually became a writer of novels and works of history.

Robertson became general manager in 1926. For three years things went very well—so well that in 1929 Oneida bought up its principal competitor, William A. Rogers Limited. Before the year was over, however, the company was being buffeted by the great depression. This time there was no speedy turnaround. In 1930 things were bad; in 1931 and 1932 they grew steadily worse. The whole labor policy of which Oneida was so proud broke down. First to go was the contingent wage because there were no profits; next came a succession of cuts in the basic wage scale; finally—and most reluctantly—the service wage based on the number of years an employee had worked for the company had to be dropped. In addition there had to be layoffs and short time. But once again the company passed through the fire without mortal injury. By 1933 it was making a

14. Walter D. Edmonds, *The First Hundred Years: 1848–1948* (Sherrill, N.Y.: Oneida Ltd., 1948), p. 58.

small profit once again, and step by step the service wage was reinstituted, the wage scale was improved, and by 1936 profit-sharing began again. In 1936 the name of the company was changed to Oneida Limited — not apparently out of any rejection of the old Community — but to avoid confusion in the marketing of its more diversified lines of products.[15]

How did all these changes affect the Kinsley family? When Pierrepont Noyes resumed command, Albert went back to his role of faithful lieutenant. In 1924 he gave up the title of general manager and became a vice-president, a post that he continued to hold until his death in 1947. Character sketches always emphasized Albert's popularity with the employees. In 1920 he arranged a merger of all the various employee organizations into the Community Associated Clubs, which conducted an outstanding health and recreational program. In recognition of this and other services, some three thousand persons on the Oneida payroll contributed toward purchasing a red Stutz roadster, a car that Albert drove for many years before finally turning it over to the Sherrill-Kenwood Volunteer Fire Department for the chief's use. Ray Noyes explained "Ab's" peculiar brand of managerial magic as "getting the biggest kick in the world out of life and business and passing on to the rest of us the same fun of working like hell, from the President to the Office Boy!"[16]

Just seven months older than Albert, Martin Kinsley had a record of service almost as outstanding. In 1924 he was made a vice-president in charge of new development. Mart was particularly involved in developing Oneida's overseas markets. In 1926 he organized the British Oneida Community, Limited with headquarters at Sheffield. He became chairman of the board of this affiliate. In a family where the men devoted themselves to business and the women to literature and art, Mart bridged the gap by developing a keen interest in antiques. The Kenwood home where Mart, Edith, and Aunt Jessie lived was soon filled with fine old pieces.

The great depression that hobbled the company for three years forced economies on the Kinsley family. Mart and Edith gave up their private home and moved into the Mansion House, and Aunt Jessie was transferred to her own apartment there. For one of the few times in her long life, Jessie's letters revealed some degree of worry about personal finances. Fortunately conditions improved before her death, but she saw somewhat less of her family than she had in earlier years. Company business took both Mart and Albert away from Kenwood for extended periods. Edith, who enjoyed the cultural opportunities of life in England, often went with Mart on these trips. In November 1937, Mart and Edith

15. Ibid., p. 16.
16. Clipping from the *Quadrangle,* collection of Jane Rich.

Mart Kinsley, 1930

began another of these residences in London. Jessie wrote to them with her usual cheerfulness. She did not feel able to do much about Christmas but she was still working on her latest braiding that she called *Street Scene.* She continued to add to her "Bedside Book." The last entry was from Tennyson's "Ulysses."

> I am part of all that I have met
> How dull it is to pause . . .
> To rust unburnished, not to shine in use.[17]

Aunt Jessie did not rust unburnished for any extended period of time. On February 10, 1938, about six weeks before her eightieth birthday,

17. *Bedside Book,* p. 22.

a thrombosis brought her life to an end. A few months earlier—perhaps anticipating what was to happen—Aunt Jessie had commented on how different Kenwood funerals were from those in the "outside world." Perhaps, as someone had suggested, it was "because of this being one big family with all of us feeling more or less like brothers and sisters." Aunt Jessie's funeral was just such a family affair. Her friends, young and old, gathered in the Mansion House. One by one they paid their tributes. Pierrepont Noyes led off; Grosvenor Allen and other men and women followed. Constance Noyes Robertson recalled how Aunt Jessie had taken her daily walks "in summer with her little white fringed cape, in winter in a brown cloak, carrying her walking stick—stopping to talk with friends, sometimes humming to herself."[18] Edith, the faithful daughter, could not get back from England, but she asked Constance Robertson to read a verse by Gerard Manly Hopkins that her mother used to recite on her walks:

> Wild air, wild-mothering air, nestling me everywhere
> My more than meat and drink, my meal at every wink.
> I say that I am bound with mercy round and round
> As if with air . . . [19]

After the service they took Aunt Jessie's body to the community cemetery where those who had gone before her were buried—John Humphrey Noyes, Catherine Baker, Lily Cragin, Myron Kinsley, Jessie Janet, Rhoda, Aunt Jane. Located not far from the Mansion House, surrounded by the golf course, it was less forbidding than most cemeteries. Indeed Dorothy Leonard, the Kenwood poet, had written a bright little couplet that Aunt Jessie had copied into her Bedside Book:

> An island in a golfing sea
> Sleep those who supped on strawberry tea.[20]

For the last two decades of her life, the best record of Aunt Jessie's activities is contained in the letters she wrote to Hope Emily Allen, a woman twenty-five years her junior. Hope was one of the most remarkable products of the Oneida environment. Jessie Kinsley had known the Allen family since her own childhood days spent in the Wallingford Community. This branch commune had been established on the Connecticut

18. Manuscript account of Jessie Kinsley's funeral.

19. *Bedside Book,* p. 18.

20. Ibid., p. 17.

farm that Henry Allen, Sr., had given to the Community when he accepted Noyes's doctrines in 1851. Allen and his wife Emily had three children, Henry Grosvenor, George, and Harriet. They were several years older than Jessie, but she knew them very well. Indeed George was one of the suitors she had turned down to marry Myron Kinsley. Hope was the daughter of Henry Grosvenor Allen, who had married Portia Underhill. Hope's brother was Grosvenor Allen, who became a key executive in the company, especially remembered for endowing Community Plate silverware with distinctive quality and beauty.

Hope Allen was a brilliant scholar. She earned her A.B. degree from Byrn Mawr College in 1901 at the age of seventeen. In 1906 she received her M.A. from the same institution. From 1908 to 1910 she did graduate work at Radcliffe. Establishing herself as an expert in medieval history and literature, Hope made several trips to England to carry on research. For a time these activities had to be curtailed because of the ill health of her parents, but after they died Hope spent most of her time in England. She became a well-known figure in the world of scholars. At the seventy-fifth anniversary convocation in honor of Bryn Mawr Alumni she was described thus: "Hope was small and slight, not much over five feet in height, pale with fair, straight hair and light blue eyes. She dressed quietly, was plain-spoken and entirely unaffected, and might easily have escaped notice in a crowd, but a second glance would surely have attracted attention, for she was a person of great independence and force of character. In the nineteen thirties she was wearing a long, black cape and a black beret. 'I saw Hope Allen this morning,' said one of the dons at Newham, 'flitting about Cambridge like the ghost of Erasmus.'"[21]

In 1929 Hope was awarded the Rose Mary Crawshay Prize of the British Academy for her book *Writings Ascribed to Richard Rolle, Hermit of Hampole, and Materials for His Biography.* In 1940 she published *The Book of Margery Kempe of Lynn,* a highly regarded study of feminine piety in medieval England. In 1946 Smith College awarded Hope the honorary degree of Doctor of Humanities (L.H.D.).[22]

Jessie Kinsley and Hope Allen were bound by both psychological and intellectual ties. After the death of her parents, Hope, who never married, must have felt the need for a close relationship with this old family friend. To "Mother Jessie" she could write long letters telling about her scholarly adventures and receive strongly supporting letters in reply. Jessie, who had great respect for scholars and authors, took vicarious satisfaction in Hope's achievements. Often Jessie would read Hope's letters to

21. Collection of Jane Rich.
22. *Who Was Who in America* (London: Adam and Charles Black).

Hope Emily Allen, 1906

other Kenwood people so they too could share in the reflected glory. Jessie was probably glad to include another daughter in her circle of affections. Hope was about the age of Jessie's own children. Born in 1883, she was two years younger than Edith, the same age as Albert, and four years older than Jessie Janet. Hope Allen's warm attachment must have helped to fill the void left in Jessie's life by the tragic death of Jessie Janet.

To carry on her side of this correspondence was an invigorating challenge for Jessie Kinsley. She sent Hope thoughtful letters, describing the life that she was leading, the books she was reading, her ideas about literature, art, and politics, and the progress of her braiding. She also wrote many pages of "noos" — as she and Hope called it — chitchat about the many Kenwood families that they knew so well. In the extracts that follow most of these "noos" items have been omitted.

LETTERS TO HOPE ALLEN, 1921–1937

Kenwood, October 8th, 1921

My dear Hope,

Now you are in London. I think of it, London, from your windows, and when the leaves rolled across Green Park and Rhoda raced with them, of Picadilly at night, and Primrose Park in the morning. There was that view from Primrose Hill in the evening, with the foreground of human sheep at rest on the long slope. Most of all the innumerable vistas where the clouds and fogs, too, sometimes helped the always old (but new to me) shape of buildings and roofs to be ineffably beautiful. I shall never cease to be glad of having lived in three distinct parts of London.

You told me the things about yourself I most wanted to hear. I felt your spirit so kind, and you helped my courage. I do have spiritual victories. What a devil-fighter your mother was. I often think of her strong nature. But you are differently strong: stronger yet and just as loving. I shall not put down all that you seem to me. You would not like me to be vocal. Besides, it's better without words.

Lily was brave about seeing Lotta and the children go[1] but gave way afterward, and we couldn't help but weep together. As for me, I find straw for bricks to build the walls when hard pressed. I know I will always find it in thankfulness, in hope and faith, too. I am glad of experience and will be tenacious of hope. Thomas a Kempis says, "Be not angry that you cannot make others as you wish them to be, since you cannot make yourself as you wish to be." What if the bluebird and the oriole mated and each insisted on the other singing his or her song, or the bluebird wouldn't sing at all? Some marriages seem like that.

Kenwood, January, 1922

Your postal from La Rochelle has just come, and you will know how very glad I am to hear you are visiting Lotta.

I do like that Clive Bell book immensely.[2] I've read a little and am saving the rest to read aloud to Edith who wants to hear it. The elasticity of my vision has been so much less than hers, and what I have has been developed by Edith, so I shall get some edification by hearing her talk

---

1. Lotta with Myron and Jane sailed for France to spend several months.

2. Clive Bell was an English critic and a member of the so-called Bloomsbury group. The book was probably *Art* (1914).

about it. And I remember reading an illuminating article in 1915, in which a writer in *Arts and Decoration,* owner of the largest collection of modern paintings in America, wrote that, of all the books that had been helpful to him, Clive Bell's had been the most helpful. Thank you again for sending it to me.

Annie Miller is now staying with me, and I have temporarily put aside my braiding,[3] and we read and walk and go visiting.

Writing is not easy for me, really. I always want to rewrite my letters and often do when I have time. I feel defects so keenly in reading what I have written. Grama Lily sometimes reads me the letters to Lotta that she is preparing to send off, and they are full of humor and meat of all sorts. Then she complains to me she cannot write.

Late January, 1922

I am hoping the preparation and strain of travel in the midst of a flu epidemic will not be too exhausting to dear Lotta. It takes all my will power to keep down these waves of apprehension and concentrate on the happy thought of these dear ones back home again.

Annie has gone. Of course, under every current of life is the thought of Violet.[4] Yet she is big, and free, too. She has a social power that I admire and marvel over. I would almost envy it if envy were right. It was quite a wonderful thing to be sharing my intimate private life with a friend. Sissy would bring us our breakfast; we, reading, talking and going about all day long like sisters. Annie's next birthday brings her to seventy, and mine to sixty-five.

Do excuse the pencil. My pen, as usual, has lost itself under bed, bureau, books, or elsewhere.

Oneida Hospital, February 27th

Sitting here beside Edith's bed, I will tell you that, at the end of twelve days, just when she was feeling gay and fine and ready to go home, came a hard set-back: a trouble that the doctor says occurs in only one in a hundred cases. Although there is so much trying disappointment in her illness, it makes her only the more loveable, if that is possible. She is a rare and wonderful daughter, and you will know that we are drawn close together.

3. Her first large braiding, finally titled *Things Not of Man's Devising.*
4. Annie's daughter, Violet Miller Sattig, died in 1921.

East River, Connecticut, June 15th

Last week I came down here to Annie. Annie with her fine chauffeur met me at New Haven. We drove through a misty, moonlighted country, haunted by sea-meadows, and our car seemed like a rolling ball on a long, silver string. More pleasant rides have ensued. Laurel is in its glory in the woody spots.

Annie has her heart nourished by all the beauty Violet loved. Everything speaks to her of Violet.

Annie's garden next to her kitchen is her daily care, her joy and her life. I have helped as much as she would let me. It is hard for her to let the perfection of every act and move that become her natural system seem possible in the hands of another. So I have not even been able to rightly peel potatoes or fix asparagus, but have set the table and unset it. The beauty in the house has its own charm and appeals to one side of me, although my clumsiness and carelessness would do ill work to precious articles in the long run. I walk on eggs with so many valuables about to knock over![5]

Kenwood, June 19th

I have returned to Kenwood to find your letter saying you won't be coming home after all. That message makes me sad. Into my scrap book I have sometime copied a Buddist prayer: "Let all creatures everywhere, all spirits and all who have taken birth, without enemies and without obstacles, overcoming sorrow and attaining cheerfulness, move forward, each in his own path." I am so glad to have you move freely after your long confinement by circumstances.[6]

September 10th

Grapes are ripening, potatoes are out of their hills; zinnias, late delphinium and phlox are gay in Edith's border. Edith has gone back to camp[7] after getting Rhoda started into school once more. Rhoda's bed is pushed to my end of the porch, but now she takes more care of me than I do of her.

I've just read *The Shropshire Lad,*[8] one of Edith's purchases, and

---

5. Annie's son-in-law was an antique dealer in New Haven, Ct.

6. Hope had been attending her father, an invalid, for years.

7. Albert and Mart had a two-family camp built on Oneida Lake, twenty miles away.

8. By the English poet A. E. Housman.

have started Hendrick Van Loon's *The Story of Mankind,* taken from the Mansion library, written for children, but a classic, I should think, with its quaint illustrations drawn by the author.

My braiding goes on so well.

September 30th

Aren't you naughty wanting to steal Marietta's petticoat for my braiding. You know I made three *Autumns*[9] before I could get that season well symbolized. Then the last one fitted splendidly into its place. The other two, somewhat made over, will be *The Vegetable Kingdom* and *Birth, Love* and *Death.* I've had an inspiration over *The Animal Kingdom,* having found just the right material to make it from. So, to my surprise, that, too, has been magically brought into shape. The two long sides are ready for borders. The other day I went to Syracuse with Edith and bought nine dollars worth of loveliness, trusting to have it prove suitable for borders. Materials, when braided, always look different than unbraided, and I feel uncertain how they will work into place. But I feel no uncertainty of ultimately coming upon the right thing and have the utmost patience. And imagine what a reward patience has had when three *Autumns* work into the scheme. The piece, so far, makes Edith enthusiastic, and that's the crown of all. At my present pace, the whole thing will be done by next spring or summer. There are forty-two small bricks and thirty-two larger ones in the border. Besides the border, there are the three large center pieces still to make. Oh, it will need many months of work to finish at my rate. I have learned moderation and how to work. I lie in bed until ten, then bathe and walk, do my room work, lunch, then braid from one to four. Another walk usually I take before dinner, and often go up to visit Aunt Jane after dinner.

October 23rd

Sometimes I think there is no happier person in the world than I, for I have found my work to do. I have my eyesight and my faculties and live in close contact with the dearest people amid loving conditions of unity and goodwill and inspiration.

Kenneth was flattering about my new work, and, oh well, I won't repeat what he said. He told Edith someday it would go all over the coun-

9. Parts of *Things Not of Man's Devising,* planned in three panels: (1) The Four Seasons; (2) Morning, Noon, Night; and (3) The Vegetable Kingdom; The Animal Kingdom; Birth, Love, and Death.

Things Not of Man's Devising, 7′ × 7′, finished December 1923 after 3 years. Photograph by Robert Kent

try. It is so large I have had to get a place on my wall for it, move furniture around, etc. The four pictures for each side are getting their borders of blue and rose color put on simultaneously, that they may grow and stretch equally and alike. If I find I cannot make it a whole, at least there will be two lovely panels, and my trial for the central pictures won't be wasted. I shall make something out of them if they cannot make a whole of my two panels.

November

You will be glad about one thing that has happened to me. Albert has liberalized me lately, and I am getting sunshine and moonshine and all the beauty of heaven and earth in my bureau drawers in *new* silks. I had asked Albert in to talk about my finances, and his whole response was for me to spend more money. Especially after seeing my big braiding, he said I should buy new silk and never scrimp on it. He is establishing a bank fund for me—for silk—so here I am, all free, though I still contrast these wonderful beauties falling to my lot with the distress of others and wonder how I am entitled to them. My big tapestry in two parts hangs on my south wall in a glory of color. Crockers, the fabric shop in Syracuse, are quick to send me samples, which is a great boon. I am also in touch with a petticoat factory in Philadelphia, where I have found ravishing changeable silk, so unfashionable now that they are not to be found in Syracuse or any of the Oneida stores. To me they are so necessary to use as a link from one color to another.

Well, I am now where you have so long wanted me to be and I wish I had gotten there sooner. I have put some weak material into my braiding, but most of it is good. There is still all the central part to do and the top and the base.

January 10th, 1923

I do thank you and Marietta for the silk. I hope you didn't snatch this waist off her back before she was through with it. I never know how I'm going to use a certain color: everything *waits*. Brown seldom gets used. I had a dream about doing a beautiful brown braiding the other night.

The lower panel of my central panels is turning out well. Edith praises it more and more.

April 26th, 1923

It has been hard for me to write during these last weeks.[10] I hope you have not been fretted by anxiety. Now Lotta says she has written you. Edith and Mart have gone off for a long ride with the bravest

10. Rhoda, Mart and Edith's only child, had died of meningitis.

hearts, so determined to get right with the world after the long and terrible pain and despair. All their world has changed. Edith centers much anxiety about me, and Mart does, too. You will know how my heart is broken anew. But I have firmer ground of spiritual strength. Every thing is still a mystery; to say, "Yes" and not "No" comes more easily than formerly. I want to be stronger than a reed for Edith and Mart to lean on.

Our maid, Annie, sails for England May 10th. I cannot tell you what a blessing she has been, one of the blessings of our hardest time. Extinguishing herself, she gave everything: service and love with gentle ways. She returns to England to get married, hoping her mate will someday like to come to America.

Spring-like weather has come and flowers are blooming.

My thoughts follow Edith and Mart through their journeying, hoping and praying that good will come out of their pain, and knowing so well that only time is a healer. We must all have hope and patience.

Rhoda weighed one-hundred and ten pounds, she was five feet two inches tall, and almost twelve years old. She would have been tall like her Grama Alice [Alice Ackley Kinsley], and, like her, she had a singing voice. Every day Edith had her at the piano to follow and to read music; she bought new songs and new operas, and these she sang so sweetly and so easily. It was beautiful to listen to, Edith said; she went easily to some high note, and Edith never, never let her strain her voice. She was always good and reasonable and loving. For fifteen days she could eat practically nothing, yet she went giving her consent and without crying to the operating table for an operation to draw fluid from her spine. The germ was of the most fatal kind. She was delirious only during the last twelve hours. One day she said to Edith, "What do you think it is, Mother, that runs over and over in my head? 'Hark, hark, the lark at heaven's gate sings and Phoebus gins arise.'" She said once, "Mama, am I going to die? I feel so sick." But this her mother vehemently denied. Then she said, "Oh, I guess I'm not half as sick as Betty was." Another time she said, "Mama, what will you do without me if I die?"

When Edith and Mart would be exhausted by sleeplessness and emotion, Albert was wonderful. I have lived to see many golden-hearted Kinsleys meet their afflictions bravely and to rise to meet the afflictions of others.

May 1st

Now work for Edith has begun, for she has had her casting table brought to the upper porch, and, after perfecting some pieces in clay, long ago begun, she has cast them in plaster.

I am jealous of time. I am making a rug for a wedding gift but I am so anxious to be working on my braiding, which has lain neglected since Rhoda's illness. How I wish I were twenty-five years younger and had long, long days full of vigor. I could braid morning and evening and see things go faster.

May 15th

Your letter comforted me. It gave me the right thought to hold on to, for, with Edith and Mart gone on their trip, my grief had become more personal than when their suffering was needing me.

You said you thought I gave Rhoda "treasures of happiness all her life through, and helped to make her one of the most fortunate of children who have ever been." So I will think of those words night and day; they are "Yes, yes," not "No." Edith will be brave but she will need me for a time, as you say. I am thankful to be as strong in spirit as I am. A circle with a great fragment gone to be filled out is a fact we will all face. Edith said she should love all children — more. Oh, how glad and thankful I am for little Erik to have come.[11]

I am reading Santayana's *Soliloquies in England*. And by mail has come G. W. Noyes' book which I am crazy to read.[12]

January 1924

How good that you went off to Liverpool after your final bout with Rolle.[13] Yet you say there is another volume, and that makes me gasp, for I had thought your leviathan about brought to shore now. Must you go on again, hauling at your monster effort? I think of the beautiful things that have slipped off your penpoint and long to have you relax.

We watch the news from England — the railroad strike and the labor party in power. They present a new combination, and every day may mean events coming into a focus of new interest.

Pierrepont, at the Sunday night meeting, discussed new standards and desires for the youth coming into work now and for those who cast in their lot with us. There would have to be an unusual standard maintained between desire for riches and desire to help others — a sort of socialism that meant equality. I thought of the leaven that a woman

11. Erik, Lotta and Albert's third child.

12. George Wallingford Noyes, *The Religious Experience of John Humphrey Noyes* (New York: Macmillan, 1923).

13. Richard Rolle, d. 1349, English mystic and religious teacher.

put into three measures of meal: the loaf of 1848 to 1880, a loaf of Pierrepont's generation, 1880 to 1920, and then of what new ingredients this loaf to come will contain: the effects of war, women's suffrage, of prohibition, of the experiment in Russia, and of all the minor things like movies, radio, new art and literature—that the leaven will not rise, I cannot imagine. I think I see now a growth of sincerity, not sentimentality, in this generation. Youth is always a little hard, but let experience work, and the new loaf will have a wonderful rise. It will need a leader of its own generation.

March 20th

Edith is back home from a New York visit, and how much that means in joys to me. The piano sings out after lunch and after dinner: sweet sounds; books are left about; Mart comes in with gusto; talk is lively at table; Edith comes to my room, and we read aloud. We are reading a book on biology by Julian Huxley.

There is an underlying torture in these spring days: this recurrence of a period so full of pain. But there is a superb courage in Edith and Mart, and some in me, too.

Spring 1924

You were in Cambridge still when your last card was written.

I was in the midst of drawing patterns for the wide borders of a new braiding[14] when I discovered moths in various places. So I left delightful things for more mundane and went about looking over closets, boxes, etc. This activity has led on to mending and planning for a dressmaker. As yet, I do not see my way out of these diggings and delvings for a week or so. One must clean one's nest and preen one's feathers, I suppose.

Edith is writing away up in her studio. She has found a way to maintain her poise against overwhelming anguish, I think. She also knows how to find and give forth pleasure. There is an outlet, too, in the piano, on which lie a pile of new music, classical and modern. Mart comes home, and they go "dogging," that is, they take one or two half-grown setters out for field practice; and many friends come in for tea.

We have two splendid new paintings, have I told you? One is by Kenneth called *The Bather*, the other by Middleton Manigault called *Adagio*. They hang on the north wall of our big parlour.

14. *A Lasting Spring.*

A Lasting Spring, 6′ × 7′, June 1924–February 1925

April 3rd

Edith is busy. She is teaching again — sometimes Rhoda's grade —
writing assiduously and involved in social affairs. Mart is busy, too —

something to do with the building of the new factory. Work is a great and powerful friend.

June 1924

I saw your letter in the Literary Supplement asking for possible unknown papers about Rolle. I wonder if you got anything from it?

Edith and Mart are just back from another ride into Pennsylvania. They asked me to go with them, but the dressmaker was here making me a muslin dress. I couldn't get her again all summer, so I said nay but made myself a loser of beauty and joy.

My braided silk landscape border is going forward. It will be months in the making. Already I can see the delight it will be to make this addition to my accomplished center.

I saw in a catalogue mention of a publication by the Victoria and Albert Museum of Miniatures of leaves and cuttings from illuminated manuscripts with twenty-six illustrations. I am wondering if this one is just lettering. Should you chance ever to go over there to the museum, perhaps you would look at it. And if there are colored plates, buy it for me. It's only two shillings. But please, don't go purposely. I have not yet found a name for this big braiding.

June

We have a child in the house. Helen Miller and her ten-year-old daughter are with us for a few weeks. Louise has her Grandmother Annie's fine, clear, dark skin and very heavy hair and something of her symmetry, with bright, blue eyes, thick, dark lashes, white teeth and beautifully chiseled lips. She has a very quick mind.

I go on and on with my big piece. This lower border is fourteen inches deep and it measures six feet long. Helen thinks my center the best work I have ever done.

Christine [Allen][15] is off to the Democratic Convention in New York as the guest of Mrs. Franklin Roosevelt. I do not at all want Al Smith for president. The one hope is for a dark horse like Davis getting the nomination. Aren't you ashamed of some of our public men?

July 18th, 1924

Beautiful, beautiful reproductions! You couldn't have chosen anything I'd rather possess than these booklets and cards. Thank you

15. Christine Allen was the wife of Grosvenor Allen, Hope Allen's brother.

again. And for your two postals unacknowledged. They made me happy, too, thinking of your new plans for your work. I feel as though you had been climbing mountains for years. There is a line from Blake I have just come upon, "great things are done when men and mountains meet" — not very Blake-ish but fitting my feeling about your work.

I have been reading Blake this morning, looking for a name for my big braiding. It is still nameless. Nothing found yet to fit.

I am feeling better this morning, too, because Aunt Jane is better. She has fine recuperative power. She was very sick. It seemed as though I could not spare her. She is like a beloved child, or sister, or mother, and, for long, our daily meetings have been reciprocal giving. She hasn't an old spirit. I would like to think she would live on and on as happily as she has this past year, which has been fruitful of work from her fingers. She has made an embroidered shawl, four sweaters, five pairs of boys' golf socks, and dozens of small baby socks and mittens.[16]

Autumn 1924

Edith and I are reading the parliamentary speeches over the Irish settlement and have not yet reached the point where MacDonald's party was beaten on a minor question. We are also reading Paine's *English Literature.*

My work is most enjoyable. I have had a reporter to interview me about it. He gave a good account of my work. I was glad it went so well. I feared a hauling out of the O. C. L. and personal details.

Spring 1925

Summer is here today. No need to wrap up in sweater or shawl as I sit here in bed writing with the windows thrown wide open. Spring is still here in the beauty of the butternut tree. Its leaves have not grown full and lush as they will later. Looking through my doorway, the poplars frame the field and distant creek banks in light, not dark green.

I was so excited by a bird last night and learned that this soaring, swooping creature, almost bat-like or swallow-like, was a night hawk catching insects.

This has been Lotta's birthday. She says she does not quite like to have it celebrated, but Edith has invited her and Albert and others in for the evening. I left them playing cards and went to the band concert. When I got back they were having coffee and cake and discussing astrology, spiritualism and Houdini. Each had a personal story to tell.

16. Aunt Jane was almost ninety-four years old.

Edith's studio has been cleaned, and she will be ready to paint over there[17] soon. I shall miss our after lunch reading but I have now started on a new braiding.[18] I like to draw, but it is hard work for me to stand reaching about making patterns. If I get a good start with color, then that works itself along, and I am off again for a year, perhaps. Hurrah!

January 14th

I was happy to get your card. There is hunger to see you here, and I am not the only one to feel it.

I have my two lower pattern pictures drawn for my *Tree of Life,* enlarged immensely from the tiny imaginations made long ago. I am all equipped to go at their production, only that Annie Miller's welcome visit has been an interruption along with Christmas holidays. And now the dressmaker is giving me a few days of her help. Before too long Edith and I start off for a six week stay in New York. Thus my poor *Tree* will be slow finishing, I fear. Really, I like the way things have dove-tailed, such as the dressmaker coming in time to fix me up for the excursion to New York. I begin to feel everything will mysteriously come my way, which is quite as bad as worrying.

February 6th

I have begun my sixth picture for the *Tree.* Many people think this is my best yet, but I hardly think so.

Soon I shall be going off to join Edith in New York. It will be nice to miss some of the rigors of February and March, for New York has a milder climate than Kenwood.

Edith and Mart have asked Dorothy Ackley to come to our house to have her baby in July.

Kenwood, July 2nd, 1927

Outdoors I lie in sunshine and shade on Edith's lawn-chair by our front hedge under the big willow. The willow is withered and dead and soon to be cut down. I have hated to see it go, but now we are ready.

I see from here most intimately our charming birds. A wren and

17. Edith had rented a small house on Middle Road in Kenwood Heights for a summer studio.

18. The braiding, *The Mansion,* was done in 1924–1925.

The Mansion, 9′ × 5′, 1924–1925

its mate are nearby in a box; two cedar wax wings have a nest in our third poplar; a beautiful spotted wood thrush has built near us and sings in the old willow; a cat bird flits softly in the hedge and sings loud enough for me to be thrilled by its songs; and a pair of red-starts are here, too.

But the best of all! This morning through the big front bay window has come the sound of Willard and Dorothy's little girl baby, born this morning, now washed and dressed, so tiny and pretty.

July 23rd, 1927

Lotta's mother still lives. It was four days ago Marion said about Lily, "She will joke with her last breath." On Monday, Lily told Marion, "This is my dying day," and she made a joke to Marion about her "last salute" when she made an unwanted noise. Her cheerfulness almost outlasts her body. I do think she is the bravest person possible. I imagine her imprisoned intellect savoring her dying, watching what it is like.

August 5th

How delighted I am with the little Albert museum book of Eliza-

bethan and Stewart embroideries. Thank you, dear Hope, for such a treasure of quaint works. I would love to see the color of these things.

I go on well with my *Tree of Life.* It's good to be at it — a rich
enjoyment.

Lily has a strong heart and cheerful spirit, although utter pros-
tration and falling away of body, beyond anything I have seen except in
my sister Mary's case. There seems to be very little suffering, and she
sleeps and sleeps without morphine.

August 11th

Gates Aerial Circus established itself on broad stubble fields in
Sherrill a week ago. The planes for two days carried over four hundred
passengers, booming over our heads. All of the boys, big and little, went
flying.

When I went to see Lily yesterday, her son, John, sat by her bed,
and her eyes were wide open. I said, "Oh, how bright you look." She
spoke, "I must look bright when my children come." And when John rose
and bowed and saluted her, she smiled and winked.

At the Community Associated Clubs park celebration yesterday,
I wandered about among the booths after buying an ice cream cone.
Overhead zoomed three airplanes. After looking over the floats, I imagined how soon our parades would be taken in the air, our band concerts
would have vast overhead audiences just as there are now hundreds of
autos clustered where, only as long ago as my husband's last year of life,
were pig sties and a cow barn. No flying machines then and only one or
two autos. Such words as "freudian," "complexes," "ectoplasm," "brain-
storm," "Rotary," "Kiwanis," "cafeteria," "sundae," "mah-jong," "flap-
per," "permanent wave," "over the top," "jazz," "bolshevism," "funda-
mentalism," and "behaviorism" were uncoined. I read a list of these
words and can only remember a few.

The big dance has come and gone. I sat in the gallery and enjoyed
it as I always do. The music, the gaiety and the color. It was midnight
when I got help to carry a tray of the refreshments around to Aunt Jane's
room, for she expressed a wish to stay up and have some. It was giggling
Jane who sat up in bed eating ice cream. She will be ninety-five next
month.

September 24th

I cannot go to the Mansion without missing Lily[19] as I pass
Lotta's rooms.

19. Lily died of cancer in September 1927.

Last week Albert asked me to go to Philadelphia and then he also asked Marion Nolan to go with us. He said he thought we had both been through a strain and a change would be nice for us. Wasn't that thoughtful of him? All during the week we were there he was generosity itself. We had perfect weather. One afternoon we went to the Sesqui-Centennial Exhibition. Part of the time Albert and a boy pushed us in a car-chair. The Sesqui is much like a big fair.

September 26th

Edith unpacked last week some lovely sea-green glass bought in Venice.[20]

That reminds me to tell you of my braiding. The parts of my *Tree of Life* are to be marked:

1. Let the waters be gathered together
2. Let the sea bring forth abundantly
3. Let the earth bring forth the living creature
4. As to man his days are grass
5. Dust thou art, to dust thou shalt return

It's going well and lots of fun.

March 6th, 1928

Yesterday I took my braiding[21] up to sit with Aunt Jane. She was full of old stories, but her voice was weak and hissing. For all my listening I only made out a word here and there: "Abby Burnham, Mr. Worden, Putney, Mr. Noyes, Wallingford, journeys" — etc. These reminiscences were only beads strung on a thin thread, not coherent for me.

As I left her room and passed through the Nursery Kitchen, three pairs of friendly hands drew me down to sit by them on the old couch. I told them of my letter and telegram from you.

Fresh work on my braided border still hangs in thin air and it needs much contemplation of material. Many hopes are dashed, but experimentation will finally find the way for sure. I'd like to be racing on with it, though there is still finishing enough at the top to keep me busy.

20. During the previous spring, Mart and Edith had traveled with friends in France, Italy, and Germany.

21. *Memory Hither Come.*

Tree of Life, 5′ × 4½′, July 1926–June 1927. Photograph by Robert Kent

Minerva Norton, 87, Emma Freeman, 91, Jessie Kinsley, 72, and Helen Barron, 83, February 1930, the "Ladies of the Nursery Kitchen"

March 13th

Sunday the boys in Henry's[22] class found a new pastime. Melting snows had hung heavy icicles from every house-ledge and gutter. With a battery of snow balls, the boys went about hitting and crashing down these shining rows. I told them that an enormous spear, fit for a giant, was hanging and tearing down one of our water pipes and then I rushed out onto the back porch to see the fun. The boys were all below. I think it was Henry who finally hit the fair blow that crashed it down, although each boy was firing thick and fast. There were no windows behind there

22. Henry G. Allen, Grosvenor's son and Hope's nephew.

to be afraid of. As they went off for more fields of ice, they called up to me, "And we haven't broken a window yet!" You know, I love to crash down icicles and was almost sorry for the boys that I had indulged myself in the sport with a long pole and had demolished all I could reach at the front of the house.

I think I ought to learn from braiding, all there is to know of peace and patience and the road to faith. My quandary over borders the other day had fine illumination. I thought I saw how to go ahead. I hopped for joy—"became a bird, and bird-like danced and shaken blossoms fell into the hands." So I am going on with hope of being aright, with assurance that each problem will bring its illumination within me. I am halfway down on the left side already.

March 18th

A white world: heavy snow is falling.

Myron came home from New York yesterday—from seeing his uncle Mart off to England. He said J. P. Morgan and a prize-fighter also sailing were each having flash-light pictures taken by reporters as he left Mart and the boat.

Today I am invited to dine with Margaret. I am glad because it is Jessie's birthday. Jessie would have been forty-one, and I like to think, like Lotta and Norma and Alice, she would have had a happy experience in motherhood. If not in that way in other ways, for like our Rhoda Kinsley and Janie, she was big-hearted and good, rather fitted to be happy. The pity about Rhoda is my not having had as full-grown a memory of her as of Jessie—to have seen her as I saw Jessie blossom. But, oh! she was a sweet child, and thinking of you in England now, and her father on his way, brings back that happy time in 1919 when we were all there.

March 26th

My birthday. Everyone says, "You don't look seventy," and certainly I don't feel seventy, so what of years—might as well ignore them.

I had a party in the afternoon. Ethel, our maid, was devoted about the food. Edith telephoned from New York in the midst of it. Albert and Jane could both come besides Josephine and Virginia. A group of children from the school came over to sing me a birthday song and brought a gift of letters. Charming letters. There were cards and flowers from others. A remarkable anniversary for me, a real event. And dear Hope, I remember the pin you say you have sent me.

Jessie Catherine Kinsley, Hope Emily Allen, and Rhoda Kinsley in London, 1919

April 14th

I have been reading numerous pages in your book every morning
— of course not the Latin. I am greatly interested and carried along. I am
sure I shall read it all with equal pleasure and with a strange feeling that it

is a part of you. Dorothy will read it with discernment and will be able to say something wisely to you about it. Excitedly I will look forward to your reviews.

I have been making a book for Albert's birthday, bigger and covered with silk than the one I made for you. It contains photos of the braidings and several of the drawings. Albert had suggested I make it for him. I had a good time doing it, but yesterday I was glad to put my effort into my big braiding again, which is coming along successfully.

Edith has some new ideas about painting, and when I go up to her studio to read to her and I see her putting these ideas into practice, I have to stop reading to watch. After all, the great thing in life is to get creative illumination, isn't it? To rejoice in them and try to work them out. According to Gilbert Murray, that is everyone's way to religion, and I remember he finished one lecture by telling how a scholar draws out of the past high thoughts and great emotions.

About that silk of Marietta's. I am fascinated by it but I doubt I should use it for a long time, having my idea for a new piece thought out in another color. If Marietta can use it in some other way that would be well, but my inner cravings scream yes and not no to such wealth and beauty. Thank her for thinking of me, will you?

April 22nd

Christine has gone to the League of Women Voters' convention in Chicago and in June she goes to Houston, Texas as a delegate at large to the Democratic Nominating Convention. She will go with Mrs. Franklin Roosevelt's party and will be entertained with an inside view of politics.

May 23rd

My braided border is going well now, and, like Aunt Elizabeth, (don't you remember how she cackled over things?) I cackle!

I'm slow at reading your book. It is almost finished in my unthorough way. Each copy of the *Literary Times* I hastily scan hoping to find a "Rolle" review. I do so want to see all of your reviews, although I cannot myself be articulate about your book. I think you'd be happy and perhaps surprised if you knew how much pleasure I have had with it.

June 4th

Aunt Jane's illness was short. After a morning seizure she lived strong of will to once more see Burton[23] who had been sent for from New York. She did see him and recognized him and then quietly slipped away. In August she would have been ninety-seven. I shall miss her and that second home she made for me where I was always welcome and where I relaxed and no gossip disturbed our spirits. We were keen at cards in our own way. How alert she was, always showing me good moves I'd missed with her knitting needle and knowing I was not unpleased to have her thus get ahead of me. If Aunt Jane had died at seventy before Myron died I should not have had this long acquaintance with her. I should have learned to love her, but admiration grew, too, in later years. Her beauty grew in all ways. Edith says physically as well as spiritually she was a grander character now than twenty or thirty years ago. Her friends had brought so many flowers to her the day before she died, as though they could not bring enough: hawthorn, tulips, lily-of-the-valley, iris, lilacs, made her vases full. She was especially pleased by the great branches of hawthorn brought in by Mrs. Drummond.

June 18th

Evenings are sometimes dull for me. I have long found that too much reading or writing or excited talk or working at my braiding means long wakefulness. Aunt Jane's room was just the outlet I needed with the pleasure of her society. Now I am looking to form new habits and may get me a radio, although I have always thought I should hate one. I wander up to find the Nursery Kitchen deserted since Mrs. Barron's illness. I pass the time sauntering about, looking for friends in their rooms. Mrs. Norton is always in her room and she is a dear woman to visit, and I find Mrs. Barron so glad to see me. I take longer walks and see a lot of Janie and Carlotta, although their rooms, so airy and nice for them, are too cold and not suited for one less vigorous.

This morning, when I went to Edith's room, I found her dressing and as I sat there Edith turned and said, "Now I am going to my studio," and her eyes shone and sparkled. And I said, "You have a morning heart, because you have something so interesting to do, and I have it, too, over my work. Aren't we fortunate!" We could not help congratulating ourselves in our good fortune in work.

I read an essay by Durer which echoed our feeling. He said, "Painting is useful when no one thinks so, for a man will have great joy if he occupies himself in that which is so rich in joys." One could put braiding into that sentence and have it true.

23. Burton L. Dunn was Aunt Jane's nephew.

July 2nd, 1928

My braiding just creeps along. A thousand bits hurried over long ago in order to show myself some effect, and really left unsewed, must now be hunted out and made perfect. Lettering to do and the final narrow border edge to braid and apply, then "finish" can be said. It was the seventh of June I had my operation last year.[24] This braiding was begun the next month, and so there will have been given a year to what is really not a work of art. But that is all my own fault. I made the design without suggestion from anyone and started off upon the work without the long digestive thought put upon many of my things. I only hope it will be suitable to the proposed situation in the directors' room and, if not, I shall want to see it taken down. Kenneth said last year of my finished *Tree of Life* that it must be a satisfaction to find each finished piece better than its fellows. I am sure he would not say that of this one which is really a map in its entirety, nothing more, a rather curious and interesting map, but I have had good times doing it.

Al Smith is the Democratic nominee. Christine has not returned from her stay in Texas yet. Holton [Noyes] says he feels Al Smith to be an honest leader. Virginia says he is nothing but a drunkard. And at the clubhouse Friday, pictures of Hoover were wildly cheered, while Al Smith's picture was seen in silence. This must be a Republican town. I shall be glad when electioneering is over.

July 19th, 1928

My piece at last is finished. This week I have been going through my "paint-box," that is, my drawers of silk and boxes and boxes of silk, scrapping up — washing brushes, as you might say — getting order back where I need it so much, so as not to waste time when I do go back to work.

July, 1928

Back home from DeRuyter Lake I am thinking of new braidings and planning and thinking of patterns, but nothing really is yet settled in my mind. So many paths are open. How I wish I was fifty — not seventy — with these thoughts. I could venture and venture on wild experiments which lure me down ever new ways. But I am certain paint isn't my me-

---

24. A benign tumor removed.

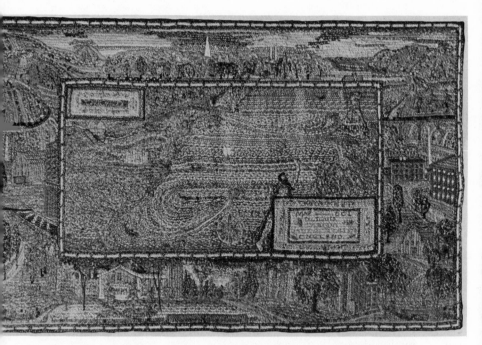

Memory Hither Come, 7′ × 6′, a map showing factories of Oneida Community, Limited in the United States, Canada, and England and Neptune pouring watery floods from a silver pitcher. The border depicts (from top clockwise) Oneida (the white, spired church), Sherrill factories, the Community Associated Club clubhouse, Sales Office, Mansion House, Knife Plant, and the Ontario and Western Railroad. Photograph by Robert Kent

dium, for I could never venture with it as I have in braids — witness the size of my braidings and the size of my paintings.

Edith makes me happy by telling me she likes *Memory Hither Come* almost best of all, and I have been so doubtful these last months of bringing it off successfully that this is a rich gift from Edith.

August 19, 1928

My small braiding for Margaret K. has gone well and is finished and given to her. Just a woodsy scene with man on horseback, a maid, a child, and numerous birds, and the verse, "When the greenwoods laugh with a voice of joy / When the painted birds laugh in the shade," by Blake. I enjoyed doing it, and it was a prelude to sew myself something I wanted to find out about before beginning a larger piece. A gift of cards of old French tapestries set going in my mind a thought for a new piece, just as one of your gifts of cards made inevitable my *Lasting Spring* which was not a copy at all. Nor would this piece be a copy—it can't. So I am drawing a new pattern. Its composition and its connection with the cards is that I shall try in my own braiding way to turn and twist the braids and fill them, if I can, full of flowers and birds and small beasts, like an inarticulate woods scene. Against this will appear various females copied from some of my little paintings. It is so good for me to have a big piece on hand, to settle down for a daily stream of work and never get pressed into a floodtide where I am tempted to overwork just to get a thing ended. Then, too, I can waken every morning with a "morning heart," because there is so much fun ahead and my work thought out.

August 30th

Last night when I went to bed and stood to look out of my doorway at the moonlight, I heard the shrill tree-toads in that butternut tree. I note every chance sound of this sort as they mark a thrilling moment to my dulled ears.

I am doing some pick-up work and at the same time getting started on my new large braiding.[25] My pick-up work is just now to make a scrapbook of all sorts of drawings of mine. Not that they are worth much labor or care, but that they may be suggestions to me. Then I hope before getting too immersed in my new braiding to catch up with pasting the year's small accumulation of photographs into my photo collection.

I am gay with hope over my drawing for a new braiding[26] but it has not turned out to be in the least like the beautiful print you gave me from the encyclopedia. I had had hopes it could be somewhat like that. About as large as a newspaper sheet, it has an inset and two borders. I am wobbly on my legs, for I have been two hours standing to draw my big pattern as they are tacked on the wall and one free hand with a long-handled brush and ink. I want to go on with my fun but have said "stop" to myself for this afternoon. The sun is near setting, and I am going for another walk as far as the bridge.

Later: the sunset seen from the bridge was beautiful, but it has grown cold, and the mercury must be down below the twenty mark. I am reminded by the sunset beauty of two things I copied into my little book

25. *Greenwood I.*
26. *Ariel's Song.*

this morning. It was funny to put them side by side—the language of a scientist and of a great poet. Michael Pupin, the scientist, wrote, "The radiation reflected, refracted and scattered by matter floating in the atmosphere is the external source of this beauty. It is an energy chaos, practically infinite in number and variety of electrical pulses sent out at random by the solar electrons. These chaotic signals are recorded by our sensations and appear in our consciousness as the beauty of the sunset. This is creative coordination." The second quotation is so familiar: "The poet's eye in fine frenzy rolling doth glance from heaven to earth, from earth to heaven, and as imagination bodies forth the forms of things unknown, the poet's pen turns them to shapes and gives to airy nothing a local habitation and a name." There are of course no "airy nothings" for the scientist, but, oh! I am so glad they are everywhere for the poets.

February 12th, 1929

My braiding begun on February first is going well so that I am full of interest in it. One never can tell about these beginnings of braidings. It is all about Ariel's song, "Come unto these yellow sands" and going on to cock-a-doodle-doo.

March 9th, 1929

Your two cards received are a delight. What a glorious ride you were having when you wrote from the latter place. I expect no ride I had in 1913 equalled it, but memory comes back of our rides in Italy, so I live them over again.

I wish you were here to tell me the story of the Phoenix, "immortal bird." I have just been reading in the *London Times Literary Supplement* a leading article about George Darley and I am fascinated by a verse quoted from a book of his just printed, *The Works and Life of George Darley:* "Laid like the young faun mossily in sun-green fields of Araby, I woke hard by the Phoenix-tree that with shadeless boughs flamed over me, an upward call by a dumb cry with moon-broad orbs of wonder, I beheld the immortal bird on high glassing the great sun in her eye; steadfast she gazed upon his fire, still her destroyer and her sire."[27] This was from George Darley's *Nepenthe,* which the reviewer calls "inspired singing". He also wrote much prose that he called "kitchen work," and you remember Mr. Abram Burt singing (do you?), "I've been roaming, I've been roaming where the meadow dew is sweet." That was George Darley, too.

27. Jessie used this verse for *The Phoenix Tree* braiding.

Did you ever hear of him before? I wonder if he is in *Ward's English Poets.* I must look at my books.

April 16th, 1929

Every morning I wake with the desire to make a braiding with horses for the life of a new picture. Horses, horses!!!?, but what will they be doing? All my scribbles turn out to be picnics, just as my little paintings used to be forever picnics. Then, while Edith painted a portrait of me and I read aloud from the Homeric hymn to Apollo, I came to the story of Telephusa and her horses. On one of her islands Apollo had decided to build a temple. She was wroth and persuaded him that the horses and mules drinking at her sacred springs would make too much noise for his worshippers. So then I made a drawing about this and hope I can turn it into something.

May 8th, 1929

This morning I have awakened with a sense that all mundane things are behind me, none left to haunt happiness in work, for spring housecleaning is over and done — even clothes and hats are in order. I have drawn five Telephusa Springs, and the choice of one of them made for a new pattern. Now to make my patterns, choose the colors, and then the truly great satisfaction of having again work in hand.

May, 1929

Your splendid letter from the Sheidegg Pass came several days ago. Yes, Annie and I went up the railroad to the foot of the glacier and there picked alpine roses. What a wonderful day! All Switzerland seemed a crown to our joy in Italy, as though one joy helped another.

It takes time to make the patterns for my braidings, for I have to erect a sort of easel of plaster board to pin my big brown papers to; also I have to stand to first draw in pencil and then with pen. I cannot work long at a time.

Did I write you how Lotta mothered four little boys for as many days or more? Sons of poor people whose house burned down a week ago yesterday. She washed and sewed evenings on piles of torn garments as only Lotta would do. I dropped in to give several quiet hours in storytelling to the boys. They were nice boys between six and ten. The three-year-old had built a fire under the bathtub to warm water while his mother was hanging out a big washing! So the fire was all up the partitions when the mother came in again.

July 5th, 1929

Rather gladly I have given up the trip to Lake Mohonk. When our outing does come, we may go a shorter distance, perhaps to Cooperstown where Marion has a great desire to go having just read novelist Cooper to her grandchildren.

My new braiding goes happily. Of this one's color I say, "Golden, golden," and yet I cannot tell if its big border will allow it to keep golden, but that is still far ahead.[28]

August 16th

Yesterday Wilber Earl and Charlie Noyes came to see me, and I read them a story and poured tea while they toasted tiny graham crackers on my little toaster, buttered and ate them until I feared they would be sick. But no, they laughed the thought to scorn, and I read on and rejoiced in my visit and visitors. They were delightfully polite and sympathetic in their appreciation of the braidings — such nice boys.

September 13th, 1929

I used to get much out of a change in travel in spite of carsickness and so forth but now I do think probably I am quite as well off with all my necessities around me, living the even routine in this healthy spot, out of doors so much and happy day by day and hour by hour. But now perhaps this will please you, for I am taking Marion Nolan for company (and ears to hear) for a week's visit to New York City. We contemplated seaside and lakeside resorts without great enthusiasm until it suddenly occured to Marion that New York is on the sea, and that was the place she most wanted to go for the week. New York is ever interesting to me. We are going to the Van Rensselaer, good rooms, good food and a quiet place.

I was so amused about Mrs. Gibb's tale of an "arthquake," and indeed you by rights should have heard of it from me, for it shook most of central and northern New York State early one morning. People on the upper floors were startled; it dislodged some hanging pictures. It awoke our maid but not Mart and Edith or me.

I have been reading some charming short stories by Anatole

---

28. *The Isles of Greece* is generally aquamarine, silver, apricot, and gold.

France, some essays by Viola Meynell, and several wild detective stories.

My big border for *Telephusa* has begun to grow from the top. I have found a place to sit out of doors with this work — or a book — day after day.

November 18th, 1929

I saw yesterday in *The New York Times* that from the British Academy you had won the Mary Crayshaw Prize of five-hundred dollars. How glad I am of that, and what a right judgment on their part to give it to you. I want words on this sheet to hop up and down with joy. When Christine [Allen] first told me over the phone, my feet hopped up and down, just as Janie's would for joy! I expect you take it soberly, but I can't do that about you. It gets to my solar plexus to have you honored after all these laborious years. "Oh sweet content! Oh sweet, oh sweet content! Work apace, apace, apace, honest labor wears a lovely face; then hey nonny-nonny!"

July, 1930

I am tempted to quote John Donne to you about how "my best treasure is time" and how my best employment of that is to "study good wishes for you in which I am by continual meditation so learned that your own good angel, when it would do you most good, might be content to come and take instruction from me." Did you have your own imaginary good angel hovering around when you were a little girl? Winged, and clothed in white, sometimes stern, but almost always tender-faced? I remember mine well. Another thing Donne says, "When letters have a convenient body of news they are letters." Otherwise are they but apparitions or ghosts of letters? If this letter is a ghost letter, still it must carry all my affection and love to you, dear one, and love of the kind that always makes me want to sign, Mother Jessie.

August 23rd, 1930

I think of these lines for my new piece of work: "Ye have been fresh and green. Ye have been filled with flowers. And ye the walks have been where maids have spent their hours." This braiding goes wonderfully, because, having worked over its mate *When the Greenwood Laughs,* not too long ago, the technique of that one is still in mind, and there is little ripping out and making over to come although the whole will be as different as possible from the other.

December 3rd, 1930

I have had two afternoons of sitting for photographic likenesses in my room with braidings for background. One quite good likeness is going to be my small Christmas greeting to my relatives and special friends, so you will get one. This saves me in all sorts of ways, for I have a long list and do not wish my purse to get too flat or my strength too taxed by Christmas needs.

There is to be no *Quadrangle* next year. Also band concerts are to be discontinued. The band concerts I shall miss when summertime comes again.[29]

Winter and zero weather, with their winds and storms, are here. I like creeping around in storms and against a wind now with my cane to help.

December 20th, 1930

A beautiful fall of snow topping and ice storm have given us the absolute picture of Christmas scenery. Looking from my bedroom window, I see the children sliding down the hills beyond the creek and the bridge. It is wonderful sliding, for they slide to the edge of the creek across the full length of the level field.

Our hard times and the needs of this neighborhood are much on Lotta's mind. She and others from Kenwood and Sherrill have met, charted all the cases, pooled the funds and organized labor to prevent suffering. There are many out of work.

Now my braiding is nearing completion and I am thinking, thinking, thinking all the time of the next one. Hence I am beginning to draw and perhaps just this morning I may have happened upon the pattern. I must show the little drawing to Edith for criticism. Edith has just finished a painted landscape of the moors, mountainous moors, which she sketched in pencil when in England or Scotland. The painting is fine, and I have persuaded her to hang it up downstairs.

January 1st, 1931

About Annie Miller, I must tell you she wrote me last week saying that since September she has lost her appetite and can hardly imagine how she kept alive since she ate so little. She moved to New York before Christmas. She wrote also that she did not yet know the underlying cause of her

29. Economies forced by the Great Depression.

Jessie Catherine Kinsley working on *Greenwood I* with *A Lasting Spring* on the wall

dropsy and she ended her letter, "Jessie, if I do not see you again on earth, we shall surely meet in another realm." I determined to go to New York with Albert.

We are having much snow. I like snowstorms. They still bring me some sort of childish joy, and I can see skiing and sliding at all hours across the creek. Starlings are outside plucking the dried fruit on the grapevine over the kitchen door and my end of the porch. If I were not so deaf I should hear their voices.

January 13th, 1931

A week or more ago I was ready to go to New York to see Annie, but a bad cold took me down, and I did not go. Of Annie I hear that she is better but very weak. So I am hoping to be able to see her before long.

I have finished my braiding begun in August and am now off on a voyage of discovery. My spirit is eager and joyous. Sometimes I think I feel as joyous as any Cortez on a peak in Darien when I begin a new piece — something untried, something to be attacked and the way found.

January 24th, 1931

When I think of Annie Miller, it is to be reminded of Christina Rossetti's poem, *No Coward Soul is Mine,* "no trembler in the world's storm-troubled sphere," for Annie's faith is so bright; she writes such fine letters although she says she doubts the outcome of her trouble because of her age. She says she is so fortunate in her rooms, her nurse, and is overwhelmed with gifts and flowers and fruit. Her callers are numerous and Kenneth comes every day.

My new rooms at the Mansion are all ready for me and are most cheerful in their new paint and paper. I like their looks.

March 1st, 1931

Painters and paperers came to our house to begin work,[30] and these are rushing days for Edith and Mart, getting their things looked over and packed and moved. Already they have moved into their rooms on the third floor of the Mansion.

30. Oneida Community, Limited bought the house and eventually converted it into a two-family house. Moving to the Mansion House, Jessie, Mart, and Edith presumably intended to save money during the Depression.

March 18th, 1931

This is Jessie's birthday—I always remember it—and today I am giving Janie a little present and Edith one. Those two with Mart and Prue and Bob go soon to England. They sail April fourth. Yesterday was dear Erik's birthday. I went to New York to see Annie Miller. She has most wonderful fortitude. I am troubled about the future for her and wonder what is back of it all. I asked Burton once. He only shook his head sadly and threw up his hands. I think he knows but wishes not to put what he knows in words. But how to live was Annie's ability. One does not, seeing her, feel death near. I read of an old saying, fifteen hundred years old: "The devil plucks me by the ear and cries, 'Live, for I cometh!'"

My rooms are charming and, to me, so satisfactory and home-like. Moving and all its odds and ends of fixing have made braiding go a bit slow, but everyone likes my new *The Innocent Moon,*[31] and now I have a drawing for another small piece made, and that shall be my knitting work until I get into good settled swing again.

May 18th, 1931

It does seem as though springtime this year has been exquisite beyond words. My spirits have revelled in its beauty. A ride recently showed rivulets in flood, and the creek to the very top of its banks. The cowslip meadows were a frosting of gold on glimmers of water, for we had a great thunder shower before we left. At the top of the East Hill—aside from the heavenly beauty of the view of our valley all in its spring glory—the heavens were wonderful in cloud effects, because another thunder storm was roaring down from the South.

Now our dear Annie has become bed-ridden and no longer has the strength to write letters. She has a new nurse who is devoted to her, one most capable in every way who reads to her a great deal.

Edith writes that Jane is already in the Slade School, and she will perhaps have French lessons with Mrs. Vincent.

May 28th, 1931

Now we are all a little pulled down by the cut in the dividends. My room rent, meals, lights, and small laundry, with my telephone charge for a quarter came to fifty cents more than my quarterly income. So I have to go very carefully but I am not yet feeling poor. I have clothes

31. A small braiding.

enough and shall pay for such small things as I need at the store and post office from my saved up sick fund.

I do not get frequent letters from Edith but I get heart-warming ones. She is busy with her painting in the studio in their house. They have had vicissitudes with their cooks. Janie wrote that the last one had an insane fit, and Edith took the second maid into the studio and kept her talking while Janie hid in the closet, Prudence peered over the banister and Mart, with the help of a Bobby, fired her.

June 4th, 1931

Annie [Miller], very frail but of indomitable spirit, insisted on Kenneth going with his pupils for a visit to London for a few weeks. Burton [Dunn] has now told me that Annie has cancer. Oh, how I hate to have her suffer.

July 23rd, 1931

Your dear letter is at hand. You say things to me about Annie's death that touch me deeply. I do want to be philosophical in meeting the incidents of life but still, of course, I am truly and naturally a sentimentalist; and so, when recently Gustave gave me a fine snapshot of Annie, I was at first afflicted by the sight of it, but so happy to have it that it sits before me now constantly.

I visited for the first time the Wampsville house of the Freemans. Herbert showed me two or three signs of Indian relics that I told him he must show to you when you come home. Also he told how several years ago in their quarry of gravel, three skeletons, supposed to be Indians, man, woman, and child, were found standing upright under the gravel. He said he had met the curator of an Albany museum who told him Indians were never known to be buried standing, though sometimes found in a sitting posture. I had read of a great find of ancient animal remains in the West, where evidence showed that they had one by one been lost in quicksand. So, I suggested the idea of quicksand, and that a family tragedy of Indians in that quarry had occurred. Herbert said there was quicksand nearby and this might be true — perhaps a mother and father rescuing their child.

I have just cut out a tribute to college education from an interesting article telling of the life of W. D. Hyde, a president and upbuilder of Bowdoin College and written by W. D. Howells: "To be at home in all lands and all ages; to count Nature a familiar acquaintance and Art an intimate friend; to gain a standard for the appreciation of other men's work and the criticism of one's own; to carry the keys of the World library in one's pocket and feel its resources behind one in whatever tasks are undertaken; to lose one's self in enthusiasm and to cooperate with others for common ends; to learn manners and form character; this is the offer of the college for the best four years of one's life." What a splendid offer, and one likes to think of those who make the best of it. And I fear, too, that it also may apply in part to education sought and desired individually in many youths now unable to go to college, for it is desire that really brings the best to one: desire — desire and the application and resourcefulness.

July 30th, 1931

Your note of the twenty-first with its enclosures is here. How interesting the clippings all are, and we do thank you for giving us this inspiring glimpse of the English quality of character and dignity, their steadfastness of temper in their party politics. Best of all has come your book. Its introduction I am now reading aloud to the ladies of the Nursery Kitchen and I mean to read the book quite through if possible.

August 13th, 1931

I am thinking of you now in Norfolk with the sea near enough to be heard in the storm, with windmills all about you, your sunporch to use on warm days, your fire to sit by, your bedroom under the roof, your blue-painted studio, and best of all, your quaint Mrs. Gibbs and other delightful people. You see, I have put together bits about you so with the photograph of your house, I can make a picture of it all.

Last evening I went out for a walk in the soft dusky air when an auto stopped beside me and Emily and Frances asked would I like a ride. That was delightful, and with Frances driving, we went off on a long ride over as bumpy roads as we could find. The reason for bumps was that Emily, long overdue for her baby, had taken castor oil and she hoped that the evening ride of bumps would find the event of birth beginning that very night.

July 3rd, 1932

Roosevelt's big plane went low over the Mansion yesterday morning as he and family flew to the Democratic convention in Chicago.[32] How it roared! Someone shook a handkerchief in response to waving from below.

---

32. Governor Franklin D. Roosevelt was en route to Chicago to accept the Democratic nomination for the presidency.

July 23rd, 1932

Yesterday morning about eight o'clock, Edith surprised me, coming in pajamas with breakfast in hand and telling me to look out at the storm threatening from the Northwest. It did look imposing, very black and threatening. "Oh, I'm glad we are not at the lake," she said. With windows closed we breakfasted together, and the storm spent itself while Edith played cards, and I had an opportunity to read her short bits I had so wanted that she should hear and talk to me about. Some of them were from the April *Capitol Periodical* (Oxford), that paper coming to me through your kindness. To me it is enjoyable both in the illustrations and the reading matter. And you will know how much sometimes it adds to my pleasure to share some interesting find, although I risk the chance that the find will not wholly suit my listener. But Edith was interested, and I much enjoyed this unexpected visit.

My new braiding, called *Nightfall,* progresses steadily. Four of my seven pictures are made, and I am now at the tantalizingly slow job of making connecting and surrounding borders for the seven pictures. I know well that if I leave all this border-making to the end it will then press and hurry me. But my pictures so far have gone well and seem to please Edith much. I am crazy to get at the next picture—the one I think of as our little Rhoda's, since I have in mind for it her winsome verse, "The clouds are made of silver smoke, they make the moon a silver cloak."

July 27th, 1932

Yesterday morning quite suddenly Helen[33] dropped away. Edith came to tell me this sad yet good news of Helen's release from complete helplessness. Helen will continue to live in the memories of so many. She had such devoted sons and daughters and grandchildren and nephews and nieces and cousins. Upright in all meanings of the word was dear Helen. In our little gatherings she was the questioner, too. She kept topics before us keenly. Her questions were often direct, to be answered, as for instance, when some European matter hung fire, "What will they do now?" "What can they do about it?" she would say. How inevitable these departures are, yet how true Thomas Hardy's quote, "Time changes everything except something in us which is always surprised by change." I always associate Swinburne's "to grow straight in the strength of thy spirit" with Helen.

33. Helen Miller Barron, sister of George N. Miller and aunt of Kenneth H. Miller, the artist.

Nightfall, 6′ × 6′, March–December 1932

September 4th, 1932

There has been joy here. Yesterday, Betty and Jerry[34] were married in Edith's and Mart's empty house. Everyone from the Mansion came to their big reception down there. Mrs. Norton and I were privileged

34. Betty Austin, Mart's niece, and her husband, Jerry Wayland-Smith.

guests at the actual wedding, which was simple and lovely with about forty of the Wayland-Smiths and Alice Austin's relatives present. I sat on the arm of big Gerard's chair later, during the reception. He had the only chair and insisted on my using that arm, and he seemed so well and like himself. The house was beautiful with flowers, and everyone in it beautiful, too. Lemonade, made with ginger-ale and mint to make it tasty, was served. A magnificent day, all doors wide open and wreathed with flowers. My braidings hung on the walls. A great crowd, but plenty of room because of all outdoors. Betty threw her bouquet down the stairway and Jane caught it. There was a throwing of confetti and a running to see the bride and groom off, then a gradual dispersal with everyone saying, "A lovely wedding." Betty and Jerry seemed a fine pair to mate. I like to think Betty did not go off to Syracuse with another suitor.

Jack Frankland has been visiting here for a few days. Such an interesting young man.

September 10th, 1932

I felt just like Aunt Elizabeth [Hawley] as I went down the hallway from the Lounge when I had read your letter from Norwich, Long Gore. Squealing with joy was not enough; I had to dance and cackle. You told me things so interesting about your work—about finding that ancient letter of the twelfth century from William the Conqueror's emissary! Dom Wilmart's copying it, the cupboard of notes, and that you may take them to Newham. And best of all, that you were able to rest at Long Gore Cottage and relax. When I reached the Nursery Kitchen, Mrs. Norton was sitting there, and just then Dorothy [Leonard] came through and sat on the couch beside us while I read your letter and shared my joy in it.

Chris [Christine Allen] has given me a wonderfully good coat lining of magnificent peacock-blue, taken out of her fur coat years ago because it was too brilliant in color. Just what I need for night skies. Again, I felt like Aunt Elizabeth, so joyous in my good fortune. I had the store in Oneida try to find me some peacock-blue as they had once before, but the color is out of style now and there was none to be had. Wasn't that good fortune to have it come from Christine?

September 18th, 1932

As I sat sewing braidings yesterday, I felt in a state of discipline— a little inclined to the blues. Forgetfulness had, with deafness to help, put me where I was afraid I had been unkind to a friend. Then I remembered how a sprained ankle, when I was a girl, seemed like a discipline. I used to think, "What can I get out of it? — This is now a spiritual sprained ankle, and what can I get out of it?" Well, this remembrance and thought sent the blues flying and gave me wisdom, too. So I went in good spirits off to the Earl's house, where Joan's class was giving Betty a wedding shower.[35] There I met my friend, and all came right. My spiritual sprain was bandaged and well in no time, and my discipline had done me good. The shower was fine and a big houseful there. Betty's presents were the usual lovely, useful things — not too much silver and glass, but some pieces of furniture, a lamp, books, and so forth. I missed Helen Barron's gift for Jerry. It would've been a fine blanket, I think.

September 26th, 1932

I am in pretty good fettle with all my bad old teeth out and no chance to do much good chewing. But I look witch-like and laugh at myself every time I happen to see myself in the glass. I have forever lost one thing: my usual expression. With weeks gone in this sunken state, and then a new plate, the old expression will hardly come back. But perhaps my new one will be better.

This being election year, Lotta is visited by Socialist speakers. Three interesting looking men were at dinner with her last evening. I imagine Norman Thomas will get a large vote this year. I saw in the New York paper that the Methodist Conference in Ohio had voted their confidence in Socialism as the coming form of government. Capitalism, they said, had failed.

October 12th, 1932

My *Nightfall* is getting on down to the seventh and last picture and pleases everyone. How glad I shall be to have you see it. I had not thought your coming home so near. December seems only a few weeks away.

October 26th, 1932

My exhibition in Utica has brought me much attention. From New York comes an invitation for an exhibition in Syracuse in April to grace a convention of occupational therapy teachers, whose annual meeting is to be in Syracuse. This invitation I am declining. From Schenectady radio station came a man to see the tapestries, that he might talk about

35. The bridal shower followed the wedding as sometimes occurred.

them at a radio lecture on tapestries to be given on October twenty-seventh. It is all a bit out of routine and a bit hard on my nerves, and I should be glad if it ends this publicity.

December 10th, 1932

I am at work on a small piece of braiding, and it goes quickly. Many ripped up pieces saved as possible treasures find their place wonderfully in this piece. It has been fairly exciting the way things fitted together. When I have a big piece started with a year's outlook ahead, I go to work and leave work calmly, but this week, with a small piece, I have been excited day by day and I press until I stop myself and go off for an extra walk.

July, 1932

I am going down to camp for a day when Mart comes home for something and goes back again. You know, roughing it has lost charm for me at lake places. I had so much of it years ago at Sylvan Beach and was more or less homesick over the hot stove, work-a-day life, though glad of my children's and husband's enjoyment. Often, Myron Sr. was not there. There was no food for the mind, no exhilarating neighbors, not much time to read, and too busy—always glad to get back home!

April 8th, 1934

I did not write to Edith and Mart in the winter or to you about my queer trouble (tintinnitis) that began for me last October out of a clear sky and has had no intermission since, night or day. But my determination has been to make the abnormal normal by thinking of all experience as life—trying to understand it, digest it, and so forth. Albert wrote to Edith about it before she left England, so she knows, but the intensity of Lotta's illness since Edith's return, and the constant need for Edith to be with her and with Albert and Myron and Jane and all the strain of this experience for us made me tell Edith that I knew she knew but would not speak about it until later. Dr. Taylor feels that Lotta will live.

July 23rd, 1934

Elizabeth Trout has written a poem about me. I feel pleased with this, don't you?

"A Tribute to an Old Lady"

You are beautiful
though faded
like a fruit lying in the sun
and charming, too,
like the Schubert "Serenade"
sung in the night.
Best of all
you are interesting
like falling stars
which make us think.
And now I envy you because you are old.

August 5th, 1934

Our business is dull again I hear. I have just come across these lines in *Two Gentlemen of Verona,* "Cease to lament for that thou canst not help and study help for that which thou lamentest."

I get on well as a rule and, having finished the big *Picnic,* am now doing a small piece. My singers sing, but I am used to them.[36]

September 3rd, 1934

It was good to think of you enjoying old friends and good research and lovely surroundings in Cambridge. I do remember Cambridge well, not as you do, but my own impressions are vivid.

I have just been reading an old *Atlantic* of September 1921, and have pleasure in all the re-reading of A. Edward Newton's *My Old Lady London.* I have a map of London on a postal card, and with it, I journey into all the parts of London he so quaintly made his way. Hither and yon we went — a happy hour for me, only that I longed that my maps would take me further, for it quite left out St. John's Wood and the Hampshire part. Also, I had finished Horace Walpole's letters recently, and in this *Atlantic* found a group of letters written by one titled Irish woman to another — her cousin in Ireland — and the letters all told of the contact she had with Walpole, of the marriage of his niece, Maria, and so forth. Lively and interesting. I have always been glad that you gave me Madame de Sévigné's letters. They were an education in regard to her time. She is so

---

36. A reference to the ringing sound in her ears, tintinnitis.

often referred to, I now feel more or less acquainted with her because of the letters.

I'm giving away a recent small braiding. It is not as good as I wish it were. Poor old braiding—it was not well-planned, though at first it seemed good. Soon I shall be making patterns for another night picture.[37]

By the way, Mrs. Oliver Harriman has written me of an exposition she and others are giving of women's work on October first, in New York, and asks that I loan braidings to be hung there. Edith is up in the Adirondacks. We will decide about this when she returns.

September 9th, 1934

I have, dear Hope, your thrilling letter with its enclosure about the wonderful manuscript, *Margery Kemp of Lynn.* How interesting. How exciting it all is! Indeed, I am glad you have the chance to go with Joan Wake[38] for a rest of two days. I can imagine your pleasure and excitement and interest in that first reading of the South Kensington find. Words can hardly be found by me to tell you how keenly I enter into the imagination of you with that manuscript, or how eager I shall be to sometime have the pleasure of reading it when it has been printed. I am glad that I can be at one with you in spirit in the interest of your work, although so little educated and getting aged.

September 23rd, 1934

I have had lovely days with Edith upstairs in their apartment and am now downstairs again. Her love and strength and vigor of spirit were good to live with. We kept out of doors on the roofdeck, although during the days I was there rain did fall. To look from there upon our dear valley with its distant hills, and, from the height, to look down upon the nearby trees and the intensely green lawn was such delight. We both had our own work. But my lower rooms and my freedom to walk abroad are renewed gifts. Edith gave me courage, for my ear trouble is harrasing. She visits me at our evening readings in the Nursery Kitchen and at other hours down here in my room.

---

37. *Bewitched.*

38. Born into a noted family of the peerage, cousins of the royal family, Joan rebelled against a purely social life. Hope persuaded her to pursue scholarly studies, and she became an authority on Northamptonshire amongst other studies. She received an honorary doctorate from Oxford.

October 6th, 1934

Dear Louise [Herrick],

To have you go and see that exhibition with all that crowd of people, to find my work and tell me about it was something to give me a quiet
spirit for the new piece I am making. It is a night piece, and I am now
busy at the top. Its subject is Walter de la Mare's line, "We followed a lady
this night, followed her far and lone. Fox and adder and weasel know the
ways that we have gone." Those are fantastic lines that suit a night piece.
And then you sent me a lovely gift. It came in perfect order and delights
me to think of for my tea-parties.[39]

Hope writes she will stay on in England until December first. At
the South Kensington Museum a lost medieval manuscript was turned up.
It has been lost since 1436 or 1438, though known in parts. The museum
called in Hope to read it to them and then they and the owner put the doc-
uments into Hope's hands to manage. Of course it is left at the museum.
She is busy getting it and her own work published by the Oxford Press.
The manuscript is the account written by a woman who travelled for years
over the Europe of her time, and Hope says it reads like a novel, while its
mysticism is interesting, too. The picture given of 1436 Europe is unusual.

October 18th, 1934

Edith and Constance[40] have had a week of attendance at a mur-
der trial in Wampsville. It is the first such trial this county has had for fifty
years, so our paper says. They went to get first-hand knowledge of court
customs and proceedings, hoping possibly for new ideas on human relationships to use in their old detective stories which they are now re-writing.

My new night braiding is getting a splendid start. It is so wonderful how subject and object — that is, my design and its native silk — come
together out of the everywhere while I am almost "slumbering on my own
right arm."

Edith and I were invited to a party at Dunc's and Connie's to eat a
pheasant that Uncle Steve had given to them. A deliciously cooked dinner
and an evening of enjoyment. Edith and Constance selected all sorts of
poetry from their favorite authors for me to read aloud. Andrew Marvel
happened to be Constance's favorite at this time, and I did so much enjoy

---

39. A box of delicate, flowered sugar lumps.

40. Constance Noyes Robertson, daughter of Corinna and Pierrepont Noyes and
wife of Miles Robertson, then the general manager of Oneida Community, Limited.

coming upon half-remembered lines in their longer context like, "but at my back I always hear time's winged chariot hurrying near."

November 11th, 1934 — Armistice Day

Fifteen years ago today, 1919, November 11th, I stood on the corner near Buckingham Palace and heard London go silent for the first time in perhaps a thousand years.

October 12th, 1935

I am at a point in my work on *The Village Vendor* where long, long strips are to be braided for its borders so I can spend my working hours out of doors taking the material to braid or sew as I sit in the sunshine.

Edith writes from Haworth[41] a grand letter.

I have just finished reading Shakespeare's *Julius Caesar* and am thinking of Mussolini and his seeming desire to be another Caesar. Also of Italy's present actions. These do not follow the play and are not lofty. Three of Cassius' lines seem prophetic: "How many ages hence shall this our lofty scene be acted o'er in states unborn and accents yet unknown?"

November 4th, 1935

I am sending you a review cut from the *New York Herald Tribune* speaking highly of Mr. Parker's book.[42]

A few clippings about earthquakes also go to you. In a letter to Edith are pasted pictures of our recent earthquake effects. I was awake at one o'clock A.M. when these shakes came, and it was a strange, weird thing to feel. One had time in the two minutes of shaking and noise to expect bricks to fall. But none did, fortunately.

January 18th, 1936

I have no news for you, so I will tell you of one of my miracles. I had been making blue flowers in my long border for *The Village Vendor,* and the right sort of blue gave out. Needing only a few more scraps of silk, I advertised on the bulletin board a notice which said, "For Women"

41. Edith was writing a book on Branwell Brontë, *A Pattern for Genius* (E. P. Dutton, 1939).

42. Robert A. Parker, *A Yankee Saint: John Humphrey Noyes and the Oneida Community* (New York: Putnam, 1935).

and did receive all and more than I needed. But the miracle was that Christine brought along rose-colored pieces that brought my heart into my mouth! For more than I needed blue, I had been needing rose color. It thrills me to have the right thing come at the right moment, and how often that happens both in finding colors and in the way certain parts of braidings seem to make themselves. I only have to fasten my thread and the effect has arrived. Gertrude Stein said to a young writer when he was in discouragement, "It will come if it is there, and you will let it come, and if you have anything you will get a sudden creative recognition. I can tell how important it is to have that creative recognition. You cannot go into the womb to form the child; it is there and comes forth whole; and there it is, and you have felt it, but it has come itself and that is creative recognition. Of course, you have a little more control over your writing than that — you have to know what you want to get, but when you know that, let it take you; and if it seems to take you off the track, don't hold back, because that is perhaps where you instinctively want to be. If you hold back and want to be always where you have been before, you will go dry."

July 20th, 1936

I have finished *The Goose Girl* today,[43] and my thoughts will be spearing around for a new idea and trying out a new pattern. I hope to find a verse to illustrate or an idea for a pattern that will come easily as *The Goose Girl* has come.

August 12th, 1936

Due to a cold I have missed much of the excitement and joy of Jane's baby coming into this world. Not much of the joy, for Albert and Edith and Mart all tell me of the event with an outgrowth of happiness. The baby was a girl with much dark hair, and her name is Rhoda Vanessa Rich.[44] It is a great happiness to me to see Edith and Mart so happy over the child. I am on tiptoe to see her.

October 13th, 1936

Just a word of welcome and to tell you how glad I shall be to see you even if your stay here is to be short. Edith returns to England on the

---

43. Between *The Village Vendor* and *The Goose Girl* three small braidings were made.

44. Jane Kinsley and Wells Rich were married in 1933. Rhoda V. Rich was Jessie's first great-grandchild.

S.S. Washington soon after your arrival. What with Mart in England, and her joining him; with Albert in Saratoga, and Jane off to live in New Jersey, this will soon leave over half of my dear family away, but I shall not be unhappy or forlorn. My deafness has long been teaching me how to live alone, and really one cannot ever call life here in the Mansion lonely where we are such close friends.

November 14th, 1936

A boisterous south wind today. I like it!

Another letter from Edith tells me of their new home on Helm Street in London. The neighborhood is quiet, and the buildings new, with steam heat, a lift, and modern fixing that includes a kitchenette, while downstairs is a fine restaurant for the tennants of the building with marvelous meals, Edith says.

Christine told me that she and Grosvenor had recently read Pierrepont's autobiography, and of its new title, *My Father's House.*[45] They so much like it all, including the new title.

Work on *The Shepherd Boy* has been held up for a few days while I have busied myself with writing Christmas notes on some of the cards that you and Edith have brought me from the British Museum at one time or another. For my family I have planned a new photograph of me: I will stand beside the braiding of *The Picnic* which is light in color. The idea is to send such a photograph to Edith and Mart. I will be wearing a new dress made for me from material that Edith chose.

Yesterday all in one mail came three envelopes from Edith. They are thrilling letters telling of the recent events in England. How she and Mart stood on corners and watched turbulent people and bought paper after paper. How Mart feared the King would abdicate, and that would affect business and so forth.[46]

December 8th, 1936

The Shepherd Boy goes slowly. Of all my various attempts to depict men, women, horses, dogs, birds, geese, houses, and hills, I find sheep and lambs the most difficult. They almost stump me. Still, the struggle goes on, and I experience every bit of the overcoming of difficulties without real discouragement. What if their first Originator found them difficult and so let them become a religious symbol?

45. Published by Farrar and Rinehart in 1937, reprinted by Holt, Rinehart, Winston in 1965.

46. The affair between Edward VIII and Mrs. Wallis Simpson had brought about a political crisis.

The Goose Girl, April–July 1936, adapted from verse by Christina Rossetti

January 21st, 1937

I go on with my usual routine of life, only that *The Shepherd Boy,* being finished, I have been doing up odds and ends such as sorting papers and letters and pasting up the accumulated photographs of 1936 into my five albums. I get tense over the album work, so I hired someone to help me, and we work together two afternoons until all is finished.

March, 1937

The newspaper gives a long account of Gerrit Miller's death and of his honors and skill in football. It was a pity that Mr. Miller had to wit-

Shepherd Boy, September 1936–January 1937, adapted from William Blake's *The Lamb*

ness the burning of the old mansion at Peterboro where so many treasures were lost. However, I am glad he had pneumonia and so was down sick only two weeks. Since my mother's quick going with that, and since witnessing Lotta's mother's lingering death, I have always felt sure that pneumonia is what Burton [Dunn] says is familiarly called, "the old peoples' friend."

After dinner in the Nursery kitchen we are still reading Pierrepont's book, *My Father's House,* and now as I look at each small boy growing up in this neighborhood, in spite of the strangeness of Pierre's Childrens' House experiences, I feel I know more of the inner mind of small boys.

Jessie Catherine Kinsley and *The Picnic*, 1936

July 18th, 1937

We have had a long hot spell of ten days or more. But yesterday's finale cooled the air. It was a tremendous thunder shower with driving rain so fierce that a flock of small boys was driven into the South Tower's lower room for shelter. They all had on bathing suits and had been allowed out in the rain. I had just gone thither to shut doors and found the boys dripping and shivering. The rain was not coming straight down but horizontally, fiercely driven by wind. I produced a towel and rubbed the shivers out of them, and soon they all pelted away down the hall and out the front door to start for their various homes.

How I wish the days would go slow, slowly and slower, for baby Rhoda's visit here is such a delight to our whole family that we can hardly bear to have her go back with Jane and Wells to New Jersey when the agents meetings are over. She is a responsive, genial, loveable, unafraid baby of eleven months — of great energetic and initiative powers. Already stands alone in her pen and says many words.

Visitors come to see our Mansion House interested by recent publications. A funny thing was that a couple who came said, that having read Carl Carmer,[47] the only thing they wanted to see here were my braidings. They saw the work and seemed interesting and intelligent, but I cannot imagine what he wrote that left that fancy in their minds.

July 25th, 1937

It is delightful to think of your long, restful stay with Joan Wake among the crags and cliffs at Land's End, which your four last cards and others received give graphic representation. And I can so well dream of the friendship between you and Joan, too. I am glad she once came here and left a little of herself behind.

August 22nd, 1937

Edith and Mart left by auto this morning for New York. Mart will sail on the *Washington* the 25th, while Edith will remain perhaps another six weeks here before she leaves to join him in England.

I called on Miss Ella, who is ninety-one, not long ago. Her spirits were as light and gay-hearted as ever, although she was much bruised in many places by another fall. "But I broke no bones," she said with a gig-

47. Carl Carmer, *Listen for a Lonesome Drum: A York State Chronicle* (Farrar and Rhinehart, 1936).

gle and added, "Grace came just in time, too, to pick me up, and when I asked Grace why she supposed an old creature like me lived on and on through so many upsets, Grace said the Lord must have something yet for me to do here. What, Jessie, do you suppose He could have for me to do?" "Just what you're doing this very minute: weeding your ills with a brave and light heart, laughing them off and making us feel your humorous courage—setting an example," I replied.

After a funeral once, someone said to me, "I have lived in the outside world and I have lived here and always I notice a difference in the atmosphere of a funeral here from any other. Perhaps it is because of this being one big family with all of us feeling more or less like brothers and sisters."

November 25th, 1937

[To Edith, Mart and Ida Kate][48]

It was near noon of November 26th, 1903, that your wedding took place, Mart and Edith. I do not suppose you need to be given this information but I just looked it up in my album again. How well I remember the year and the day. I have had out the old albums to look at you both, you with your much ruffled dress, Edith, and long veil, and Mart in the group of attendants. Remember how you scudded out the door of the back parlor into the library and thence down the cellar stairs and through the cellar to your waiting carriage behind the Ice House? Albert made a fake wait with another horse and carriage at the front of the Mansion where were gathered the rice throwers. How much has happened to us all since that day. I copy below what Alexander Woolcott writes of the things we did not know about twenty-five years ago. He did not know of an inferiority complex. He'd never heard of one. He never heard of daylight saving, nor of rayon, nor of the Soviets, nor of jazz, nor of insulin, or of broccoli. He'd never seen a one-piece bathingsuit or read a gossip column. He'd never heard of an inhibition. He'd never heard a radio or seen a talking picture, nor listened to the whirr of an electric ice-box. He'd never seen an animated cartoon nor a cement road or a neon light. Nor had he seen a wristwatch or a filling station. How much he had to learn! When I read these unknown things to Mrs. Norton, she asked if I thought there were yet more changes or new discoveries and inventions yet to come. "Oh, yes," I said, "Perhaps even more unexpected ones than these."

48. Ida Kate Burnham, Chester Burnham's older daughter, who had been invited to go to England with Mart and Edith.

"Well, it seems to me we have more than we can digest now," and she sighed. But imagination with me looks forward to unimagined things with keen interest, although not thinking another twenty-five years looms ahead for either Mrs. Norton or for me.

December 8th, 1937

Dearest people — Mart, Ida, and darling Edith,

This may prove to be my Christmas letter. How can I be sure it will be put on a fast boat? I hope you get the pictures that were taken of me before Christmas, and that you, dearest Edith, will remember to think of the large picture as my Christmas gift to you and Mart. I am not trying to do much giving this Christmas, as it requires shopping, mailing, and writing. All these are hard with my troublesome arm. (A sadness comes with the thought of not giving.)

The *Street Scene* border gets made little by little.

I am wondering, Edith, if the Dr. Williams of your library was Dr. Harold Williams who died in 1928, and of whom Maurice Baring, editor of *The London Times,* wrote lines I put in my small red quotation book.[49] I have so loved these lines and have thought of them in connection with Albert:

> He kept the bitter bread, and gave away
> the shining salt, to all who came his way.

All, all love, down to the well, up to the sky.

Mother

49. In February 1938 Albert and Edith had this privately printed under the title *Bedside Book.*

A LASTING SPRING

was composed in 10-point Compugraphic Times Roman with two points of leading
by Metricomp Studios,
with display type in VGC Treasury Open by Dix Typesetting Co., Inc.;
printed on 55-pound, acid-free Glatfelter Antique Cream,
Smythe-sewn and bound over boards in Joanna Arrestox B,
also adhesive bound with laminated paper covers printed by Philips Offset,
by Maple-Vail Book Manufacturing Group, Inc.;
and published by

SYRACUSE UNIVERSITY PRESS
SYRACUSE, NEW YORK 13210

47790043

DATE DUE

APR 2 8 2010